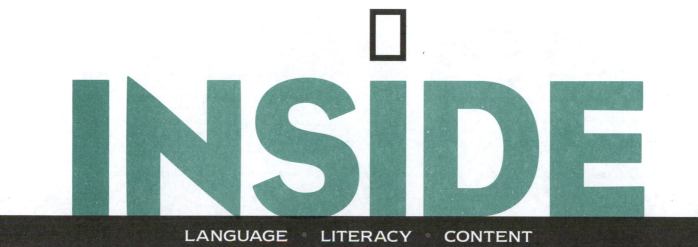

INSIDE

LANGUAGE · LITERACY · CONTENT

NATIONAL GEOGRAPHIC LEARNING | CENGAGE Learning·

Acknowledgments

Grateful acknowledgment is given to the authors, artists, photographers, museums, publishers, and agents for permission to reprint copyrighted material. Every effort has been made to secure the appropriate permission. If any omissions have been made or if corrections are required, please contact the Publisher.

Sandy Asher: "Pas de Trois" by Sandy from *Heart to Heart: New Poems Inspired by Twentieth-Century American Art,* edited by Jan Greenberg. Copyright © by Sandy Asher. Reprinted by permission of the author.

National Geographic Society: Adaptation of "The Power of a Radically Affordable Irrigation Pump" by Sandra Postel from *National Geographic Newswatch.* Copyright © 2012 by the National Geographic Society. Reprinted by permission of the National Geographic Society.

Excerpt from "How Crisis Mapping Saved Lives in Haiti" from the blog by Patrick Meier. Copyright © 2010 by the National Geographic Society. Reprinted by permission of the National Geographic Society.

Russell & Volkening, Inc.: Excerpt from *Harriet Tubman: Conductor on the Underground Railroad* by Ann Petry. Copyright © 1955 by Ann Petry, renewed 1983 by Ann Petry. Reprinted by permission of Russell & Volkening as agents for the author's estate.

Scholastic, Inc.: Excerpt from *Call Me Maria,* by Judith Ortiz Cofer. Copyright © 2004 by Judith Ortiz Cofer. Reprinted by permission.

Photography

Cover, Back Cover ©Patrick Endres/Visuals Unlimited/Corbis. **7** ©Caro/Alamy. **8** ©Matthew Wakem/Aurora Photos. **15** ©Borderlands/Alamy. **16** ©Phil Schermeister/Corbis. **23** ©Stephanie Maze/National Geographic. **45** ©Jeremy Enlow/BlueMoon Stock/Alamy. **52** ©Michael Fay/National Geographic Stock. **53** ©Mark Newman/Lonely Planet Images/Getty Images. **59** ©Harald Sund. **60** ©Brent Stirton/Staff/Getty Images News/Getty Images. **66** Courtesy International Development Enterprises. **78** ©Martin Gray/National Geographic. **85** ©Margo Silver/Photonica World/Getty Images. **86** ©HMS Group Inc./Getty Images. **92** ©Mario Tama/Getty Images News/Getty Images. **93** ©Wilco van Herpen. **98** ©Joe Raedle/Getty Images. **99** ©Courtesy Ushahidi. **100** ©Erin Oberholtzer/U.S. Navy via Getty Images. **113** ©AP Photo/Koji Sasahara. **120** ©John Kobal Foundation/Moviepix/Getty Images. **121** ©Bettmann/Corbis. **128** ©Joan Marcus Photography. **129** ©Wayne Eastep/Photographer's Choice/Getty Images. **149** ©M. Timothy O'Keefe/Alamy. **128** ©Danita Delimont/Alamy. **156** ©Bridgeman Art Library. **163** ©Institute for Exploration/University of Rhode Island & Mystic Aquarium. **164** ©Danita Delimont/Alamy. **170, 171** ©Corey Ford/Stocktrek Images/Getty Images. **182** ©Hulton Archive/Getty Images. **189** ©AFP/Getty Images. **196** ©Gerard Malie/AFP/Getty Images. **203** ©Glenn Leblanc/Photolibrary/Getty Images. **214** Compliments of NASA Orbital Debris Program Office. **215** ©Digital Vision/Getty Images. **221** ©Trip/Art Directors & TRIP/Alamy. **222** ©Compliments of NASA. **225** ©Ernst Haas/Getty Images. **229** ©Owaki/Kulla/Terra/Corbis. **236** (r) ©AP Photo. **236** (l) NASA/JPL/USGS. **237** NASA. **245** ©Getty Images. **248** ©Muntz/Taxi/Getty Images. **249** ©Paul Spinelli/Getty Images. **255** Ernst Haas/Getty Images. **262** ©Imagno/Hulton Archive/Getty Images. **256** age fotostock/SuperStock.

Illustration

30–31, 33 Oscar Ortiz. **66** Mo Ulicny. **133–134, 136, 137** Nathan Aardvark.

Fine Art

271 *Number 6,* 1948, Jackson Pollock, Oil on paper. Reproduction, including downloading of Pollock works is prohibited by copyright laws and international conventions without the express written permission of Artists Rights Society (ARS), New York.

For product information and technology assistance, contact us at
Cengage Learning Customer & Sales Support, 888-915-3276

For permission to use material from this text or product, submit all requests online at **www.cengage.com/permissions**
Further permissions questions can be emailed to
permissionrequest@cengage.com

National Geographic Learning | Cengage Learning
1 Lower Ragsdale Drive
Building 1, Suite 200
Monterey, CA 93940

Cengage Learning is a leading provider of customized learning solutions with office locations around the globe, including Singapore, the United Kingdom, Australia, Mexico, Brazil, and Japan. Locate your local office at **www.cengage.com/global**.

Visit National Geographic Learning online at **ngl.cengage.com**
Visit our corporate website at **www.cengage.com**

Printer: Quad Graphics, Taunton, MA

ISBN: 978-12854-38948 (Practice Book)
ISBN: 978-12854-38993 (Practice Book Teacher's Annotated Edition)

ISBN: 978-12857-55069 (Practice Masters)
Teachers are authorized to reproduce the practice masters in this book in limited quantity and solely for use in their own classrooms.

Printed in the United States of America
20 21 22

INSIDE

LANGUAGE · LITERACY · CONTENT

Contents: Reading

Contents: Reading, continued

Contents: Reading, continued

Contents: Reading, continued

Contents: Grammar

Unit 1

Unit 2

Unit 3

Unit 4

Contents: Grammar, continued

Proofreader's Marks

Mark	Meaning	Example
≡	Capitalize.	I love new york city.
/	Do not capitalize.	I'm going shopping at my favorite Store.
⊙	Add a period.	Mr Lopez is our neighbor.
?	Add a question mark.	Where is my black pen
↓	Add an exclamation point.	Look out
ᵛ ᵛ	Add quotation marks.	You are late, said the teacher.
⋏	Add a comma.	Amy how are you feeling today?
⋏	Add a semicolon.	This shirt is nice however, that one brings out the color of your eyes.
◇	Add a colon.	He wakes up at 6 30 a.m.
⊼	Add a dash.	Barney he's my pet dog has run away.
{ }	Add parentheses.	I want to work for the Federal Bureau of Investigation FBI.
=	Add a hyphen.	You were born in mid September, right?
ᵛ	Add an apostrophe.	I m the oldest of five children.
#	Add a space.	She likes him alot.
⌒	Close up a space.	How much home work do you have?
⋀	Add text.	My keys are on the table.
℮	Delete.	I am going too my friend's house.
⌒℮	Change text.	We have to too much garbage.
⊓	Transpose words, letters.	Did you see thier new car?
(SP)	Spell out.	Today he is turning 16 (SP)
⌗	Begin a new paragraph.	"I win!" I shouted. "No you don't," he said.
(ital)	Add italics.	The Spanish word for table is mesa. (ital)
(u/s)	Add underlining.	Little Women is one of my favorite books.

xi

Mind Map

Use the mind map to show your ideas about the things that make a place feel like home. As you read the selections in this unit, add new ideas you learn about what makes people feel at home.

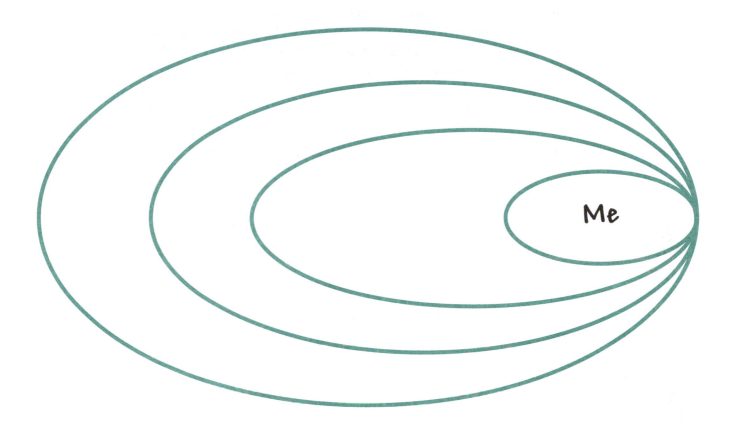

Academic Vocabulary

Think about what it means to be an **immigrant** . What are some things that might change when you move to a new country? Use the word **immigrant** in your answer.

_____

_____

_____

_____

Reading Strategy: Synthesize

A. Read the passage.

> My friend Maria and I both like school. We do not live near each other, so we go to different schools. Maria's school is two blocks from her house, so she walks to school. My school is several miles away from my home. Unlike Maria, I take a bus. Another difference is that Maria wears a uniform to school, but I do not. I am glad that I do not wear a uniform, but sometimes I wish I could walk to school.
>
> Maria and I both have a lot of homework each night. Maria listens to music when she does her homework, but I must have quiet. Even though we are different in that way, there are ways that we are similar. We do our homework at the same time. We like to sit at a desk to do our work. Maria and I do well in school. That is why we like it so much!

B. Answer the questions.

1. Draw a conclusion to explain why the author takes a bus to school.

   _____

   _____

2. Form a generalization to explain why Maria and the author do well in school.

   _____

3. What does the passage tell you about the writer and Maria?

   _____

   _____

   _____

Focus on Vocabulary

Use Context Clues: Multiple-Meaning Words

▶ Follow these steps to figure out the meaning of words you do not know.

1. Look at the word. Think about what the sentence is about.
2. Look at the other words in the sentence.
3. Read the sentences nearby to find more clues or hints.
4. Use the clues to think of a meaning that makes sense.
5. Check the inferred meaning in a dictionary to make sure it is correct.

> **Dictionary Information**
>
> **back** (bak) *noun* **1** the rear part of the human body below the neck *adverb* **2** in reply or in return
>
> **bank** (bangk) *noun* **1** a container or place for storing money **2** the rising ground along the edge of a river, lake, or sea
>
> **bit** (bit) *noun* **1** a short period of time *verb* **2** the past tense and past participle of *bite*
>
> **hard** (härd) *adjective* **1** not soft **2** difficult, needing much effort

A. Read the passage. Write the meaning of each underlined word.

> We rode on a bus to visit my grandparents. I was tired, but the bumpy ride made it too <u>hard</u> to sleep. I asked Dad when we would get there. He smiled and said, "Be patient. We will be there in a <u>bit</u>." Late in the afternoon, the bus finally stopped. I saw Grandpa walking toward the bus, waving at us. I waved <u>back</u> and laughed.

hard _____

bit _____

back _____

B. Read the passage. Write the meaning of each underlined word.

> My parents took me down to the river for a picnic. We sat on the <u>bank</u> and ate. I <u>bit</u> into my apple. It was sweet and juicy. The river was calm and quiet. I could feel the warm sun shining on my <u>back</u>. I am glad my parents took me there.

bank _____

bit _____

back _____

Academic Vocabulary

Use the word *bank* to write about a place. Give **context** clues to show the word's meaning.

_____

_____

_____

Build Background

Critical Viewing Guide

▶ **Take Notes**

A. View the video. Take notes on at least three things that you learned.

_____

_____

_____

_____

_____

_____

_____

▶ **Analyze the Video**

B. Review your notes to help answer these questions.

1. Write two sentences to explain what was in the video.

_____

_____

_____

2. What was the most interesting thing you learned?

_____

_____

_____

3. What did the video tell about the journey of an **immigrant**? Why is it important for **immigrants** to learn about their new home?

_____

_____

_____

Learn Key Vocabulary

Name _____

Growing Together: Key Vocabulary

A. Study each word. Circle a number to rate how well you know it. Then complete the chart.

Rating Scale	**1** I have never seen this word before.	**2** I am not sure of the word's meaning.	**3** I know this word and can teach the word's meaning to someone else.

▲ Life in a new country can be a big **change** for an **immigrant**.

Key Words	Check Understanding	Deepen Understanding
❶ angry (**an**-grē) *adjective* Rating: 1 2 3	You laugh and smile when you are **angry**. Yes No	When a cat is angry, it _____ _____ _____ _____ _____ .
❷ change (**chānj**) *noun* Rating: 1 2 3	A new season often means a **change** in the weather. Yes No	An example of a change in weather is _____ _____ _____ _____ _____ .
❸ curious (**kyoor**-ē-us) *adjective* Rating: 1 2 3	A **curious** person wants to learn new things. Yes No	If you are curious about the work of an author, you might _____ _____ _____ _____ .
❹ immigrant (**i**-mu-grunt) *noun* Rating: 1 2 3	An **immigrant** lives his or her entire life in the same place. Yes No	One reason an immigrant comes to a new country is because _____ _____ _____ _____ .

Name _____

If you are **curious** about another culture, there are many ways you can **learn** about it. ▶

Key Words	Check Understanding	Deepen Understanding
❺ learn (lurn) *verb* Rating:　1　2　3	Reading is a good way to **learn** about something. Yes　　　　No	To learn more about United States history, you could _____ _____ _____ _____ .
❻ leave (lēv) *verb* Rating:　1　2　3	A bear will **leave** its den to find food. Yes　　　　No	After I leave school each day, I _____ _____ _____ _____ .
❼ ordinary (or-du-nair-ē) *adjective* Rating:　1　2　3	A beautiful work of art might be called **ordinary**. Yes　　　　No	An ordinary dog can do things such as _____ _____ _____ _____ .
❽ strange (strānj) *adjective* Rating:　1　2　3	People often feel surprised when something **strange** happens. Yes　　　　No	When I see a strange animal, I _____ _____ _____ _____ .

B. Use one of the Key Vocabulary words. Write about a time when you experienced something new.

_____

_____

_____

Name _____

Growing Together: Reading Strategies Log

Complete at least one row of the Reading Strategies Log for each section of "Growing Together."

Text I Read	Strategy I Used	How I Used the Strategy
Page: 18 **Text:** There is only one tree in my yard.	**Plan** ☐ **Monitor** ☐ **Visualize** ☐ ☐ _____	Planning helped me predict that the story would be about the tree.
Page: _____ **Text:** _____	**Plan** ☐ **Monitor** ☐ **Visualize** ☐ ☐ _____	
Page: _____ **Text:** _____	**Plan** ☐ **Monitor** ☐ **Visualize** ☐ ☐ _____	

Selection Review

Growing Together

Key Vocabulary

angry	learn
change	leave
curious	ordinary
immigrants	strange

A. Read the paragraphs.
Write a Key Vocabulary word in each blank.
Reread the paragraphs to make sure the words make sense.

My family and I had to _____ our home and go to a new country. I did not want to move

to a _____ place where I did not know anyone. I did not want to talk about it because I felt

_____ . I did not want _____ in my life. It was like starting over! I would have to

_____ everything again!

After a few weeks in this new country, I felt better. I started asking questions about it because I

wanted to know more. I was _____ about this new country. Now when I meet other kids

who are _____ , I tell them not to worry. In a short time, even the oddest things will seem

_____ .

B. Write complete sentences to answer these questions about "Growing Together."

1. Summarize how Carmen's father helps her through a difficult time.

_____

_____

_____

_____

_____

_____

2. Over time, Carmen will adjust to her new home. What would you say to Carmen to help her
adjust?

_____

_____

_____

_____

_____

Vocabulary Study

Use Context Clues

Dictionary Information

bat (**bat**) *noun* **1** a wooden club used in games **2** a flying mammal

key (**kee**) *noun* **1** a small instrument used to open a lock **2** something that helps solve a problem

side (**sid**) *noun* **1** one of the halves of an object or body **2** one of two or more teams or groups

▶ Use the steps below to figure out the meaning of each word. Then write the context clues that explain the word's meaning.

1. Think about what the sentence is about. Look at the other words in the sentence.
2. Think about what the word means.
3. Look up the word in a dictionary. Copy the definition that makes sense in the sentence.
4. Then write the context clues that helped you figure out the meaning.

1. The <u>key</u> to solving the puzzle is to use all of the pieces.

   key _____

   Context Clues _____

2. I used a <u>key</u> to unlock the door to my house.

   key _____

   Context Clues _____

3. The left <u>side</u> of my body hurt when the ball hit me.

   side _____

   Context Clues _____

4. Mia wants to be on Trevon's <u>side</u> because his team usually wins.

   side _____

   Context Clues _____

5. A <u>bat</u> flies at night because it is looking for food.

   bat _____

   Context Clues _____

6. I used the <u>bat</u> to hit the ball out of the park.

   bat _____

   Context Clues _____

Name _____

Analyze Narrator's Point of View

A. Read the passage. Analyze the passage to figure out the narrator's point of view. Underline the words that help you know the point of view.

> It was my first day at a new school. I sat there all alone. Everyone around me was laughing and talking with friends. I wanted to talk with them, but I was afraid. I missed my friends from home. A girl named Ana came over to talk to me. Ana just moved here from the same town as I. She said she was scared when she first came here. Then she made some friends and felt better. I felt less afraid after talking to Ana.

B. Reread the passage. What is the narrator's point of view? Write the words that tell how you know. Describe the thoughts and feelings of the narrator.

_____

_____

_____

C. Write about a time when you were afraid to do something, but you did it anyway. Write the story using the third-person point of view.

_____

_____

_____

_____

_____

_____

_____

_____

_____

_____

Academic Vocabulary

Name _____

Growing Together: Academic Vocabulary Review

Academic Vocabulary

analyze	immigrant
context	purpose
explain	summarize

A. Write the Academic Vocabulary words next to their definitions.

Meaning	Word
1. parts near a word that help you understand the meaning	
2. to cover the main points briefly	
3. someone who comes to live in a new country	
4. to break down information into parts to understand it	
5. a reason for doing something	
6. to make an idea clear, so people can understand it	

B. Write an Academic Vocabulary word to complete each sentence.

1. Sara and Anwar will _____ the book they read for the class.

2. My _____ for practicing dribbling is to get better at passing a basketball.

3. Vanya will _____ to us why her family left their country to move here.

4. An _____ may travel many miles to get to a new country.

5. Mei and Kai will _____ the parts of the plot to understand the story better.

6. I used the _____ of the sentence to understand the new word.

C. Use at least two of the Academic Vocabulary words. Write about a time you visited or moved to a new place.

_____

_____

_____

_____

Critical Viewing Guide

▶ **Take Notes**

A. View the video. Take notes on at least three things that you learned.

_____

_____

_____

_____

_____

_____

_____

▶ **Analyze the Video**

B. Review your notes to help answer these questions.

1. Write two sentences to explain what was in the video.

_____

_____

_____

_____

2. What was the most interesting thing you learned?

_____

_____

_____

3. What did the video tell about how **immigrants** adjust to life in a new country?

_____

_____

_____

Learn Key Vocabulary

Name _____

Kids Like Me: Key Vocabulary

A. Study each word. Circle a number to rate how well you know it. Then complete the chart.

Rating Scale	**1** I have never seen this word before.	**2** I am not sure of the word's meaning.	**3** I know this word and can teach the word's meaning to someone else.

▲ Eating food from around the world is a great **opportunity** to **appreciate** other **cultures**.

Key Words	Check Understanding	Deepen Understanding
❶ adjust (u-**just**) *verb* Rating: 1 2 3	Circle the synonym for **adjust**. adapt remain	A person might have to adjust to situations such as _____ _____ _____ _____ .
❷ appreciate (u-**prē**-shē-āt) *verb* Rating: 1 2 3	Circle the synonym for **appreciate**. enjoy dislike	A person can show that he or she appreciates a friend by _____ _____ _____ _____ .
❸ culture (**kul**-chur) *noun* Rating: 1 2 3	Circle the synonym for **culture**. nature customs	Some examples of things that make up a group's culture are _____ _____ _____ _____ .
❹ different (**di**-fu-runt) *adjective* Rating: 1 2 3	Circle the synonym for **different**. similar unlike	Some things that might be different in another country are _____ _____ _____ _____ .

It is important for farmers to **understand** the **value** of what they sell. ▶

Key Words	Check Understanding	Deepen Understanding
❺ opportunity (ah-pur-**tü**-nu-tē) *noun* **Rating:** 1 2 3	Circle the synonym for **opportunity**. chance village	You have opportunities at school to _____ _____ _____ _____ _____ .
❻ relative (**re**-lu-tiv) *noun* **Rating:** 1 2 3	Circle the synonym for **relative**. friend family	Relatives often gather together for _____ _____ _____ _____ _____ .
❼ understand (un-dur-**stand**) *verb* **Rating:** 1 2 3	Circle the synonym for **understand**. comprehend struggle	You demonstrate that you understand something by _____ _____ _____ _____ .
❽ value (**val**-yū) *noun* **Rating:** 1 2 3	Circle the synonym for **value**. strength ideal	One value of a good friendship is _____ _____ _____ _____ _____ .

B. Use at least one of the Key Vocabulary words. Write about an experience that taught you about another culture.

_____

_____

_____

Name _____

Kids Like Me: Reading Strategies Log

Complete at least one row of the Reading Strategies Log for each section of "Kids Like Me."

Text I Read	Strategy I Used	How I Used the Strategy
Page: 34 **Text:** their native country is South Korea	☐ **Make Connections** ☐ **Ask Questions** ☐ **Determine Importance** ☐ _____	I know someone from South Korea. I can make connections between what I know about her culture and what I read.
Page: _____ **Text:** _____	☐ **Make Connections** ☐ **Ask Questions** ☐ **Determine Importance** ☐ _____	
Page: _____ **Text:** _____	☐ **Make Connections** ☐ **Ask Questions** ☐ **Determine Importance** ☐ _____	

Kids Like Me

Key Vocabulary

adjust	opportunity
appreciate	relatives
culture	understands
different	values

A. Read the paragraph.
Write a Key Vocabulary word in each blank.
Reread the paragraph to make sure the words make sense.

> Elisa has the _____ to study in the United States. Her mother and other _____ all think it's a great idea. A good education is one of her family's _____ . Elisa will learn about a country that is very _____ from her own. She will explore a new _____ . Elisa _____ that it might be a hard year. "I will have to _____ to life on my own," she says. Her Tía Elena tells her, "Yes, but think how much you will _____ home."

B. Write complete sentences to answer these questions about "Kids Like Me."

1. What makes it hard for some teens to **adjust** to life in the United States?

_____

_____

_____

_____

_____

_____

2. What advice would you give to someone who is new to the United States?

_____

_____

_____

_____

_____

_____

Vocabulary Study

Use Context Clues

▶ Follow these steps for each item below.

1. Read the sentence. Look at the underlined multiple-meaning word.
2. Think about what the word means. Look up the definition in a dictionary.
3. Use other words in the sentence as context clues to figure out which meaning fits in the sentence. Write the correct definition.
4. Then complete each sentence.

1. A tall post fell during the storm.

   post _____

   A person might walk into a post if _____.

2. Miss Jackson will post student art in the hall.

   post _____

   To post a note on a door, I can use _____.

3. Do not place a hot pan on the kitchen counter.

   place _____

   A person might place a book _____.

4. The lake is a good place for fishing.

   place _____

   My favorite place to visit is _____.

5. The newspaper report described an accident.

   report _____

   I would like to write a report about _____.

6. After school, report to Mr. Henderson for football practice.

   report _____

   I might have to report to the principal's office if _____.

Literary Analysis

Analyze Text Structure: Compare and Contrast

A. Read the passage. Think about how Stella's life in the United States compares and contrasts to her life in Poland.

> Stella was born in Poland. She lived with her family in a small house near the Oder River. Both of Stella's parents were teachers. They didn't make very much money. Stella's parents taught their children the value of learning. Stella went to school and worked hard. They went to church and to dances that were held in local halls.
>
> In 1915 Stella came to the United States with her mother, her father, and her brothers and sisters. Her parents came to this country to find a better life. They found jobs that paid more money. They lived in a house that was bigger than their house in Poland. Stella knew it was important to study and work hard. Stella had lots of fun, too. Her family went to dances. They listened to Polish music and ate Polish food. It reminded them of home!

B. Use the Venn Diagram below to compare and contrast Stella's life in Poland with her life in the United States.

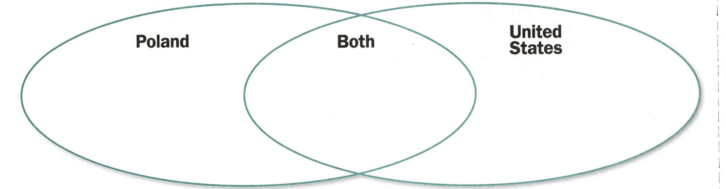

Poland   **Both**   **United States**

C. Compare and contrast Stella's life with your own.

_____

_____

_____

_____

_____

_____

_____

_____

Academic Vocabulary

Kids Like Me: Academic Vocabulary Review

A. Use your own words to tell what each Academic Vocabulary word means.

Word	My Definition
1. **compare**	
2. **context**	

B. Write an Academic Vocabulary word to complete each sentence.

1. To figure out the meaning of a word, you can use _____ clues in the text nearby.

2. When you look for how two things are alike and different, you _____ them.

C. Use at least one Academic Vocabulary word. Write about a custom you share with your family and one you have learned about from friends or others.

_____

_____

_____

_____

_____

_____

Build Background

Critical Viewing Guide

▶ **Take Notes**

A. View the video. Take notes on at least three things that you learned.

_____

_____

_____

_____

_____

_____

_____

_____

▶ **Analyze the Video**

B. Review your notes to help answer these questions.

1. Write two sentences to explain what was in the video.

_____

_____

_____

2. What was the most interesting thing you learned?

_____

_____

_____

3. Why would **immigrants** want to live together in communities?

_____

_____

_____

_____

Learn Key Vocabulary

Name _____

Familiar Places: Key Vocabulary

A. Study each word. Circle a number to rate how well you know it. Then complete the chart.

Rating Scale	**1** I have never seen this word before.	**2** I am not sure of the word's meaning.	**3** I know this word and can teach the word's meaning to someone else.

▲ The **population** of a city is divided into many different **communities**.

Key Words	Check Understanding	Deepen Understanding
❶ agree (u-**grē**) *verb* Rating: 1 2 3	☐ to be excited ☐ to have the same ideas	Example: _____ _____ _____ _____ _____
❷ community (ku-**myū**-nu-tē) *noun* Rating: 1 2 3	☐ a place where people live and work ☐ a store where people buy things	Example: _____ _____ _____ _____ _____
❸ familiar (fu-**mil**-yur) *adjective* Rating: 1 2 3	☐ already known ☐ strange or extraordinary	Example: _____ _____ _____ _____ _____
❹ festival (**fes**-tu-vul) *noun* Rating: 1 2 3	☐ a competition or sporting event ☐ a special event or party	Example: _____ _____ _____ _____

Name _____

> ### Did You Know?
> The word **tradition** comes from an Old French word that means "surrender" or "handing down."

Key Words	Check Understanding	Deepen Understanding
5 native (**nā**-tiv) *adjective* Rating: 1 2 3	☐ something that you don't understand ☐ something you know well because of where you were born	Example: _____ _____ _____ _____ _____
6 neighborhood (**nā**-bur-hood) *noun* Rating: 1 2 3	☐ the area in which people live ☐ a single building	Example: _____ _____ _____ _____ _____
7 population (pah-pyu-**lā**-shun) *noun* Rating: 1 2 3	☐ the number of tall buildings in a city ☐ the number of people who live somewhere	Example: _____ _____ _____ _____ _____
8 tradition (tru-**di**-shun) *noun* Rating: 1 2 3	☐ an activity people share for many years ☐ a person's favorite food	Example: _____ _____ _____ _____ _____

B. Use one Key Vocabulary word to write about a celebration that you share with your family, friends, or the people in your community.

_____

_____

_____

Familiar Places: Reading Strategies Log

Complete at least one row of the Reading Strategies Log for each section of "Familiar Places."

Text I Read	Strategy I Used	How I Used the Strategy
Page: 50 **Text:** Some foods feel more like home, though.	☐ **Make Inferences** ☐ **Synthesize** ☐ _____	Making inferences helped me understand how food can make people feel closer to home.
Page: _____ **Text:** _____	☐ **Make Inferences** ☐ **Synthesize** ☐ _____	
Page: _____ **Text:** _____	☐ **Make Inferences** ☐ **Synthesize** ☐ _____	

Selection Review

Familiar Places

Key Vocabulary

agrees	native
community	neighborhoods
familiar	population
festival	traditions

A. Read the paragraph.
Write a Key Vocabulary word in each blank.
Reread the paragraph to make sure the words make sense.

Everyone _____ that it is important to live in a comfortable place with _____ things.

People want to feel a sense of _____ in their _____ . The _____ of a place may

change, but if people preserve the _____ from their _____ lands, they will always feel

at home. One way to make people feel welcome is to have a _____ or celebration.

B. Write complete sentences to answer these questions about "Familiar Places."

1. How can sharing **traditions** help bring people together?

_____

_____

_____

_____

_____

_____

2. What food, clothing, and music would make you feel more comfortable in a new place?

_____

_____

_____

_____

_____

_____

Vocabulary Study

Name _____

Use Context Clues

▶ Follow the steps below to figure out the meaning of each word.

1. Read the word in context.
2. Look up the word in a dictionary.
3. Copy the definition that makes sense in the sentence.
4. Then complete each sentence.

1. Vince will study for his math test.

    study _____

    I have to study a lot to _____ .

2. My dad went into the study to read the newspaper.

    study _____

    A study will most likely be filled with _____ .

3. I watched the little girl roll down the hill.

    roll _____

    It would be difficult to roll a _____ .

4. The teacher calls the roll every morning.

    roll _____

    A roll is useful for _____ .

5. Sarah turned on the light so she could see down the basement steps.

    light _____

    I have to turn on a light to _____ .

6. The box was light because it only contained feathers.

    light _____

    Some things that are not light are _____ .

Literary Analysis

Analyze Text Structure: Main Idea

A. Read the passage. Underline the sentence that gives the main idea about the topic.

> **What Is Culture?**
> Many different things make up culture. These include language, clothes, food, beliefs, holidays, and even ways of greeting someone. How families raise their children is another part of culture. Culture also consists of art, laws, and manners. For example, in some countries it is not polite to show the bottoms of your feet. All of these things help make up culture. Can you think of other things that make up your culture?

B. Reread the passage. Write the topic and the main idea. Then tell how the main idea is related to the topic.

Topic _____

Main Idea _____

_____

The main idea relates to the topic in this way:

_____

_____

C. Choose a topic related to culture in the United States. Write a passage about it. Be sure to write at least one sentence that tells the main idea.

_____

_____

_____

_____

_____

_____

_____

_____

Academic Vocabulary

Name _____

Familiar Places: Academic Vocabulary Review

A. Draw a line to match each Academic Vocabulary word with its meaning.

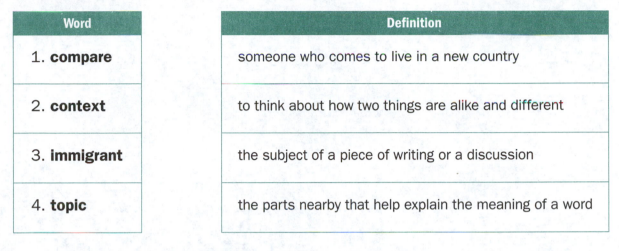

Word	Definition
1. **compare**	someone who comes to live in a new country
2. **context**	to think about how two things are alike and different
3. **immigrant**	the subject of a piece of writing or a discussion
4. **topic**	the parts nearby that help explain the meaning of a word

B. Read each statement. Circle **Yes** or **No** to answer.

1. **Context** helps you understand what a new word means.   **Yes**   **No**

2. An **immigrant** can only visit a new country for a short time.   **Yes**   **No**

3. When you **compare**, you look at what is the same and different.   **Yes**   **No**

4. The **topic** of a discussion is its subject.   **Yes**   **No**

C. Use at least one of the Academic Vocabulary words. Write about a time you visited a new place and found something familiar.

_____

_____

_____

_____

_____

from Call Me María

by Judith Ortiz Cofer

Oscar Ortiz

1   My grandmother comes into the kitchen where I am sitting down at the table reading a magazine. It is a dark winter day. Rain and sleet have been predicted. **Abuela** shakes her head as she looks out the window of our basement apartment. All the feet that pass by are wearing boots. She pours herself a cup of coffee and sits down across from me. She sighs as if her heart is breaking. She shivers and pulls her sweater around her shoulders. Papi comes in whistling. It is his day off. He will spend it with friends he knew from when he was a boy in the **barrio**. They will go to the park, even if it's raining or cold, and talk about the good times they had as children.

2   Abuela says, shivering, "María, let me tell you about my Island in the sun. The place where I was born. A **paradise**."

In Other Words
Abuela Grandmother
barrio Spanish neighborhood
paradise perfect place

3　　Papi, frowning as he struggles to put on his boots, says, "I know, I know your paradise. I lived there once, remember? In San Juan, I couldn't see the sun behind the buildings. I'll take **the island of Manhattan** anytime, if what I want is a paradise made of concrete."

4　　Abuela, ignoring him, tapping my hand as she speaks.

5　　I am trying to stay out of it, hiding behind my magazine: "*Ay, bendita hija.* When I was growing up on my Island, everyone treated each other nicely, like family. We shared what we had, and if you were poor, your neighbors helped you. *La familia, los amigos, el amor,* that's what mattered. People were not always angry; people were not cold like they are here in this cold place, these are cold people . . . the sun shines every day on my Island."

In Other Words
the island of Manhattan New York City
bendita hija blessed daughter
La familia, los amigos, el amor Family, friends, love

6 Papi, sounding angry: "The familia on your Island made fun of me, called me *el gringo* because my Spanish sounded funny to their ears. They laughed when I complained that the mosquitoes were eating me alive. Fresh American blood, they joked, to fatten up our hungry bugs. I couldn't wait to come home to my country where people **understand** what I say, and the mosquitoes treat everyone the same."

7 Abuela, paying no attention to Papi, moving her chair closer to mine: "When I was your age on my Island there was no crime, no violence, no drugs. The children respected the adults. We obeyed the teachers, the priests, the Pope, the governor, and our parents. The sun shines every day. On my Island . . ."

> **"The sun shines every day. On my Island..."**

8 Papi: "I once had my wallet stolen in the **plaza of your pueblo**, Señora. I used to watch the news in the bedroom, while everyone else sat hypnotized by the romantic **telenovelas** in the living room. On my screen was the same world I see on our TV here: drugs, guns, angry people, and violence. Only difference—the bad news was in Spanish."

9 Abuela, not listening. Looking into her cup as if she were watching a movie: "The sun shines every day. On my Island . . ."

10 Papi, in a mocking tone of voice: "The sun shines every day, that's true. While I was unhappy, missing my friends here, while I was lonely, the sun shone every day and it was 110 degrees in the shade."

11 Abuela: "On my Island . . ."

12 Before she can finish her sentence, the lights flash on and off, and then we hear the gasping sounds of electrical things shutting down and darkness. A roll of thunder shakes the glass window. We hear the sound of feet running on the sidewalk above our heads. Abuela gets a candle from a kitchen drawer, places it on the table, and lights it. There is another roll of thunder and the sound of pouring rain. I hear Papi opening the pantry door to get his flashlight. The telephone begins to ring. I run to get it, grateful that it has interrupted a **culture** clash I have been hearing all of my life. It is the old battle between Island Puerto Rican and mainland Puerto Rican. It is what finally drove my parents apart.

13 On the telephone, I hear Doña Segura's shaky voice asking me in Spanish if Papi can come see about a smell like gas in her apartment. Everyone else is away for the day. She is blind. She does not even know that it is dark. Abuela nods. I know she will go stay with Doña Segura.

14 Papi, already dressed for his day of freedom, listens to me tell Doña Segura that she will be right up. I look at my father by the light of the candle. Both of us sigh **in unison**, a big, deep, melodramatic, Puerto Rican sigh. Abuela's candle is blown out by our breath. Then there is the sound of three people laughing together in the dark.

Key Vocabulary
- **understand** *v.*, to know
- **culture** *n.*, the ideas and way of life for a group of people

In Other Words
el gringo American
plaza of your pueblo area in front of your house
telenovelas soap operas; TV shows
in unison at the same time

Close Reading, continued

▶ Read for Understanding

A. What kind of text is this? How do you know?

_____

B. Write a sentence that tells the topic of the selection.

_____

_____

▶ Reread and Summarize

C. On **Practice Book** pages 30–33, circle the 3–5 most important words in each section. Make notes about why you chose each word. Why is the word important in the section?

1. Section 1: (paragraphs 1–3)

_____

_____

2. Section 2: (paragraphs 4–6)

_____

_____

3. Section 3: (paragraphs 7–11)

_____

_____

4. Section 4: (paragraphs 12–14)

_____

_____

D. Use your topic sentence from above and your notes to write a summary of the selection.

_____

_____

_____

ⓓ Reread and Analyze

E. Analyze the pictures you form in your mind as you read.

1. Reread paragraph 5 on **Practice Book** page 31. What pictures do these words form in your mind? How do they help you understand the text? The illustrator, Oscar Ortiz, is from Puerto Rico. How do you think his background helped him visualize the story? Underline words and phrases to support your answers. Use evidence from the text to support your answer.

_____

_____

_____

_____

2. Underline other words on **Practice Book** pages 30–33 that help you visualize Abuela's Puerto Rico. Explain what pictures these words form in your mind.

_____

_____

F. Analyze how the pictures you form in your mind create emotional responses.

1. Reread paragraph 6 on **Practice Book** page 32. What pictures did you form in your mind as you read? Which words in the text bring those pictures to your mind? How do those pictures make you feel? Underline the words and phrases that support your answer. Use evidence from the text to support your answer.

_____

_____

_____

2. On **Practice Book** pages 30–33, underline other words and phrases that help you visualize Papi's Puerto Rico. Explain how the pictures you form in your mind make you feel.

_____

_____

▶ **Reread and Analyze**

G. Analyze the text by making inferences.

1. Reread paragraphs 7–8 on **Practice Book** page 32. Why is Abuela's description of Puerto Rico different from Papi's description of Puerto Rico? Underline words and phrases to support your answers. Use evidence from the text to support your answer.

_____

_____

_____

2. Choose another paragraph on **Practice Book** pages 30–33 and make an inference to fill in missing information in the text. Explain how your inference helped you understand what you read.

_____

_____

H. Analyze the text by making inferences. Use what is in the text, what you already know, and what you have personally experienced.

1. Reread paragraph 10 on **Practice Book** page 32. How did you use your own experience to help you understand the text? How did you combine your experience with what you read to make an inference? What inference did you make? Underline the words and phrases that support your answer. Use evidence from the text to support your answer.

_____

_____

_____

2. Choose another paragraph on **Practice Book** pages 30–33 and make an inference based on what you already know or what you have personally experienced. Explain how your inference helped you to understand what you read.

_____

_____

▶ Discuss and Write

I. Synthesize your ideas about the passage based on what you visualized and inferred.

1. Discuss with your classmates how your visualizations and inferences added to your understanding of the text. Tell how the pictures you formed and the prior knowledge and experiences you used helped you understand Abuela and Papi's disagreement.

_____

_____

_____

2. Write a paragraph comparing and contrasting what you visualized when you read the two descriptions of Puerto Rico. Then make inferences about how the characters feel about Puerto Rico and why their ideas of the same place are different. Use the questions below to organize your thoughts.

   • What do you visualize when you read each description of Puerto Rico?

   • From the text, what can you infer about each character's feelings about Puerto Rico?

   • Why are their memories and feelings about Puerto Rico so different? Make an inference.

_____

_____

_____

_____

_____

▶ Connect with

J. Discuss the Guiding Question: What defines home?

1. How does Abuela define her home in Puerto Rico?

_____

_____

2. How do you think Papi would define home?

_____

_____

Academic Vocabulary Review

Academic Vocabulary

analyze	immigrant
compare	purpose
context	summarize
explain	topic

A. Circle the word that best fits into each sentence.

1. The **(purpose / context)** of the assignment is to practice identifying plant parts.

2. Rita and Max will (**compare / summarize**) leaves from different plants.

3. The teacher chose a (**topic / context**) for our science reports.

4. We will (**context / analyze**) directions to understand them better.

B. Write a definition for each word. Then write whether it is a person, a thing, or an action.

Word	Definition	Person, Thing, or Action
1. **analyze**		
2. **compare**		
3. **context**		
4. **immigrant**		
5. **purpose**		
6. **summarize**		
7. **topic**		
8. **explain**		

C. What do you think is the most important thing to explain to an **immigrant** in this country?

_____

_____

_____

_____

Key Vocabulary Review

A. Read each sentence. Circle the word that best fits into each sentence.

1. A (**community** / **culture**) is a place where people live, work, and carry out their daily lives.

2. My best friend's (**relative** / **native**) country is Mexico.

3. A big meal at Thanksgiving is a (**value** / **tradition**) in her family.

4. If you do not (**understand** / **change**), ask your teacher for help.

5. He was (**curious** / **angry**) about what causes thunderstorms.

6. I'll need a (**strange** / **different**) book to find information about George Washington.

7. A trip to Spain will be a good (**opportunity** / **agree**) to learn about another culture.

8. Jen will have to (**learn** / **adjust**) to her new town.

B. Use your own words to write what each Key Vocabulary word means. Then write an example for each word.

Word	My Definition	Example
1. **agree**		
2. **change**		
3. **culture**		
4. **festival**		
5. **immigrant**		
6. **ordinary**		
7. **population**		
8. **relative**		

Name _____

Unit 1 Key Vocabulary

adjust	change	different	learn	opportunity	strange
agree	community	familiar	leave	ordinary	tradition
angry	culture	festival	native	population	understand
appreciate	curious	immigrant	neighborhood	relative	value

C. Answer the questions in complete sentences.

1. What is a place that is **familiar** to you?

   _____

   _____

2. Describe a **neighborhood** where you would like to live.

   _____

   _____

3. Describe what happens at a **festival** .

   _____

   _____

4. Describe a sudden **change** in weather that you have seen.

   _____

   _____

5. Describe the **population** of your hometown.

   _____

   _____

6. What is something that you hope to **learn** this year?

   _____

   _____

7. How might you help an **immigrant** who is new to your school?

   _____

   _____

8. What will you do today when you **leave** school?

   _____

   _____

Mind Map

Use the mind map to show different kinds of **resources** and how people use them. As you read the selections in this unit, add new ideas you learn about **resources** .

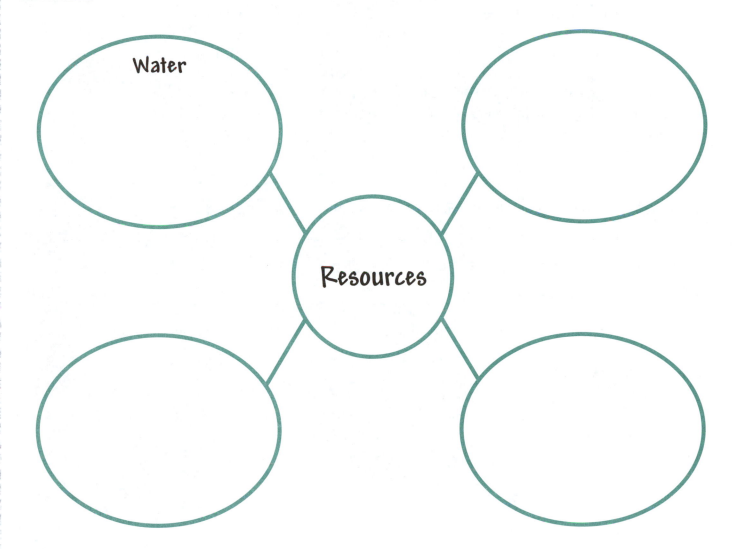

Water

Resources

Academic Vocabulary

Think about a **resource** you use every day. What are some ways you could use less of this **resource** ? Use the word **resource** in your answer.

_____

_____

_____

_____

Focus on Reading

Analyze Events and Ideas

A. Read the passage. Look for the characters' response to story events. Then answer the questions.

> **The Sky People Strike Again**
>
> Connie and her friends were at the park. They heard thunder. Connie told them not to worry. "It's the Sky People bowling," she explained.
>
> Connie's friends all laughed. They never believed her stories. Suddenly there was another roar of thunder. Then a loud voice yelled from above, "Strike!" It was one of the Sky People. His bowling ball was a giant ball of lightning. He had just knocked down 10 rain clouds. "Now do you believe me?" Connie asked. Her friends nodded their heads.

1. Who are the characters? _____

2. What do the characters believe about Sky People in the beginning of the story? _____
_____

3. Which characters react to plot events? _____

4. How do these characters react? _____

B. Read the passage. Look for the topic, main idea, and details. Then answer the questions.

> **Thunderstorm Safety**
>
> Do you know what to do during a thunderstorm? If you are outside, you should seek shelter in a school or another building. Do not use electronics, such as phones, computers, or televisions. If you cannot get inside, stay away from poles, posts, or trees. Try to stay low. If you are in a car, do not leave it.

1. What topic is introduced? _____

2. What is the main idea? _____

3. What details does the writer give about the main idea? _____
_____

4. What examples does the author give to elaborate on electronics? _____

Academic Vocabulary

What science or history **topic** would you like to know more about? Explain why.

_____

_____

Focus on Vocabulary

Name _____

Relate Words: Synonyms

▶ Read the passages. Follow these steps.

1. Whenever you read, take time to learn new words.
2. Put words into categories to help you understand their exact meanings and what they imply.
3. Use a Synonym Scale to rank synonyms in order of their strength. Think about the impact the strength of the word has on meaning and tone.

A. Follow the directions above. Make a Synonym Scale for the underlined words.

> Mr. Handles stood outside. "It's raining!" he shouted. He was very excited. Now the crops would survive. His wife hurried outside to see. Miss Owens bolted from the house, still holding a dishtowel. Mr. Cooper ran out with his boy sitting on his shoulders.

Synonym Scale

_____   _____   _____

What category do the underlined words belong to? _____

Which word implies the fastest movement? _____

What does this word choice tell you? _____

B. Follow the directions above. Make a Synonym Scale for the underlined words.

> I help my mother plant flowers in the spring. The flowers have lovely colors. Daffodils and sunflowers are both pretty. They are a yellow color just like the sun. The roses are gorgeous with soft, red petals. I love to touch them!

Synonym Scale

_____   _____   _____

What category do the underlined words belong to? _____

Which word implies something is the most attractive? _____

What does this word choice tell you? _____

Academic Vocabulary

A whale, a dolphin, and a crab all belong in the same **category** because _____

_____ .

Build Background

Name _____

Critical Viewing Guide

▶ Take Notes

A. View the video. Take notes on at least three things that you learned.

_____

_____

_____

_____

_____

_____

_____

_____

▶ Analyze the Video

B. Review your notes to help answer these questions.

1. Write two sentences to explain what was in the video.

_____

_____

_____

2. What was the most interesting thing you learned?

_____

_____

_____

3. What did you learn about water in China? Write about how this important **resource** is used.

_____

_____

_____

_____

_____

Learn Key Vocabulary

The Secret Water: Key Vocabulary

A. Study each word. Circle a number to rate how well you know it. Then complete the chart.

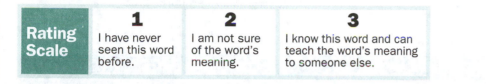

| Rating Scale | **1** I have never seen this word before. | **2** I am not sure of the word's meaning. | **3** I know this word and can teach the word's meaning to someone else. |

The lack of **available** water is a big **problem** in some **villages**. ▶

Key Words	Check Understanding	Deepen Understanding
❶ available (u-vā-lu-bul) *adjective* **Rating:** 1 2 3	☐ extremely large ☐ ready to use	List other words that describe *available*: _____ _____ _____ _____ _____
❷ perfect (**pur**-fikt) *adjective* **Rating:** 1 2 3	☐ just right ☐ needing improvement	List other words that describe *perfect*: _____ _____ _____ _____ _____
❸ plan (plan) *noun* **Rating:** 1 2 3	☐ an idea about how to do something ☐ a mistake or error	List other words that describe *plan*: _____ _____ _____ _____ _____
❹ problem (**prah**-blum) *noun* **Rating:** 1 2 3	☐ a long story that is told more than once ☐ something that needs to be solved	List other words that describe *problem*: _____ _____ _____ _____ _____

Key Vocabulary, continued

Did You Know?
There is an African proverb that says, "It takes a **village** to raise a child." This means that everyone in a community is responsible for its children.

Key Words	Check Understanding	Deepen Understanding
❺ secret (sē-krut) *adjective* **Rating:** 1 2 3	☐ hidden from others ☐ announced by a teacher	List other words that describe *secret*: _____ _____ _____ _____ _____
❻ statue (sta-chü) *noun* **Rating:** 1 2 3	☐ a famous painting ☐ a model of a person or thing	List other words that describe *statue*: _____ _____ _____ _____ _____
❼ village (vi-lij) *noun* **Rating:** 1 2 3	☐ a very small town ☐ a city near the sea	List other words that describe *village*: _____ _____ _____ _____ _____
❽ worry (wur-ē) *verb* **Rating:** 1 2 3	☐ to celebrate ☐ to feel afraid about what may happen	List other words that describe *worry*: _____ _____ _____ _____ _____

B. Use at least two Key Vocabulary words. Write about a time when you overcame a challenge.

_____

_____

_____

Analyze Plot

As you read "The Secret Water," look for the events that lead to the solution.
Complete the Problem-and-Solution Chart.

Problem:	The villagers must walk over a steep mountain to get water.

Event 1:

Event 2:

Event 3:

Solution:

Name _____

The Secret Water

Key Vocabulary

available	secret
perfect	statue
plan	village
problem	worried

A. Read the paragraphs.
Write a Key Vocabulary word in each blank.
Reread the paragraphs to make sure the words make sense.

Shu Fa lived in a mountain _____ . Everyone had to walk a long distance for water. One day Shu Fa picked a turnip that looked _____ for lunch, and water poured from the hole it left behind! Shu Fa thought this would solve the village's _____ . Now water would be _____ for everyone. However, the Voice of the Mountain told Shu Fa she could not take the water or tell anyone about it. If she told anyone about the _____ water, she would be punished.

Shu Fa _____ about the people who worked hard to get water. When Shu Fa's uncle was hurt, she smashed the turnip to get the water. The Voice of the Mountain made her live in the river as punishment. Her uncle came up with a _____ . He carved a _____ that looked just like Shu Fa. The Voice of the Mountain thought the statue was Shu Fa.

B. Write complete sentences to answer these questions about "The Secret Water."

1. How can you tell that the Voice of the Mountain is powerful?

_____

_____

_____

_____

_____

2. What else could Shu Fa have done to trick the Voice of the Mountain?

_____

_____

_____

_____

_____

Vocabulary Study

Create Word Categories

▶ Follow the steps below to create word categories.

1. Think about each set of words.
2. Decide how they connect to the same topic to form a category.
3. Write the name of the category on the line. Then write another word in this category.

1. **strawberry, banana, orange** _____

   Another word in this category is _____ .

2. **chalk, pencil, crayon** _____

   Another word in this category is _____ .

3. **race car, speedboat, missile** _____

   Another word in this category is _____ .

4. **math, science, reading** _____

   Another word in this category is _____ .

5. **bird, airplane, kite** _____

   Another word in this category is _____ .

6. **whale, shark, goldfish** _____

   Another word in this category is _____ .

7. **sun, stars, moon** _____

   Another word in this category is _____ .

8. **snow, ice cream, ice cubes** _____

   Another word in this category is _____ .

9. **tennis, football, baseball** _____

   Another word in this category is _____ .

Academic Vocabulary

Name _____

The Secret Water: Academic Vocabulary Review

A. Draw a line to match each Academic Vocabulary word with its meaning.

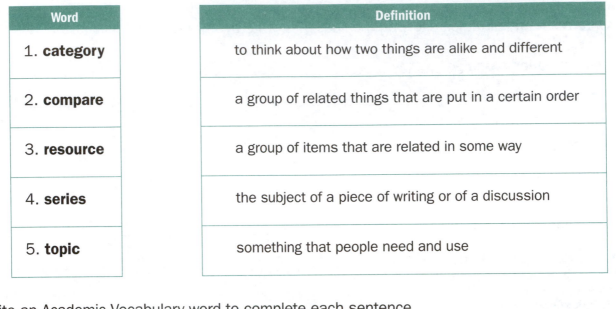

Word	Definition
1. **category**	to think about how two things are alike and different
2. **compare**	a group of related things that are put in a certain order
3. **resource**	a group of items that are related in some way
4. **series**	the subject of a piece of writing or of a discussion
5. **topic**	something that people need and use

B. Write an Academic Vocabulary word to complete each sentence.

1. Water is a _____ all people need. We cannot live without water.

2. Our class watched a _____ of six science videos about water.

3. We will _____ what we learned on the videos with what we learned in class.

4. We grouped the different ways water is used and made a _____ for each group.

5. Our class had many good discussions on the _____ of water.

C. Choose two Academic Vocabulary words. Write a complete sentence using each word.

_____

_____

_____

_____

_____

_____

_____

Build Background

Critical Viewing Guide

▶ Take Notes

A. View the images. Take notes on at least three things that you learned.

_____

_____

_____

_____

_____

_____

_____

▶ Analyze the Images

B. Review your notes to help answer these questions.

1. Write two sentences to explain what was in the images.

_____

_____

_____

2. What was the most interesting thing you learned?

_____

_____

_____

3. What did the images show about water? Write about the different ways you use this **resource** .

_____

_____

_____

_____

Learn Key Vocabulary

Name _____

How Do We Use Water?: Key Vocabulary

A. Study each word. Circle a number to rate how well you know it. Then complete the chart.

▲ People, animals, and **crops** all need water to stay **alive**.

Rating Scale	**1** I have never seen this word before.	**2** I am not sure of the word's meaning.	**3** I know this word and can teach the word's meaning to someone else.

Key Words	Check Understanding	Deepen Understanding
❶ alive (u-**liv**) *adjective* Rating: 1 2 3	Something that is **alive** does not need food or water. Yes No	I can tell that a rock is not alive because _____ _____ _____ _____ _____ .
❷ amount (u-**mount**) *noun* Rating: 1 2 3	You can determine the **amount** of money you need by reading the price tag. Yes No	I have the largest amount of homework for _____ _____ _____ . _____ _____ .
❸ crop (krop) *noun* Rating: 1 2 3	Corn is a type of **crop** grown in the United States. Yes No	To grow properly, crops need _____ _____ _____ _____ _____ .
❹ depend (di-**pend**) *verb* Rating: 1 2 3	A soccer player can **depend** on her teammates. Yes No	A friend depends on you to be _____ _____ _____ _____ _____ .

Name _____

Water is a very important **resource.** People all over the **globe depend** on it. ▶

Key Words	Check Understanding	Deepen Understanding
❺ **globe** (glōb) *noun* **Rating:** 1 2 3	A **globe** is shaped like a cube. **Yes** **No**	I use a globe to _____ _____ _____ _____ _____ .
❻ **material** (mu-**tear**-ē-ul) *noun* **Rating:** 1 2 3	Water is a **material** you can use to make clothing. **Yes** **No**	I can use many materials to make an art project including _____ _____ _____ _____ .
❼ **rainfall** (**rān**-fawl) *noun* **Rating:** 1 2 3	If the amount of **rainfall** in a month is very high, it has rained a lot. **Yes** **No**	People who measure rainfall include _____ _____ _____ _____ _____ .
❽ **resource** (rē-sors) *noun* **Rating:** 1 2 3	Water is a natural **resource.** **Yes** **No**	It is important to save natural resources because _____ _____ _____ _____ .

B. Use one of the Key Vocabulary words to write about why water is important.

_____

_____

_____

Analyze Main Idea and Details

As you read "How Do We Use Water?" look in each section for details that support the main idea. Complete the Main-Idea Chart.

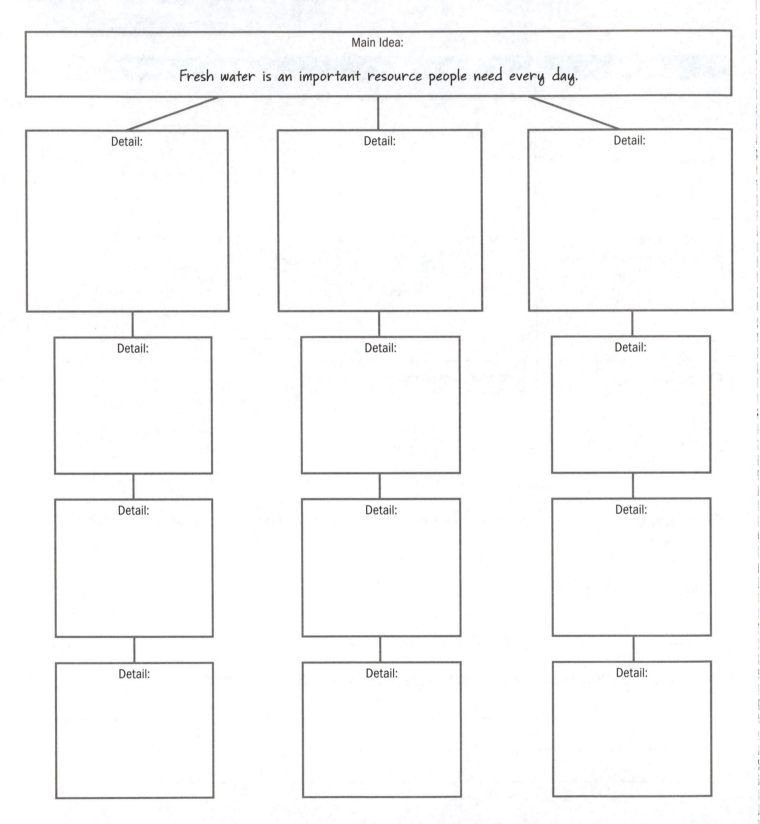

Main Idea:

Fresh water is an important resource people need every day.

Detail:

Detail:

Detail:

Detail:

Detail:

Detail:

Detail:

Detail:

Detail:

Detail:

Detail:

Detail:

How Do We Use Water?

Key Vocabulary

alive	globe
amount	materials
crops	rainfall
depend	resource

A. Read the paragraph.
Write a Key Vocabulary word in each blank.
Reread the paragraph to make sure the words make sense.

Every living thing on Earth needs water. If you look at a _____, you can see that Earth is mostly covered with water. People would not be _____ without it. But what if we run out? Some years are dry. During those years, the _____ of _____ is very low. We must find ways to save this important _____. Farmers cut back on water for _____. Builders cut back on water used to make _____ such as concrete. Can we _____ on you to save water, too? Saving water is a job for everyone.

B. Write complete sentences to answer these questions about "How Do We Use Water?"

1. Why is it important to protect fresh water **resources**?

_____

_____

_____

_____

_____

_____

2. What could you do to reduce the **amount** of water you use?

_____

_____

_____

_____

_____

_____

Vocabulary Study

Use Synonyms

▶ Follow the steps below to use synonyms.

1. Read each sentence.
2. Use a thesaurus to find a synonym with a stronger connotative meaning for each underlined word.
3. Rewrite the sentence with the synonym.

1. I <u>ran</u> down the street to catch the bus.

_____

2. I <u>looked</u> through the microscope at the plant cells.

_____

3. The movie was <u>scary</u> because it was about monsters.

_____

4. An African elephant is a <u>big</u> animal.

_____

5. My mother's banana bread is <u>good</u>.

_____

6. The race car <u>moved</u> around the track and almost crashed.

_____

7. A <u>nice</u> person will help you when you need it.

_____

8. I was <u>glad</u> when my team won the game.

_____

9. Tami won first place in the <u>game</u>.

_____

10. The boy will <u>try</u> to carry the rocks.

_____

Academic Vocabulary

Academic Vocabulary

category	specific
support	topic

How Do We Use Water?: Academic Vocabulary Review

A. Write a synonym for each Academic Vocabulary word. Choose from the words in the chart below.

Word	Choose from these words			Synonym
1. **category**	certain	group	alone	
2. **support**	defend	target	break	
3. **specific**	loose	detailed	about	
4. **topic**	frame	plans	subject	

B. Rewrite each sentence. Replace the underlined words with an Academic Vocabulary word.

1. Be <u>detailed</u> about the plans you make for the next meeting.

   _____

2. You should make a list of each <u>group</u> you want to discuss.

   _____

3. Rico and Jade <u>defend</u> the decision to make summer school longer.

   _____

4. Have you chosen a <u>subject</u> for your next science report?

   _____

Critical Viewing Guide

▶ **Take Notes**

A. View the video. Take notes on at least three things that you learned.

_____

_____

_____

_____

_____

_____

_____

▶ **Analyze the Video**

B. Review your notes to help answer these questions.

1. Write two sentences to explain what was in the video.

_____

_____

_____

2. What was the most interesting thing you learned?

_____

_____

_____

3. Write about the ways that water **resources** can be used for fun.

_____

_____

_____

_____

Learn Key Vocabulary

Name _____

Water at Work: Key Vocabulary

A. Study each word. Circle a number to rate how well you know it. Then complete the chart.

Rating Scale	**1** I have never seen this word before.	**2** I am not sure of the word's meaning.	**3** I know this word and can teach the word's meaning to someone else.

▲ Water can be used to **generate electricity**.

Key Words	Check Understanding	Deepen Understanding
❶ arrive (u-**rīv**) *verb* Rating: 1 2 3	Circle the synonym for **arrive**. enter leave	Why is it important to arrive at school on time? _____ _____ _____ _____
❷ electricity (i-lek-**tri**-su-tē) *noun* Rating: 1 2 3	Circle the synonym for **electricity**. power thunder	What are some ways that we use electricity? _____ _____ _____ _____
❸ flow (flō) *verb* Rating: 1 2 3	Circle the synonym for **flow**. freeze move	What is an example of a body of water that flows? ___ _____ _____ _____
❹ generate (je-nu-rāt) *verb* Rating: 1 2 3	Circle the synonym for **generate**. make feed	What kinds of natural resources can we use to generate power? _____ _____ _____

Name _____

Because rivers **flow** quickly, it is important to enjoy the water **safely.** ▶

Key Words	Check Understanding	Deepen Understanding
❺ goods (goodz) *noun* **Rating:** 1 2 3	Circle the synonym for **goods.** ideas products	What are some goods that you can find at your local market? _____ _____ _____ _____
❻ power (pow-ur) *noun* **Rating:** 1 2 3	Circle the synonym for **power.** force humor	Share an example of an everyday thing that uses power. _____ _____ _____ _____
❼ safely (sāf-lē) *adverb* **Rating:** 1 2 3	Circle the synonym for **safely.** loudly carefully	What should you do to ride a bicycle safely? _____ _____ _____ _____ _____
❽ treat (trēt) *verb* **Rating:** 1 2 3	Circle the synonym for **treat.** change dry	Why do certain places treat water? _____ _____ _____ _____ _____

B. Use one of the Key Vocabulary words to write about a way you can save energy.

_____

_____

_____

Name _____

Analyze Main Idea and Details

As you read "Water at Work," look in each section for details that support the main idea. Complete the Main-Idea Diagram.

Main Idea:	Millions of people depend on water from the Columbia River.

Detail:
Detail:
Detail:
Detail:
Detail:

Water at Work

Key Vocabulary

arrives	goods
electricity	power
flows	safely
generate	treated

A. Read the paragraph.
Write a Key Vocabulary word in each blank.
Reread the paragraph to make sure the words make sense.

The Columbia River _____ through two states. Barges move along the river and carry

_____ . The river flows through the Dalles Dam. It turns machines that _____ enough

_____ to provide _____ for two cities. The river's water can be _____ to

provide fresh water for people. People can then _____ drink the water. The Columbia River

helps many people along its banks before it _____ at the sea.

B. Write complete sentences to answer these questions about "Water at Work."

1. How might the way people use water in Pasco affect the water in Longview?

_____

_____

_____

_____

_____

_____

_____

2. Why is it important to protect river resources?

_____

_____

_____

_____

_____

_____

_____

Vocabulary Study

Synonyms and Antonyms

▶ Follow the steps below to show how words relate to each other.

1. Read the antonyms at the ends of each scale.
2. Think of other words that relate to each word.
3. Write them in order on the scale.

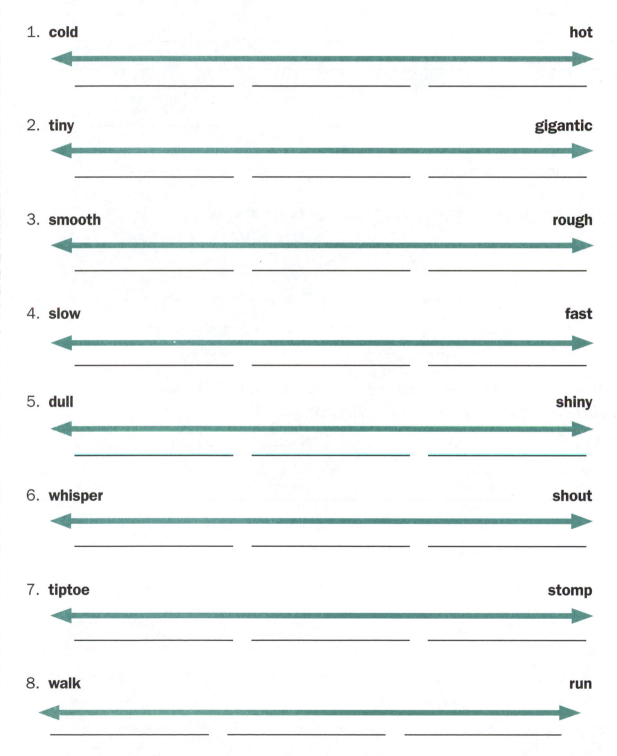

1. **cold**   **hot**

  ←——————————————————————→

  _____ _____ _____

2. **tiny**   **gigantic**

  ←——————————————————————→

  _____ _____ _____

3. **smooth**   **rough**

  ←——————————————————————→

  _____ _____ _____

4. **slow**   **fast**

  ←——————————————————————→

  _____ _____ _____

5. **dull**   **shiny**

  ←——————————————————————→

  _____ _____ _____

6. **whisper**   **shout**

  ←——————————————————————→

  _____ _____ _____

7. **tiptoe**   **stomp**

  ←——————————————————————→

  _____ _____ _____

8. **walk**   **run**

  ←——————————————————————→

  _____ _____ _____

Academic Vocabulary

Name _____

Water at Work: Academic Vocabulary Review

Academic Vocabulary

category	resource
compare	support
relate	topic

A. Use your own words to tell what each Academic Vocabulary word means.

1. **category:** _____

2. **compare:** _____

3. **relate:** _____

4. **resource:** _____

5. **support:** _____

6. **topic:** _____

B. Answer the questions in complete sentences.

1. How do students show **support** for their sports teams? Give examples.

   _____

   _____

   _____

   _____

   _____

2. Many sports teams name themselves after animals such as tigers and bears.
   Why do you think these teams want to **relate** to animals?

   _____

   _____

   _____

   _____

   _____

3. **Compare** life in school to life outside of school.

   _____

   _____

   _____

   _____

   _____

Irrigation Pumps

April 18, 2012
by Sandra Postel

CAN SAVE | POOR FARMERS

1   One of the more useful tools ever developed for the world's poor farmers is a device called a treadle pump.

2   The treadle pump looks and operates much like an exercise machine that you'd find in a gym. But the farmers who use these devices are not trying to lose pounds; they're trying to gain them.

3   More than 850 million people in the world today are hungry most of the time. Oddly enough, many of these people live on farms. These farm families go hungry because they do not have the resources to make their land produce enough food to meet their needs.

A woman in Bangladesh uses a treadle pump to irrigate a rice field on her own farm. ▶

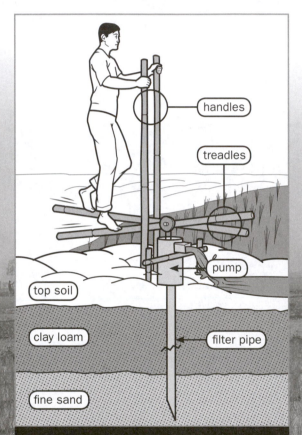

handles

treadles

pump

top soil

clay loam

filter pipe

fine sand

Human-powered treadle pump

4   For many of them, the missing resource is water. And that's where the treadle pump **comes in.**

5   Traveling through Bangladesh some years ago, I saw vast areas of brown, **barren** land. It was January, which is the dry season in this country. The **amount** of **rainfall** is not enough for farmers to grow **crops**. Without access to irrigation water, small farmers leave their land unplanted, which in turn leaves them hungry and poor.

6   But northeast of Dhaka, the fields were green and filled with activity. Men and women, children and parents, were operating treadle pumps.

7   The operator of the treadle pump pedals up and down on two poles called treadles. This action sucks water up through a shallow well. The water then **flows** into an irrigation ditch that travels into the fields to water crops.

8   For a total investment of about $35, Bangladeshi farmers can irrigate half an acre (about 1.5 school gymnasiums) during the dry season. They can grow enough to support their families. They can also sell food at the market. The technology of a treadle pump is relatively simple and it does not cost very much money, making it "radically affordable" compared to other irrigation technologies.

9   Many small farms are owned by women.

"The treadle pump can radically change the lives of women . . ."

So the treadle pump can radically change the lives of women by providing an opportunity for them to run their small farms. To help poor women buy their own pumps, a nonprofit organization called KickStart established a Mobile Layaway program. This program allows women farmers to pay for a pump by sending small payments through their mobile phones. Paying a little bit at a time, many women are able to pay for a pump within ten weeks.

10   In March, 2012 U.S. Secretary of State Hillary Clinton presented KickStart with the first-ever Innovation Award for the Empowerment of Women and Girls. Secretary Clinton said, "If you just stop and think that 60 to 70 percent of the small-holder farmers in the world are women, this [project] has **enormous potential.**"

11   People who use treadle pumps don't have to do the hard work of treadling forever. As they **move up the income ladder**, they can turn to a labor-saving irrigation system, perhaps powered by diesel or solar energy. With extra time, women may start a business. Girls will attend school. Unleashed from poverty and hunger, the entrepreneurial spirit will soar.

12   The power of a water pump—designed for its "radical affordability"—should not be underestimated.

Key Vocabulary
- **amount** *n.*, the total number, the quantity
- **rainfall** *n.*, the total rain that comes down
- **crops** *n.*, plants that farmers grow
- **flow** *v.*, to move freely

In Other Words
comes in is important
barren empty
enormous potential many possibilities
move up the income ladder make more money

▶ Read for Understanding

A. What kind of text is this? How do you know?

_____

_____

B. Write a sentence that tells the topic of the selection.

_____

_____

▶ Reread and Summarize

C. On **Practice Book** pages 66–67, circle the 3–5 most important words in each section. Make notes about why you chose each word. Why is the word important?

1. Section 1: (paragraphs 1–4)

_____

_____

2. Section 2: (paragraphs 5–7)

_____

_____

3. Section 3: (paragraphs 8–10)

_____

_____

4. Section 4: (paragraphs 11–12)

_____

_____

D. Use your topic sentence from above and your notes to write a summary of the selection.

_____

_____

_____

▶ Reread and Analyze

E. Analyze how the author introduces the main idea.

1. Reread paragraph 1 on **Practice Book** page 66. What idea is introduced in this paragraph? Underline words and phrases to support your answer. Use evidence from the text to support your answer.

   _____

   _____

   _____

2. Reread another paragraph on **Practice Book** pages 66–67 and underline the sentence that introduces the main idea of that paragraph. Explain how you determined it was the main idea.

   _____

   _____

F. Analyze how the author explains the main idea.

1. Reread paragraphs 5–6 on **Practice Book** page 67. What more do these paragraphs tell you about the main idea? Underline the words and phrases that support your answer. Use evidence from the text to support your answer.

   _____

   _____

   _____

2. On **Practice Book** pages 66–67, underline other words and phrases that explain the main idea. Describe what more they tell about the main idea.

   _____

   _____

▶ Discuss and Write

G. Synthesize your ideas about the main idea of the article.

1. With the class, discuss how the writer explained the main idea. List the explanations you discuss.

_____

_____

_____

_____

_____

2. Choose one of the explanations that you listed. Write a paragraph about how the writer explained the main idea with it. Use the questions below to organize your thoughts.

   • What explanation did the writer use?

   • What did it explain about the main idea?

   • How did it help you to better understand the main idea?

_____

_____

_____

_____

_____

▶ Connect with

H. Discuss the Guiding Question: How do we depend on Earth's resources?

1. Why is water so important to these farmers?

_____

2. Why must these farmers depend on an irrigation system rather than rainfall?

_____

3. How do you think the lives of these farmers would change if more treadle pumps were available?

_____

Academic Vocabulary Review

Academic Vocabulary

category	series
compare	specific
relate	support
resource	topic

A. Circle the word that best fits into each sentence.

1. A group of related items put in a certain order is called a (**topic** / **series**).

2. When you (**support** / **compare**) an idea, you give reasons for it.

3. When you (**resource** / **relate**) two things, you think about how they are connected.

4. Something that is (**topic** / **specific**) is detailed.

B. Use your own words to write a definition for each Academic Vocabulary word. Then write a synonym for each word.

Word	My Definition	Synonym
1. **specific**		
2. **relate**		
3. **resource**		
4. **topic**		

C. Imagine that a teacher gives you the following assignment. Rewrite the assignment. Replace each underlined word or phrase with an Academic Vocabulary word.

Choose from the <u>groups</u> and select two <u>exact</u> items. <u>Think about how</u> the two items <u>are alike and different</u>. Then write the details of your study.

_____

_____

_____

_____

_____

_____

_____

Key Vocabulary Review

A. Read each sentence. Circle the word that best fits into each sentence.

1. In some parts of the country, windmills (**treat / generate**) electricity.

2. Water is a (**resource / worry**) that people need.

3. One family has a (**secret / goods**) source of water that they keep for themselves.

4. The farmer has planted many (**goods / crops**) this season.

5. There is plenty of water (**alive / available**) to us.

6. If you don't pay attention, water will (**flow / arrive**) out of the tub.

7. Jack has a (**problem / plan**) to save energy.

8. It is important to be safe around (**electricity / village**) so you don't get a shock!

B. Use your own words to write what each Key Vocabulary word means.
Then write a synonym for each word.

Word	My Definition	Synonym
1. **alive**		
2. **amount**		
3. **goods**		
4. **material**		
5. **power**		
6. **statue**		
7. **treat**		
8. **worry**		

Name _____

Unit 2 Key Vocabulary

alive	crop	generate	perfect	rainfall	statue
amount	depend	globe	plan	resource	treat
arrive	electricity	goods	power	safely	village
available	flow	material	problcm	secret	worry

C. Answer the questions in complete sentences.

1. What is a **problem** that you have solved?

_____

_____

2. What is the first thing you do when you **arrive** at school?

_____

_____

3. Does your area get a lot of **rainfall**?

_____

_____

4. Why might you use a **globe**?

_____

_____

5. On whom do you **depend**?

_____

_____

6. Why is water important to a **village**?

_____

_____

7. Describe your **perfect** day.

_____

_____

8. Why is it important to behave **safely** near water?

_____

_____

Mind Map

Use the mind map to show different **forces** of nature. Explain what happens during each **force** of nature and how people deal with it. As you read the selections in this unit, add new ideas you learn about **forces** of nature.

Force of Nature	What Happens	How People Deal with It
Earthquake	• Ground shakes • •	• Rescue workers bring food and blankets • •
	• • •	• • •
	• • •	• • •

Academic Vocabulary

People prepare for a possible **force** of nature in order to stay safe. Why is it important to prepare for a **force** of nature? Use the word **force** in your answer.

_____

_____

_____

_____

Focus on Reading

Determine Viewpoints

A. Read the fiction passage. Underline the dialogue, thoughts, and other words that convey Matthew's viewpoint.

> **A Stormy Day**
>
> It was after four, but Mrs. Drake said that students could not go home until the storm was over. She tried to keep them busy. Matthew felt trapped and protested, "C'mon, Mrs. Drake! Can't we play in the snow?"
>
> "Absolutely not," she replied handing him a book.
>
> Matthew tried to read, but he kept looking out the window, building a snowman in his mind. The snow swirled around, not seeming to land. Suddenly, Matthew's father walked through the door with snow still clinging to his coat.

Use the words you underlined to explain Matthew's viewpoint.

_____

_____

_____

B. Read the narrative nonfiction passage. Underline words, thoughts, and actions that convey the author's viewpoint.

> **Snow Days**
>
> When I was in sixth grade, a blizzard shut down schools, businesses, and roads for days. School was still closed after it finally stopped snowing. I hoped it stayed that way for a long time. I took full advantage of this unexpected vacation. When I wasn't building a family of snowmen, I was playing video games in my pajamas. I thought life couldn't get any better. But then, my mom made the announcement I had been dreading.

Use the underlined words to explain the author's viewpoint.

_____

_____

_____

Academic Vocabulary

Create a plan for what you would do during a snowstorm. Write your ideas here.

_____

_____

Focus on Vocabulary

Name _____

Use Word Parts

Suffix	Meaning	Example
-ful	full of	hopeful
-ive	having the qualities of	creative
-ly	in a certain way	quietly
-ment	an action or process	payment

▶ Read the passages. Follow these steps.

1. Look at each underlined word. Then look at words nearby for clues to the word's meaning.
2. Break down the word into meaningful parts.
3. Think about the meaning of each part.
4. Put the meanings together to define the whole word. See if the meaning makes sense.

A. Follow the directions above. Write the meaning of each underlined word.

> A tornado is a powerful storm. It has a huge funnel-shaped cloud that turns around and around. The winds of a tornado are destructive. It can knock down trees, tear roofs from buildings, and even pick up a car! You should go someplace safe to protect yourself from a tornado. An underground room is the best place. A room without windows is another safe place.

powerful _____

destructive _____

underground _____

someplace _____

B. Follow the directions above. Write the meaning of each underlined word.

> A blizzard is a strong winter storm that has wind and snow. It can snow heavily in a blizzard. During the Blizzard of 1978, a snowstorm dumped more than 40 inches of snow in parts of the northeastern United States. The snow was almost as tall as a second grader! Schools were closed for days. This created excitement for children. It was also a sad time. The storm caused many deaths and ruined many homes.

heavily _____

snowstorm _____

excitement _____

Academic Vocabulary

I would **define** a "storm" as _____

_____ .

Build Background

Critical Viewing Guide

▶ **Take Notes**

A. View the video. Take notes on at least three things that you learned.

_____

_____

_____

_____

_____

_____

_____

▶ **Analyze the Video**

B. Review your notes to help answer these questions.

1. Write two sentences to explain what was in the video.

_____

_____

_____

2. What was the most interesting thing you learned?

_____

_____

_____

3. Give examples from the video that showed the **force** of a volcano.

_____

_____

_____

_____

Learn Key Vocabulary

Name _____

Volcano!: Key Vocabulary

A. Study each word. Circle a number to rate how well you know it. Then complete the chart.

Rating Scale	1	2	3
	I have never seen this word before.	I am not sure of the word's meaning.	I know this word and can teach the word's meaning to someone else.

▲ A **volcano** can **erupt** only when it is **active**.

Key Words	Check Understanding	Deepen Understanding
❶ active (**ak**-tiv) *adjective* **Rating:** 1 2 3	☐ likely to move or show action ☐ slow or lazy	To stay active, I _____ _____ _____ _____ _____ .
❷ dangerous (**dān**-ju-rus) *adjective* **Rating:** 1 2 3	☐ moving at a slow speed ☐ not safe	If you see something that is dangerous, you should _____ _____ _____ _____ .
❸ erupt (i-**rupt**) *verb* **Rating:** 1 2 3	☐ to trickle or run slowly ☐ to shoot out suddenly	When a volcano erupts, _____ _____ _____ _____ _____ .
❹ force (fors) *verb* **Rating:** 1 2 3	☐ to push ☐ to hold steady	An example of something you might have to force is _____ _____ _____ _____ .

Name _____

Key Words	Check Understanding	Deepen Understanding
❺ layer (lā-ur) *noun* Rating: 1 2 3	☐ a section that is on top of or under another ☐ a large area made up of many sections	You might wear many layers of clothing if _____ _____ _____ _____ _____ .
❻ surface (sur-fus) *noun* Rating: 1 2 3	☐ something that you know for sure ☐ the outside of something	Many things live below the surface of the ocean, such as _____ _____ _____ .
❼ volcano (vol-kā-nō) *noun* Rating: 1 2 3	☐ a planet in the solar system ☐ an opening in the earth from which lava, ash, and steam escape	If I saw steam coming from a volcano, I would _____ _____ _____ _____ .
❽ warning (wor-ning) *noun* Rating: 1 2 3	☐ a sign that something bad may happen ☐ something that is heating up	If a fire starts in my home, I can give a warning to others by _____ _____ _____ . .

B. Use at least two of the Key Vocabulary words. Write about how you could stay safe during a bad storm, an earthquake, or a volcanic eruption.

_____

_____

_____

Analyze Text Structure: Cause and Effect

A. Read the passage. Look for clues that show cause and effect.

> Santa Ana winds often cause wildfires to burn out of control in California. These winds come from the desert regions to the east. During the fall of each year, high pressure builds over the desert. This causes the air to begin moving to the low-pressure areas near the west coast. As it moves through the mountains toward the coast, the air grows hotter and the winds build speed. When the winds reach California, they dry out plant life. The dry vegetation adds fuel to California wildfires.

B. Reread the passage. Think about how Santa Ana winds form. Then think about the effects of these winds. Complete the Cause-and-Effect Chain.

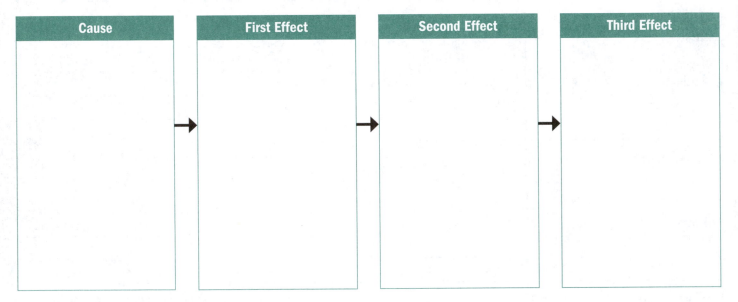

Cause	First Effect	Second Effect	Third Effect

C. Write about one event that happened to you and the effects of that event.

_____

_____

_____

_____

_____

_____

_____

Selection Review

Volcano!

Key Vocabulary

active	layers
dangerous	surface
erupt	volcano
force	warning

A. Read the paragraph.
Write a Key Vocabulary word in each blank.
Reread the paragraph to make sure the words make sense.

Liquid rock flows beneath Earth's crust, or _____ . Pressure can _____ the liquid up through Earth's _____ until it oozes out of a crack. This is how a _____ forms. A volcano is one of nature's most amazing features. It can blow up, or _____ , without any _____ . It can be _____ to live near an _____ volcano. You never know when something big will happen!

B. Write complete sentences to answer these questions about "Volcano!"

1. What does an **active** **volcano** do?

_____

_____

_____

_____

_____

_____

2. What are some reasons that a **volcano** is **dangerous**?

_____

_____

_____

_____

_____

_____

_____

Vocabulary Study

Use Word Parts

▶ Follow the steps below to figure out the meaning of each underlined word.

1. Break down the word into meaningful parts.
2. Think about the meaning of each part.
3. Put the meanings together to define the whole word.
4. Write an explanation of how you defined each word.

1. We put the flag on the <u>flagpole</u> in front of our school. _____

   Explanation: _____

2. I stood under the <u>waterfall</u> and got wet. _____

   Explanation: _____

3. As the ship sank, people climbed into <u>lifeboats</u>. _____

   Explanation: _____

4. The <u>sunlit</u> forest was very pretty. _____

   Explanation: _____

5. The <u>wastebasket</u> was full of trash. _____

   Explanation: _____

6. I like to watch the fish swim in the <u>fishbowl</u>. _____

   Explanation: _____

7. My father stopped the car at the <u>stoplight</u>. _____

   Explanation: _____

8. Jenny picked a <u>blueberry</u> from the bush and ate it. _____

   Explanation: _____

Academic Vocabulary

Volcano!: Academic Vocabulary Review

Academic Vocabulary

create	narrative
define	report

A. Write the Academic Vocabulary word next to the correct definition.

Definition	Word
1. to make something new	
2. to describe what happens during an event	
3. to tell what something means	
4. something that tells a story	

B. Circle the Academic Vocabulary word that best fits in each sentence.

1. Ana chose to (**report** / **define**) on the causes of volcanoes.

2. Joe wants to (**define** / **create**) a poster that shows the inside of a volcano.

3. For my (**create** / **narrative**) writing topic, I will tell the story of how I broke my arm.

4. Max will use a dictionary to (**define** / **narrative**) the words *crater* and *plume*.

C. Use each Academic Vocabulary word in a sentence.

1. **create** _____

2. **define** _____

3. **narrative** _____

4. **report** _____

Build Background

Critical Viewing Guide

▶ **Take Notes**

A. View the video. Take notes on at least three things that you learned.

_____

_____

_____

_____

_____

_____

_____

▶ **Analyze the Video**

B. Review your notes to help answer these questions.

1. Write two sentences to explain what was in the video.

_____

_____

_____

2. What was the most interesting thing you learned?

_____

_____

_____

3. What did the video show about hurricane damage? What would you try to save if a **force** like Hurricane Katrina struck?

_____

_____

_____

Learn Key Vocabulary

Fleeing Katrina: Key Vocabulary

A. Study each word. Circle a number to rate how well you know it. Then complete the chart.

Rating Scale	**1** I have never seen this word before.	**2** I am not sure of the word's meaning.	**3** I know this word and can teach the word's meaning to someone else.

▲ A **hurricane** can cause people to **evacuate** their homes.

Key Words	Check Understanding	Deepen Understanding
❶ evacuate (i-**va**-kyū-āt) *verb* **Rating:** 1 2 3	☐ to leave or get out ☐ to dig something up	List 3 other words that are related to *evacuate*: _____ _____ _____ _____
❷ fortunate (**for**-chu-nut) *adjective* **Rating:** 1 2 3	☐ similar to a fort or hiding place ☐ lucky	List 3 other words that are related to *fortunate*: _____ _____ _____ _____
❸ future (**fyū**-chur) *noun* **Rating:** 1 2 3	☐ what will happen in the time to come ☐ what has happened already	List 3 other words that are related to *future*: _____ _____ _____ _____
❹ hurricane (**hur**-u-kān) *noun* **Rating:** 1 2 3	☐ a violent shaking of the earth ☐ an ocean storm with strong winds	List 3 other words that are related to *hurricane*: _____ _____ _____ _____

In a **severe** storm, river water can rise and spill over a **levee**, causing a flood. ▶

Key Words	Check Understanding	Deepen Understanding
❺ levee (**le**-vē) *noun* **Rating:** 1 2 3	☐ a large pile of leaves ☐ a structure that keeps a river from flooding	List 3 other words that are related to *levee*: _____ _____ _____ _____ _____
❻ necessity (ni-**se**-su-tē) *noun* **Rating:** 1 2 3	☐ an item that someone needs ☐ an item that can be found in a city	List 3 other words that are related to *necessity*: _____ _____ _____ _____ _____
❼ severe (su-**vear**) *adjective* **Rating:** 1 2 3	☐ very serious or dangerous ☐ funny or joking	List 3 other words that are related to *severe*: _____ _____ _____ _____ _____
❽ untouched (un-**tucht**) *adjective* **Rating:** 1 2 3	☐ not hurt or changed ☐ sad or lonely	List 3 other words that are related to *untouched*: ____ _____ _____ _____ _____

B. Use at least two of the Key Vocabulary words. Write about how you think people can help victims of natural disasters.

_____

_____

_____

Analyze Author's Viewpoint

A. Complete the Attribute Web as you read "Fleeing Katrina."

Acts:	Feels:

Samantha Perez

Other Details:	Says: 1. I don't live anywhere.

Fleeing Katrina

Key Vocabulary

evacuate	levee
fortunate	necessities
future	severe
hurricanes	untouched

A. Read the paragraph.
Write a Key Vocabulary word in each blank.
Reread the paragraph to make sure the words make sense.

Samantha and her family knew that a _____ storm was heading their way. They had

experienced _____ , with their high winds and heavy rainfall. When it was time to leave, or

_____ , they packed the car with _____ . Samantha's home was flooded when

the _____ holding back the water broke. The house was a disaster, but her prom dress was

_____ . Samantha knows she is _____ that no one in her family was injured. She will

help her family rebuild their home and their plans for the _____ .

B. Write complete sentences to answer these questions about "Fleeing Katrina."

1. What would you grab if you suddenly had to **evacuate** your home?

_____

_____

_____

_____

_____

_____

2. What can people who live in coastal areas do to prepare for **hurricanes**?

_____

_____

_____

_____

_____

Vocabulary Study

Use Word Parts

▶ Follow the steps below to figure out the meaning of each word.

Suffix	Meaning
-hood	quality of
-ity	state of
-less	without
-ly	in a certain way
-ness	state of

1. Cover the suffix in each word.
2. Think about the meaning of the base word.
3. Uncover the suffix. Use the chart to help write the meaning of each word.
4. Then write the word in a sentence that shows its meaning.

1. **childhood** _____

   Sentence: _____

2. **closely** _____

   Sentence: _____

3. **harmless** _____

   Sentence: _____

4. **emptiness** _____

   Sentence: _____

5. **creativity** _____

   Sentence: _____

6. **falsely** _____

   Sentence: _____

7. **fearless** _____

   Sentence: _____

8. **silliness** _____

   Sentence: _____

Academic Vocabulary

Academic Vocabulary

define	locate
explanation	narrative

Fleeing Katrina: Academic Vocabulary Review

A. Write a synonym for each Academic Vocabulary word.

Word	Choose from these words:			Synonym
1. **define**	explain	study	understand	
2. **locate**	lose	look	find	
3. **narrative**	weak	telling	clear	
4. **explanation**	reason	problem	compare	

B. Complete each sentence with an Academic Vocabulary word.

1. Through _____ writing, people tell amazing stories about surviving storms.

2. Rick looks at a map to _____ the path of the storm.

3. Ms. Vasquez asked us to find the meaning of *hurricane* in a dictionary and _____ it in our own words.

4. This article gives a good _____ for how to prepare for a hurricane.

C. Use at least two Academic Vocabulary words. Write about a day at school.

_____

_____

_____

_____

_____

Build Background

Critical Viewing Guide

▶ Take Notes

A. View the images. Take notes on at least three things that you learned.

_____

_____

_____

_____

_____

_____

_____

▶ Analyze the Images

B. Review your notes to help answer these questions.

1. Write two sentences to explain what was in the images.

_____

_____

_____

2. What was the most interesting thing you learned?

_____

_____

_____

3. What did the images show about the power of an earthquake? Write about why it is important to prepare for a **force** of nature.

_____

_____

_____

Learn Key Vocabulary

Name _____

Earthquake: Key Vocabulary

A. Study each word. Circle a number to rate how well you know it. Then complete the chart.

Rating Scale	**1** I have never seen this word before.	**2** I am not sure of the word's meaning.	**3** I know this word and can teach the word's meaning to someone else.

A severe storm or an **earthquake** can cause houses or other structures to **collapse**. ▶

Key Words	Check Understanding	Deepen Understanding
❶ carefully (**kair**-foo-lē) *adverb* Rating: 1 2 3	If something is delicate, you should handle it **carefully**. Yes No	When is it important to do something carefully? _____ _____ _____ _____
❷ collapse (ku-**laps**) *verb* Rating: 1 2 3	It is safe to be near a building when it **collapses**. Yes No	When have you seen a building that you thought might collapse? Describe the building. _____ _____ _____ _____
❸ confused (kun-**fyūzd**) *adjective* Rating: 1 2 3	If you are **confused** by a question, you will be able to answer it easily. Yes No	Describe something that confused you. _____ _____ _____ _____
❹ earthquake (**urth**-kwāk) *noun* Rating: 1 2 3	An **earthquake** can damage roads and buildings. Yes No	What do you think it feels like to be in an earthquake? _____ _____ _____ _____

Key Vocabulary, continued

A natural disaster can leave people **confused**, **frightened**, and without **shelter**. ▶

Key Words	Check Understanding	Deepen Understanding
❺ equipment (i-**kwip**-munt) *noun* Rating: 1 2 3	Workers need the correct **equipment** to rebuild a house. Yes No	What kind of equipment do you need for one of your hobbies or activities? _____ _____ _____ _____
❻ frightened (**frī**-tund) *adjective* Rating: 1 2 3	It is important to be brave when you are **frightened**. Yes No	If you were frightened, what might you say? _____ _____ _____ _____
❼ prepare (pri-**pair**) *verb* Rating: 1 2 3	A good way to **prepare** for a math test is to go to the movies with friends. Yes No	Describe how you prepare for the first day of school. _____ _____ _____ _____
❽ shelter (**shel**-tur) *noun* Rating: 1 2 3	A house does not provide **shelter** from rain. Yes No	What kind of shelter might an animal find in a forest? _____ _____ _____ _____

B. Use at least two of the Key Vocabulary words. Write about a time when you experienced severe weather.

_____

_____

_____

Analyze Characters' Viewpoints

As you read "Earthquake," complete the Character Description Chart.

Character	What the Character Does	What the Character Says and Thinks
narrator and her family		not hurt, just stunned
PoPo		
MaMa		
Policeman		

Earthquake

Key Vocabulary

carefully	equipment
collapsed	frightened
confused	prepare
earthquake	shelter

A. Read the paragraph.
Write a Key Vocabulary word in each blank.
Reread the paragraph to make sure the words make sense.

On April 18, 1906, a powerful _____ hit San Francisco. People ran into the streets. "What is going on?" they cried, feeling _____ . Buildings fell down, or _____ . People felt scared and _____ by the events. They had to get ready, or _____ , to leave their homes for safer places. Firefighting _____ clogged the streets. People had to move _____ through the rubble, watching every step. It was a relief to reach the tents set up for _____ .

B. Write complete sentences to answer these questions about "Earthquake."

1. What do the family members do to evacuate their home?

_____

_____

_____

_____

_____

_____

2. Where would you go to be safe after an **earthquake**?

_____

_____

_____

_____

_____

_____

Vocabulary Study

Name _____

Use Word Parts

Suffix	Meaning	Changes
-able	able to be	a verb to an adjective
-ness	state of	an adjective to a noun
-ty	state of	an adjective to a noun
-y	having the quality of	a noun into an adjective

▶ Follow the steps below to figure out the meaning of each word.

1. Cover the suffix in each word.
2. Think about the meaning of the base word.
3. Uncover the suffix. Use the chart to help write the meaning of each word.
4. Then write the word in a sentence that shows its meaning.

1. **darkness** _____

   Sentence: _____

2. **certainty** _____

   Sentence: _____

3. **fitness** _____

   Sentence: _____

4. **fruity** _____

   Sentence: _____

5. **reusable** _____

   Sentence: _____

6. **activity** _____

   Sentence: _____

7. **readable** _____

   Sentence: _____

8. **rainy** _____

   Sentence: _____

Academic Vocabulary

Earthquake: Academic Vocabulary Review

A. Use your own words to tell what each Academic Vocabulary word means.

Word	My Definition
1. **define**	
2. **discuss**	
3. **element**	
4. **force**	

B. Rewrite each sentence. Replace the underlined word(s) with an Academic Vocabulary word.

1. One <u>basic part</u> of my report is the list of the biggest earthquakes in ten years.

   _____

2. He gave the class a list of words about earthquakes. We have to <u>tell the meaning of</u> each word.

   _____

3. Today we will <u>talk about</u> the famous San Francisco earthquake.

   _____

4. The <u>power</u> of the storm knocked down trees.

   _____

How Crisis Mapping Saved Lives in Haiti

BY PATRICK MEIER

1   The National Geographic Society has a long history of **crisis mapping** disasters. But what happened in Haiti on January 12, 2010 would forever change the very concept of a crisis map. A devastating **earthquake** struck the country's capital that Tuesday afternoon. I was overwhelmed with emotions when I heard the news just an hour later. Over 100,000 people were feared dead. Some very close friends of mine were doing research in Port-au-Prince at the time and I had no idea whether they had survived the earthquake. So I launched **a live** crisis map of Haiti. But this was an emotional reaction rather than a calculated plan with a detailed strategy. I was in shock and felt the need to do something, anything. It was only after midnight that I finally got an **SMS** reply from my friends. They had narrowly escaped a **collapsing** building. But many, many others were not near as lucky. I continued mapping.

Key Vocabulary
- **earthquake** *n.*, a sudden shaking of the Earth
- **collapse** *v.*, to fall down

In Other Words
crisis mapping making maps of places that need help during
a live an online
SMS short message service; text message

2   This is what the map looked like after midnight on January 13th. What was I mapping exactly? Tweets. I had found a dozen Haitians tweeting live from Port-au-Prince shortly after the earthquake. They were describing scenes of devastation but also hope.

Crisis map
Each dot shows where tweets came from and how many there were.

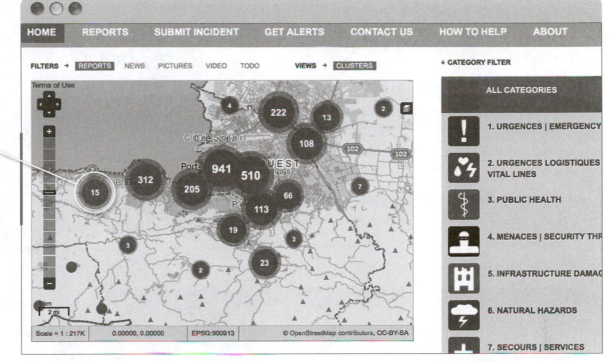

3   I added these Twitter users to my inbox and began mapping the most urgent Tweets (those that had enough geographic information to be mapped). The following night, several friends joined me in the living room of my dorm to help map Haiti's needs.

4   But within a couple days, we couldn't keep up with the vast amount of information being reported via both social media and mainstream media. So I reached out to friends at The Fletcher School (Tufts University) where I was **doing my PhD**. By the end of the week, we had trained over 100 graduate students on how to monitor social and mainstream media for relevant, mappable content. These **"digital humanitarians"** began to manually monitor hundreds and hundreds of online sources for information on Haiti almost **24/7**. The Ushahidi Haiti Crisis Map became a live map with some 2,000 individual reports added during the entire project.

5   Soon enough, we began receiving thousands of text messages. Many volunteers joined the cause after hearing about the need for volunteers via Facebook.

Geography Background
During a disaster people use crisis maps to identify where help is needed. Ushahidi is a nonprofit company that provides software that anyone can use to share information during a crisis.

In Other Words
doing my PhD completing advanced studies
"digital humanitarians" people using technology to help others
24/7 every hour of the day and night

6   On January 19th, just a week after the earthquake, someone from the U.S. Coast Guard emailed us with the following question:

> I am compiling reports from Haiti for the U.S. Coast Guard and Joint Task Force Command Center. Is there someone I can speak with about how better to use the information in Ushahidi?

Several days later, we set up **a dedicated Skype chat with** the Coast Guard to fast-forward the most urgent (and actionable) content that was being added to the Haiti Crisis Map. We were also contacted by an American Search and Rescue team in Port-au-Prince who urgently needed **GPS** coordinators for the locations of trapped individuals.

7   On January 22nd, the U.S. Marine Corps got in touch with us via email.

8   > I am with the U.S. Marine Corps. I am stateside assisting the 22 MEU [Marine Expeditionary Unit] coming off the U.S.S. Bataan [on the Haitian Coast]. We want to use your data to bring aid to the people of Haiti right now. The **USMC** is focusing on Leogane, Grand Goave, and Petit Goave. Is there a way to import your data into **Google Earth or GIS**? We want to make this work for the people of Haiti . . . please let me know **ASAP**!

Haitians unload water from a U.S. military helicopter on January 21, 2010 after the earthquake.

In Other Words
a dedicated Skype chat with
  an online video chat only for
GPS global mapping
USMC United States Marine Corps
Google Earth or GIS online
  mapping services
ASAP as soon as possible

9 Five days later, the same contact from the U.S. Marine Corps shared the following by email (which we got permission to make public):

10 I can not overemphasize to you what the work of the Ushahidi/Haiti has provided. It is saving lives every day. I wish I had time to **document to you** every example, but there are too many and our operation is moving too fast. Here is one from the 22 MEU: 'We had data on an area outside of Grand Goave needing help. Today, we sent an assessment team out there to validate their needs and everything checked out. While the team was out there, they found two old women and a young girl with serious injuries from the earthquake; one of the women had critical respiratory issues. They were **evacuated**.'

11 Your site saved these people's lives. I say with confidence that there are 100s of these kinds of stories. The Marine Corps is using your project every second of the day to get aid and assistance to the people that need it most. We did have a **tech barrier** that we had to surmount. The Marines downrange have Google Earth and your site does not work on the ship for them. So, I had Georgia Tech create a bridge from your site to Google Earth.

12 But it is YOUR data and YOUR work that is putting aid and assistance directly on the target and saving lives. Our big gap right now is locating **NGOs** and where they are working. Your site is helping with that. Keep up the good work!! You are making the biggest difference of anything I have seen out there in the open source world.

13 These incredible efforts following the Haiti earthquake demonstrated a huge potential for the future of humanitarian response. Student volunteers in Boston working online with the **Diaspora** using free mapping technology from Africa could help save lives in another country thousands of miles away without ever setting foot in said country. In time, these reactive and organic volunteer-driven efforts in Haiti, and those that followed that same year in Chile, Pakistan, and Russia, led to the launch of the award-winning Standby Volunteer Task Force (SBTF), a global network of 850+ volunteers in more than 80 countries around the world who use their live mapping skills to support humanitarian [and] human rights development and media organizations.

Key Vocabulary
- **evacuate** *v.*, to leave, to get out

In Other Words
document to you provide proof of
tech barrier problem with technology
NGOs Non-Governmental
Organizations that provide assistance
Diaspora scattering of people

▶ Read for Understanding

A. What kind of text is this? How do you know?

_____

_____

_____

B. Write a sentence that tells the topic of the selection.

_____

_____

▶ Reread and Summarize

C. On **Practice Book** pages 98–101, circle the 3–5 most important words in each section. Make notes about why you chose each word. Why is the word important in the section?

1. Section 1: (paragraphs 1–5)

_____

_____

2. Section 2: (paragraphs 6–8)

_____

_____

3. Section 3: (paragraphs 9–12)

_____

_____

4. Section 4: (paragraph 13)

_____

_____

D. Use your topic sentence from above and your notes to write a summary of the selection.

_____

_____

_____

⬤ Reread and Analyze

E. Analyze how the author conveys viewpoint by using phrases like "I thought" or "I feel."

1. Reread paragraph 1 on **Practice Book** page 98. What does the author think and feel? What does this convey about the author's viewpoint? Underline words and phrases to support your answers. Use evidence from the text to support your answer.

   _____

   _____

   _____

2. Underline another sentence on **Practice Book** pages 98–99 that shows what the author thinks or feels. Explain how it conveys the author's viewpoint.

   _____

   _____

F. Analyze how the author conveys his viewpoint by his actions, or what he does.

1. Reread paragraph 4 on **Practice Book** page 99. What does the author do? What do these actions convey about the author's viewpoint? Underline the words and phrases that support your answer. Use evidence from the text to support your answer.

   _____

   _____

   _____

2. On **Practice Book** pages 98–99, underline other words and phrases that show actions that convey the author's viewpoint. Explain what the author's viewpoint is.

   _____

   _____

⬤ Reread and Analyze

G. Analyze the viewpoint of the author who wrote the email from the U.S. Marine Corps.

1. Reread the first three sentences in paragraph 10 on **Practice Book** page 101. What does this quotation say to convey viewpoint? Underline words and phrases to support your answers. Use evidence from the text to support your answer.

   _____

   _____

   _____

2. Underline other words and phrases in paragraphs 10–12 on **Practice Book** page 101 that convey the author's viewpoint. Explain what the author's viewpoint is.

   _____

   _____

H. Analyze how the author's word choice conveys viewpoint.

1. Reread the first three sentence in paragraph 13 on **Practice Book** page 101. What words or phrases convey the author's viewpoint? What do these words or phrases tell you about the author's viewpoint? Underline the words and phrases that support your answer. Use evidence from the text to support your answer.

   _____

   _____

   _____

2. On **Practice Book** pages 98–101, underline other words and phrases that convey the author's viewpoint. Explain what the author's viewpoint is.

   _____

   _____

▶ Discuss and Write

I. Synthesize your ideas about the authors' viewpoints.

1. With the class, discuss how the author of the article and the author of the email conveyed their viewpoints. List what the authors said and did as well as examples of their word choices.

_____

_____

_____

2. Choose one of the authors' viewpoints. Write a paragraph about how the author's viewpoint is conveyed. Use the questions below to organize your thoughts.

   • What is the author's viewpoint?

   • What does the author say? Give 2 examples of word choice that conveys viewpoint.

   • What does the author think and feel? Give 2 examples.

   • What does the author do? Give 2 examples.

_____

_____

_____

_____

_____

▶ Connect with

J. Discuss the Guiding Question: How should people deal with the forces of nature?

1. How can mapping technology help people deal with and recover from earthquakes?

_____

2. In what other situations can this technology be used to help people?

_____

_____

Unit 3 Review

Name _____

Academic Vocabulary Review

Academic Vocabulary

create	element	locate
define	explanation	narrative
discuss	force	report

A. Circle the best Academic Vocabulary words to complete the paragraph.

> We need to (**discuss / create**) the travel plans we made for tomorrow. The weather (**report / element**) on television explained that heavy rain will fall. The explanation for the weather is a hurricane to the south. The report made it clear that the rain will last all day. The bad weather could (**define / create**) problems for drivers. Do you think we should change our plans?

B. Use your own words to tell what each Academic Vocabulary word means. Then write a synonym.

Word	My Definition	Synonym
1. **create**		
2. **element**		
3. **define**		
4. **locate**		

C. Complete each sentence.

1. To **define** a word you don't know, you _____

_____ .

2. At the school meeting, we will **discuss** _____

_____ .

3. When I do **narrative** writing, I like to _____

_____ .

4. The newspaper had an **explanation** of the _____

_____ .

Key Vocabulary Review

A. Read each sentence. Circle the Key Vocabulary word that best fits into each sentence.

1. The strong winds of the (**earthquake** / **hurricane**) damaged many houses.

2. This is one of the only (**untouched** / **active**) forests left in the country.

3. The girl looked for (**shelter** / **surface**) from the rain.

4. The fire alarm sounded a (**necessity** / **warning**) siren.

5. I was (**confused** / **fortunate**) about how to answer the question.

6. He was too (**active** / **frightened**) to go into the dark room alone.

7. The old building may (**evacuate** / **collapse**).

8. The (**levee** / **layer**) will keep the river from flooding.

B. Use your own words to write what each Key Vocabulary word means.
Then write a synonym for each word.

Word	My Definition	Synonym
1. **carefully**		
2. **dangerous**		
3. **erupt**		
4. **evacuate**		
5. **force**		
6. **layer**		
7. **prepare**		
8. **severe**		

Unit 3 Key Vocabulary

active	dangerous	evacuate	future	necessity	surface
carefully	earthquake	force	hurricane	prepare	untouched
collapse	equipment	fortunate	layer	severe	volcano
confused	erupt	frightened	levee	shelter	warning

C. Answer the questions in complete sentences.

1. What do you hope will happen in the **future**?

   _____

   _____

2. What would you do if you saw a **volcano**?

   _____

   _____

3. In your opinion, what is a basic **necessity**?

   _____

   _____

4. What kind of **equipment** do you need to do your favorite activity?

   _____

   _____

5. What do you feel **fortunate** to be able to do?

   _____

   _____

6. Share an example of something that looks different on the **surface** than it is inside.

   _____

   _____

7. What would you do in an **earthquake**?

   _____

   _____

8. What is a good way to stay **active**?

   _____

   _____

Mind Map

Use the mind map to show your ideas about **classic** characters.
As you read the selections in this unit, add new ideas you learn about
classic characters.

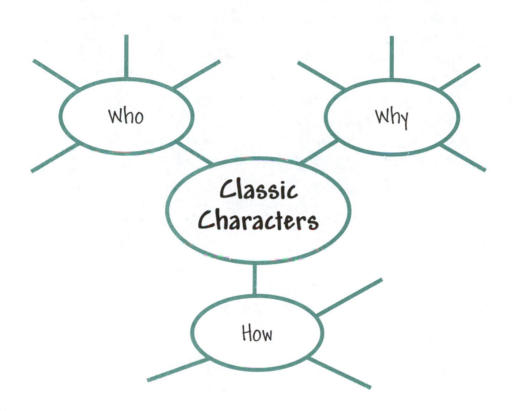

Academic Vocabulary

Think about a **classic** story you have read or heard. What made the story
interesting to you? Use the word **classic** in your answer.

_____

_____

_____

Focus on Reading

Name _____

Elements of Fiction: Plot, Characters, and Setting

Read the passage. Look for clues that show the **elements** of fiction.

> Long ago when dragons roamed the earth, a hunter made a paper dragon for his son. He placed the dragon on a shelf in his home. He told his son that the dragon would protect them. The little boy felt calm each night as he went to sleep. He knew the paper dragon would keep him safe.
>
> The dragon was sad because he sat alone on the shelf. He wanted to go out and see the world. The dragon could not move because he was made of paper.
>
> One day, the hunter's son tied some string to the dragon and took him off the shelf. The son took the dragon outside to fly him like a kite. Suddenly the dragon was high in the sky! He flew up and down and all around.
>
> Then the string broke. The dragon did not fall. He could feel his wings get stronger and stronger. He was flying! Now the dragon could fly around the world. The boy was sad to see the dragon go, but he was happy to see him fly.

Write complete sentences to answer these questions about the passage.

1. What is the setting?

   _____

2. Describe the characters. How do they change in response to story events?

   _____

   _____

3. What are the conflicts?

   _____

4. What is the turning point?

   _____

5. What is the resolution?

   _____

Academic Vocabulary

What **elements** might you use to make a paper dragon?

_____

_____

_____

Focus on Vocabulary

Use Word Parts

Prefix	Meaning	Example
dis-	opposite	disappear
im-	not	improper
over-	too much	overreact
re-	again	redo
un-	not	untrue

▶ Read the passages. Follow these steps.

1. Look at the surrounding words for clues to the new word's meaning.
2. Break the word into parts. **Identify** word parts you know.
3. Think about the meaning of each word part. Use a dictionary if you need to.
4. Put the meanings of the word parts together to understand the whole word. Check that the meaning makes sense in the passage.

A. Follow the directions above. Write the meaning of each underlined word.

> Julio was <u>unhappy</u>. He wanted to stay up late and watch a scary movie on TV. His mother <u>disagreed</u>. She said, "It will be <u>impossible</u> for you to get up for school tomorrow if you stay up late!" Julio stomped off to his room, but then he <u>reappeared</u> with a calendar. "Tomorrow is Saturday, Mama," he said. Julio's mother smiled. "We can watch together," she said.

unhappy _____

disagreed _____

impossible _____

reappeared _____

B. Follow the directions above. Read the passage. Write the meaning of each underlined word.

> Many wonderful stories have been written about Nessie, the monster of Loch Ness. People who think she is a real monster love to read these stories over and over. Other people think Nessie is the product of <u>overactive</u> imaginations. They are <u>dissatisfied</u> when they visit Loch Ness but never see Nessie.

overactive _____

dissatisfied _____

Academic Vocabulary

A monster would be easy to **identify** because_____

_____

_____ .

Build Background

Critical Viewing Guide

▶ **Take Notes**

A. View the video. Take notes on at least three things that you learned.

_____

_____

_____

_____

_____

_____

_____

_____

_____

▶ **Analyze the Video**

B. Review your notes to help answer these questions.

1. Write two sentences to explain what was in the video.

_____

_____

_____

2. What was the most interesting thing you learned?

_____

_____

_____

3. What did the video tell about **classic** characters? Describe your favorite **classic** character from the video.

_____

_____

_____

_____

Learn Key Vocabulary

Frankenstein: Key Vocabulary

A. Study each word. Circle a number to rate how well you know it. Then complete the chart.

Rating Scale	**1** I have never seen this word before.	**2** I am not sure of the word's meaning.	**3** I know this word and can teach the word's meaning to someone else.

▲ This **creature** looks like an **evil** monster from a movie. It is really a giant squid **scientists** caught in the ocean.

Key Words	Check Understanding	Deepen Understanding
❶ **create** (krē-āt) *verb* Rating: 1 2 3	You can use clay to **create** a sculpture. Yes No	When I want to create art, I _____ _____ _____ _____ _____ .
❷ **creature** (krē-chur) *noun* Rating: 1 2 3	A dragon is an imaginary **creature**. Yes No	At the zoo, you can see creatures such as _____ _____ _____ _____ _____ .
❸ **destroy** (di-stroi) *verb* Rating: 1 2 3	If a volcano erupts, it can **destroy** a village. Yes No	It is wrong to destroy another person's work because _____ _____ _____ _____ .
❹ **evil** (ē-vul) *adjective* Rating: 1 2 3	An **evil** person helps others. Yes No	I can tell when a character in a story is evil because _____ _____ _____ _____ .

Name _____

Did You Know?

Benjamin Franklin was a **scientist** who was curious about electricity and lightning. He performed an **experiment** when he flew his kite in a thunderstorm.

Key Words	Check Understanding	Deepen Understanding
❺ experiment (ik-**spair**-u-munt) *noun* **Rating:** 1 2 3	It is important to follow directions when you perform an **experiment**. Yes No	A scientist performs an experiment when _____ _____ _____ _____ _____ .
❻ hideous (**hi**-dē-us) *adjective* **Rating:** 1 2 3	A **hideous** picture might scare somebody. Yes No	You might wear a hideous mask if _____ _____ _____ _____ _____ .
❼ lonely (**lōn**-lē) *adjective* **Rating:** 1 2 3	When people are **lonely**, they usually feel happy. Yes No	When I am lonely, I _____ _____ _____ _____ _____ .
❽ scientist (**sī**-un-tist) *noun* **Rating:** 1 2 3	A **scientist** might use a microscope. Yes No	Scientists are important because _____ _____ _____ _____ _____ .

B. Use at least two Key Vocabulary words. Write about a time when you felt afraid.

_____

_____

_____

Analyze Character Development

Use a Beginning-Middle-End Chart to tell how Dr. Frankenstein changes as the plot unfolds. List examples to show how story elements cause him to change.

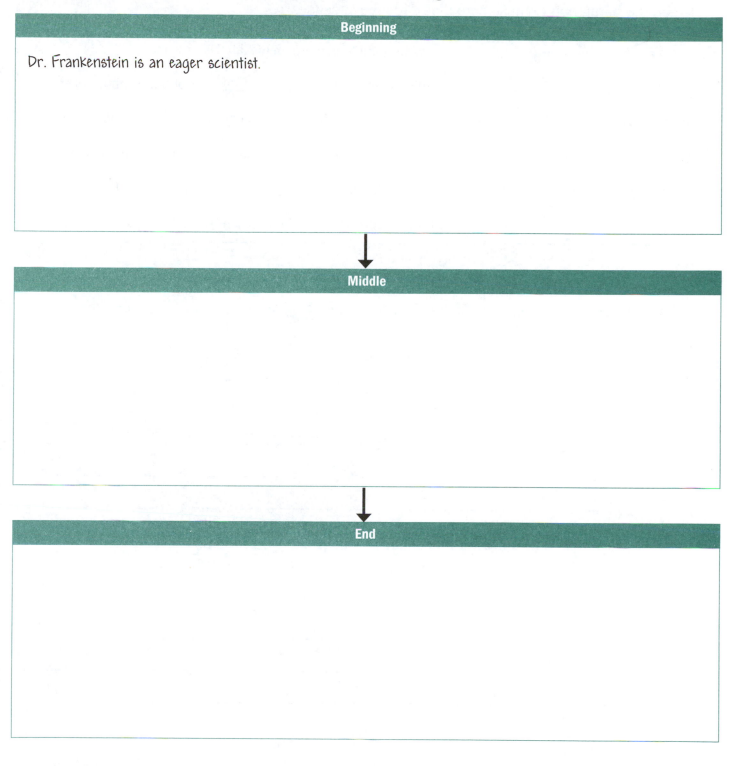

Beginning

Dr. Frankenstein is an eager scientist.

↓

Middle

↓

End

Selection Review

Frankenstein

A. Read the paragraph.
Write a Key Vocabulary word in each blank.
Reread the paragraph to make sure the words make sense.

Victor Frankenstein was a _____ who spent long hours in his lab. During one _____ ,

he _____ something shocking. Frankenstein made a _____ out of bones and body parts

from graveyards. The monster was so _____ that Frankenstein could not stand to look at him.

The monster felt sad and _____ because he did not have any friends. Frankenstein made a wife

for the monster, but he was too frightened to bring her to life. He _____ her instead.

The _____ monster was so angry that he killed Frankenstein's family.

B. Write complete sentences to answer these questions about "Frankenstein."

1. Why did Victor Frankenstein think the **creature** was "**evil**"?

_____

_____

_____

_____

_____

_____

2. The passage tells how the **creature** and his feelings change over time.
Describe a time when your feelings changed.

_____

_____

_____

_____

_____

_____

Vocabulary Study

Use Word Parts

Prefix	Meaning	Example	Word Meaning
in-	not	inactive	not active
de-	do the opposite	defrost	to take the frost off something
bi-	two	bicolored	two-colored

▶ Follow the steps below to figure out the meaning of each word.

1. Look at the chart. Locate the meaning of the prefix.
2. If you don't know the base word, look it up in a dictionary.
3. Put the meanings of the word parts together. Write a definition.
4. Then complete the sentence.

1. **deconstruct** _____

   A person might have to <u>deconstruct</u> a table because _____ .

2. **incomplete** _____

   My work would be <u>incomplete</u> if _____ .

3. **deform** _____

   A strong wind can <u>deform</u> _____ .

4. **inactive** _____

   A student might be <u>inactive</u> in gym class if _____ .

5. **bilingual** _____

   A <u>bilingual</u> person can help someone _____ .

6. **incapable** _____

   If I am <u>incapable</u> of lifting something heavy, I _____ .

7. **decompose** _____

   Plants <u>decompose</u> after _____ .

8. **indirect** _____

   An <u>indirect</u> route takes longer because _____ .

Academic Vocabulary

Name _____

Frankenstein: Academic Vocabulary Review

A. Write the word or phrase that has the same meaning as the Academic Vocabulary word.

Word	Choose from these words:			Synonym
1. **classic**	arrange	old but good	new time	
2. **element**	piece	entire	idea	
3. **identify**	allow	forget	recognize	
4. **locate**	point	find	release	
5. **theme**	reason	details	message	

B. Write an Academic Vocabulary word to complete each sentence.

1. An _____ is a basic part of a whole.

2. If you find something that is lost, you _____ it.

3. If something is _____ , it is old but good.

4. When you find out what something is, you _____ it.

5. The main message of a story is its _____.

C. Use two Academic Vocabulary words in a sentence.

_____

_____

_____

Critical Viewing Guide

▶ **Take Notes**

A. View the video. Take notes on at least three things that you learned.

_____

_____

_____

_____

_____

_____

_____

▶ **Analyze the Video**

B. Review your notes to help answer these questions.

1. Write two sentences to explain what was in the video.

_____

_____

_____

2. What was the most interesting thing you learned?

_____

_____

_____

3. Explain why **classic** horror characters have changed through the years.

_____

_____

_____

_____

Learn Key Vocabulary

Name _____

Film Fright: Key Vocabulary

A. Study each word. Circle a number to rate how well you know it. Then complete the chart.

Rating Scale	**1** I have never seen this word before.	**2** I am not sure of the word's meaning.	**3** I know this word and can teach the word's meaning to someone else.

▲ **Classic** horror **characters** such as Frankenstein's Monster and the Wolf Man have brought **terror** and fun to movie screens for years.

Key Words	Check Understanding	Deepen Understanding
❶ actor (**ak**-tur) *noun* **Rating:** 1 2 3	☐ a person who works in an emergency room ☐ a person who acts in a movie or play	List other words that describe an *actor*: _____ _____ _____ _____
❷ character (**kair**-ik-tur) *noun* **Rating:** 1 2 3	☐ someone who lives next door ☐ someone in a story	List other words that describe a *character*: _____ _____ _____ _____
❸ classic (**kla**-sik) *adjective* **Rating:** 1 2 3	☐ something that is old and broken ☐ something that is old but good	List other words that describe *classic*: _____ _____ _____ _____
❹ fascinated (**fa**-su-nā-tud) *adjective* **Rating:** 1 2 3	☐ very interested ☐ scared	List other words that describe *fascinated*: _____ _____ _____ _____

Name _____

A **successful** scary movie makes the audience feel frightened and **fascinated**. ▶

Key Words	Check Understanding	Deepen Understanding
❺ original (u-**rij**-u-nul) *adjective* **Rating:** 1 2 3	☐ one of many ☐ the first of its kind	List other words that describe *original*: _____ _____ _____ _____ _____
❻ process (**prah**-ses) *noun* **Rating:** 1 2 3	☐ a procedure followed to get a certain result ☐ someone who does something for a job	List other words that describe *process*: _____ _____ _____ _____ _____
❼ successful (suk-**ses**-ful) *adjective* **Rating:** 1 2 3	☐ difficult or stressful ☐ having a good result	List other words that describe *successful*: _____ _____ _____ _____ _____
❽ terror (**tair**-ur) *noun* **Rating:** 1 2 3	☐ extreme fear ☐ a calm feeling	List other words that describe *terror*: _____ _____ _____ _____ _____

B. Use one of the Key Vocabulary words to write about a movie or story that frightened you.

_____

_____

_____

Prepare to Read

Name _____

Analyze Media

A. Use your Critical Viewing Guide from the video "Meet Movie Monsters" and what you read in "Film Fright" to complete the Compare Media Chart.

"Meet Movie Monsters"
Monster movies are the most popular horror film.

"Film Fright"
Dracula and Frankenstein were two of the most successful horror movies of the time.

What I Now Understand About Monster Movies
Monster movies are popular because they were so successful early on.

B. On a piece of paper, write a paragraph to explain what you now understand about monster movies. Use examples from the video and selection. How did viewing and reading about monster movies develop your understanding of the topic?

Selection Review

Film Fright

Key Vocabulary

actor	original
character	process
classic	successful
fascinate	terror

A. Read the paragraph.
Write a Key Vocabulary word in each blank.
Reread the paragraph to make sure the words make sense.

Many _____ movies are remade. The _____ versions are great, but modern special effects make them even better. It is difficult to create a _____ horror film. An _____ can spend hours putting on makeup so his _____ looks real. The _____ takes a long time. Directors also use camera tricks to _____ audiences. They want everyone who sees their movies to feel shock, fear, and _____ .

B. Write complete sentences to answer these questions about "Film Fright."

1. What do you think would be the hardest part of being an **actor** in a monster movie?

_____

_____

_____

_____

_____

_____

_____

2. What **classic** movie monster is most **fascinating** to you, and why?

_____

_____

_____

_____

_____

_____

_____

Vocabulary Study

Name _____

Root	Origin	Meaning
dict	Latin	tell
gram	Greek	write
scrib	Latin	write
sect	Latin	cut
tele	Greek	far

Use Latin and Greek Roots

▶ Follow the steps below to figure out the meaning of each word.

1. Define each word.
2. Use the chart to the right and a dictionary if you need to.
3. Then answer each question with a complete sentence.

1. **dictate** _____

Why did the teacher <u>dictate</u> the assignment?

_____

2. **telephone** _____

When is a <u>telephone</u> useful?

_____

3. **cardiogram** _____

Why would someone need a <u>cardiogram</u>?

_____

4. **telescope** _____

What could you see through a <u>telescope</u>?

_____

5. **diagram** _____

What might a <u>diagram</u> of a human body include?

_____

6. **dissect** _____

What tool do you need to <u>dissect</u> a watermelon?

_____

7. **describe** _____

How would you <u>describe</u> your school?

_____

Name _____

Analyze Rhythm in Poetry

A. Read the poem aloud. Listen for the rhythm in the poem.

> **Monster Music**
> The mummy played the violin,
> Count Dracula played the flute.
> Frankenstein played the clarinet,
> while wearing a green-striped suit.
>
> The werewolf banged on the drums with sticks,
> King Kong strummed the guitar.
> Bigfoot found a wooden spoon
> and made music on an old jar.

B. With a partner, read the poem again. Clap out the rhythm. Locate each strong beat.

1. What is the poem about?

_____

_____

2. What is the mood of the poem?

_____

_____

3. How does the rhythm add to the mood of the poem?

_____

_____

C. Write a short poem. Read the poem aloud. Clap out the rhythm, and locate each strong beat. What is the poem about?

_____

_____

_____

_____

_____

_____

Academic Vocabulary

Name _____

Film Fright: Academic Vocabulary Review

A. Write the Academic Vocabulary word next to the correct definition.

Definition	Academic Vocabulary Word
1. to find something	
2. to find out what something is or to show what it is	
3. something that is old but good	
4. something that is part of a category of related things	
5. to think about how two things are connected	

B. Read each pair of statements. Underline the statement that is true or correct.

1. a. You can **identify** an actor if you know his or her face.

   b. If you **identify** an actor, it means he or she is funny.

2. a. Only a few people like **classic** films.

   b. **Classic** films are films that have been popular for a long time.

3. a. To **relate** a book to a movie, you look for ways they are different.

   b. To **relate** a book to a movie, you think about ways they are alike.

4. a. A map can help you **locate** places you want to visit.

   b. If you **locate** a book, you think about the characters in the story.

5. a. Horror films are **specific** movies about monsters and other scary things.

   b. If you want to see a **specific** kind of movie, you want to see any movie.

Critical Viewing Guide

▶ Take Notes

A. View the images. Take notes on at least three things that you learned.

_____

_____

_____

_____

_____

_____

_____

▶ Analyze the Images

B. Review your notes to help answer these questions.

1. Write two sentences to explain what was in the images.

_____

_____

_____

2. What was the most interesting thing you learned?

_____

_____

_____

3. Why do you think people enjoy **classic** plays?

_____

_____

_____

_____

Learn Key Vocabulary

Name _____

Mister Monster: Key Vocabulary

A. Study each word. Circle a number to rate how well you know it. Then complete the chart.

Rating Scale	**1** I have never seen this word before.	**2** I am not sure of the word's meaning.	**3** I know this word and can teach the word's meaning to someone else.

▲ A great play will leave the **audience** feeling **amazed**.

Key Words	Check Understanding	Deepen Understanding
❶ amazed (u-**māzd**) *adjective* **Rating:** 1 2 3	Circle the synonym for **amazed**. **terrified** **surprised**	I was amazed when _____ _____ _____ _____ _____ .
❷ apply (u-**plī**) *verb* **Rating:** 1 2 3	Circle the synonym for **apply**. **refuse** **request**	If I apply for a job, I need to talk about my skills, such as _____ _____ _____ _____ .
❸ audience (**aw**-dē-unts) *noun* **Rating:** 1 2 3	Circle the synonym for **audience**. **viewers** **performers**	I would like to be in the audience for _____ _____ _____ _____ _____ .
❹ commercial (ku-**mur**-shul) *noun* **Rating:** 1 2 3	Circle the synonym for **commercial**. **advertisement** **product**	In my opinion, a commercial should _____ _____ _____ _____ _____ .

Name _____

Your **response** to a play may depend on the actors, but many important things happen **offstage.** ▶

Key Words	Check Understanding	Deepen Understanding
❺ **disappear** (dis-u-**pear**) *verb* **Rating:** 1 2 3	Circle the synonym for **disappear**. vanish perform	I saw something disappear when _____ _____ _____ _____ _____ .
❻ **mascot** (**mas**-kot) *noun* **Rating:** 1 2 3	Circle the synonym for **mascot**. character coach	A team's mascot should _____ _____ _____ _____ _____ .
❼ **offstage** (awf-**stāj**) *adverb* **Rating:** 1 2 3	Circle the synonym for **offstage**. hidden displayed	When they are offstage, the actors _____ _____ _____ _____ _____ .
❽ **response** (ri-**sponts**) *noun* **Rating:** 1 2 3	Circle the synonym for **response**. silence reply	If an audience enjoys a performance, their response should be _____ _____ _____ _____ .

B. Use one of the Key Vocabulary words to write about a time when you performed for an audience.

_____

_____

_____

Analyze Character and Plot

A. As you read the "Mister Monster," complete the Plot Diagram.

Characters: Ms. Rosario _____

Setting: _____

Turning point: _____

_____

Event: _____

_____

Event: _____

_____

Event: _____

_____

Event: _____

_____

Resolution: _____

_____

Conflict: _____

_____

B. How does Ms. Rosario change as the plot moves toward a resolution?

_____

_____

Selection Review

Mister Monster

A. Read the paragraph.
Write a Key Vocabulary word in each blank.
Reread the paragraph to make sure the words make sense.

Dear Dr. Frankenstein,

I _____ for a job to act in a television _____ . I was so nervous! Ygor went onto

the stage first, as I waited _____ to try out for the part. Guess what? I got the job! The product

is a kitchen cleaner. I get to say, "With one look at me, your grease will _____ forever." My boss

is _____ by the _____ from viewers. The _____ loves me! They even want to

make me the company _____ . Who ever thought a monster would represent a kitchen cleaner?

Your monster, Frankie

B. Write complete sentences to answer these questions about "Mister Monster."

1. How might Dr. Frankenstein feel about Mister Monster's movie offers?

_____

_____

_____

_____

_____

2. If you could be a team **mascot** , which team would you choose? Why?

_____

_____

_____

_____

_____

_____

Vocabulary Study

Name _____

Use Word Parts

Prefix	Meaning	Example	Word Meaning
im-	not	impatiently	not patiently
mis-	wrongly	mistakenly	done wrongly
over-	a lot or too much	overjoyed	having a lot of joy

▶ Follow the steps for each item below.

1. Underline the prefix in each word.
2. Use the chart and a dictionary if you need to. Define each word part.
3. Put the meanings of the word parts together. Write a definition.
4. Complete the sentence.

1. **oversleep** _____

   If I oversleep on a school day, then _____ .

2. **mislead** _____

   If a road sign misleads me, then _____ .

3. **imperfect** _____

   Even though the king was imperfect, he _____ .

4. **overeat** _____

   When I overeat, _____ .

5. **mistreat** _____

   It is wrong to mistreat _____ .

6. **misunderstand** _____

   If I misunderstand a question, then _____ .

7. **impatient** _____

   Everyone gets impatient when _____ .

8. **overload** _____

   If I overload my backpack, then _____ .

9. **immature** _____

   I tell my brother that he is immature when he _____ .

Academic Vocabulary

Name _____

Mister Monster: Academic Vocabulary Review

A. Use your own words to tell what each Academic Vocabulary word means.

Word	My Definition
1. **classic**	
2. **element**	
3. **identify**	
4. **structure**	
5. **theme**	

B. Answer the questions in complete sentences.

1. We will use a **classic** horror story for our play. Why is a **classic** a good choice?

_____

_____

2. What **elements** of a scary movie make it frightening to you?

_____

3. Think about the **structure** of your day. List the things you do in order.

_____

_____

4. How could you **identify** people in your class who like dogs more than cats?

_____

_____

5. Think of a story you have read. Describe the **theme** of the story.

_____

_____

FROM Frankenstein

BY MARY SHELLEY

1   The **creature** finished speaking, and fixed his looks upon me in expectation of a reply. But I was bewildered, perplexed and unable to collect my thoughts sufficiently to understand the full extent of what he asked of me. He continued—

2   "You must create a female for me, with whom I can live as a real and feeling human being. This you alone can do; and I demand it of you as a right which you must not refuse to grant to me."

3   The latter part of his tale had **rekindled** in me the anger that had died away while he told me about his peaceful life among the cottagers, and, as he said this, I could no longer **suppress** the rage that burned within me.

4   "I do refuse it," I replied; "and no torture you inflict shall ever make me change my mind. You may make me the most miserable of men, but you shall never make me dishonorable in my own eyes. If I were to create another like yourself, together your wickedness might **desolate** the world! Be gone! I have answered you; you may torture me, but I will never do what you ask."

Literature Background

Mary Shelley wrote her novel *Frankenstein* in 1818. A Swiss scientist named Dr. Frankenstein assembles a human being from parts he obtains from dead bodies and brings it back to life by using electricity.

Key Vocabulary
- **creature** *n.*, a living thing

In Other Words
rekindled brought back
suppress stop
desolate destroy; ruin

5   "You are in the wrong," replied the **fiend**; "and, instead of threatening, I am content to reason with you. I am hateful because I am miserable. Does not **all mankind shun** me and hate me? Even you, my creator, would tear me to pieces, and think it a victory; remember that, and tell me why I should feel sorry for man more than he feels sorry for me? You would not call it murder if you could force me beneath the ice into the water below and **destroy** my being, the work of your own hands. Shall I respect man when he despises me? If others were able to live with me in mutual kindness, then, instead of injury, I would **bestow every benefit upon him** with tears of gratitude at his acceptance. But that cannot be; the human senses are impossible barriers to living in this mutual kindness. Yet I will not submit to their hatred and be their slave. I will **revenge my injuries**: if I cannot inspire love, I will cause fear; and chiefly towards you my greatest enemy, because my creator, do I swear everlasting hatred. Be careful: I will work at your destruction, and not stop until I destroy your heart, so that you shall curse the hour of your birth."

Key Vocabulary
- **destroy** v., to take apart, to ruin

In Other Words
fiend monster
all mankind shun everyone ignore
bestow every benefit upon him be a great friend
revenge my injuries hurt those who hurt me

6 A fiendish rage **animated him** as he said this; his face was wrinkled into contortions too horrible for human eyes to **behold**; but presently he calmed himself and proceeded—

7 "I intended to reason. These human feelings cause me great harm, and you don't realize that you have caused them. If any human being felt emotions of kindness towards me, I should return them an hundred and an hundred **fold**; for that one human being's sake, I would make peace with the whole kind! But I now indulge in dreams of happiness that can never come true. What I ask of you is reasonable and moderate; I demand a creature of another sex, as **hideous** as myself; this satisfaction is small, but it is all

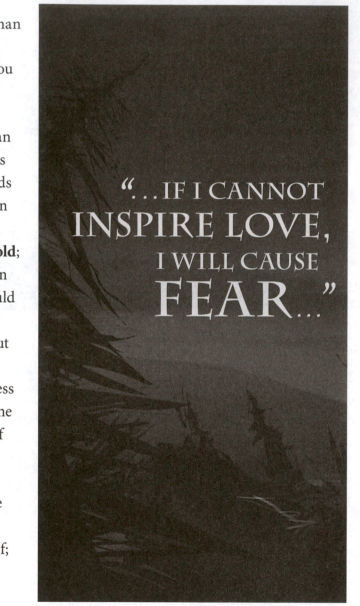

"...IF I CANNOT INSPIRE LOVE, I WILL CAUSE FEAR..."

that I can receive, and it shall content me. It is true we shall be monsters, cut off from all the world; but on that account we shall be more attached to one another. Our lives will not be happy, but they will be harmless, and free from the misery I now feel. Oh! my creator, make me happy; let me feel gratitude towards you for this one benefit! Let me see that I can share these feelings with some existing thing; do not deny me my request!"

8 I was moved. I shuddered when I thought of the possible **consequences** of granting his request; but I felt that there was some justice in his argument. His tale, and the feelings he now expressed, proved him to be a creature **of fine sensations**; and did I not as his maker owe him all the portion of happiness that it was in my power to give to him?

Key Vocabulary
● **hideous** adj., very ugly

In Other Words
animated him gave him more energy
behold look at
fold times
consequences results
of fine sensations who had feelings

Read for Understanding

A. From what kind of text is this passage taken? How do you know?

_____

_____

B. Write a sentence that tells the topic of the selection.

_____

_____

Reread and Summarize

C. On **Practice Book** pages 134–137, circle the 3–5 most important words in each section. Make notes about why you chose each word. Why is the word important in the section?

1. Section 1: (paragraphs 1–4)

_____

_____

2. Section 2: (paragraph 5)

_____

_____

3. Section 3: (paragraphs 6–7)

_____

_____

4. Section 4: (paragraph 8)

_____

_____

D. Use your topic sentence from above and your notes to write a summary of the selection.

_____

_____

_____

▶ Reread and Analyze

E. Analyze how the writer develops character by looking at how the characters think, act, and feel.

1. Reread paragraphs 3–4 on **Practice Book** page 134. How does the creator feel? What does he think about the creature's request? Underline words and phrases to support your answers. Explain how the text evidence supports your answer.

_____

_____

_____

2. Underline other words and phrases on **Practice Book** pages 134–135 that show what the creator thinks and feels. Explain what this shows about the creator's character.

_____

_____

F. Analyze how the writer describes the characters by showing how they think and act towards other characters.

1. Reread paragraph 5 on **Practice Book** page 135. According to the creature, what does his creator think of him? What does the creature think of his creator? What action is the creature willing to take? Underline the words and phrases that support your answer. Use evidence from the text to support your answer.

_____

_____

_____

2. Underline other words and phrases on **Practice Book** pages 134–135 that show what the creature thinks and feels. Explain what it shows about the creature.

_____

_____

▶ **Reread and Analyze**

G. Analyze how the two characters change the way they think, act, and feel as the plot unfolds.

1. Reread paragraph 8 on **Practice Book** page 136. How has the creator changed the way he thinks and feels about the creature? Underline words and phrases to support your answers. Use evidence from the text to support your answer.

_____

_____

_____

2. Underline other words and phrases on **Practice Book** page 136 that show the creator has changed. Explain what this shows about how the creator has developed.

_____

_____

H. Analyze how the writer uses dialogue to reveal how a character changed.

1. Reread paragraph 7 on **Practice Book** page 136. What does the creature say to his creator? How is this different from what he said to him before? Why do you think he changed? Underline the words and phrases that support your answer. Use evidence from the text to support your answer.

_____

_____

_____

2. On **Practice Book** page 136, underline other words and phrases that reveal changes in the creature. Explain what this shows about how the creature has developed.

_____

_____

▶ Discuss and Write

I. Synthesize your ideas about character.

1. With the class, discuss how the characters changed as the plot unfolded. List the characters' actions, thoughts, and feelings.

_____

_____

_____

2. Choose one of the characters. Write a paragraph about how the character developed throughout the story. Use the questions below to organize your thoughts.

  · What does the character think and feel at the beginning of the story? Give 2 examples.

  · How does he act at the beginning of the story?

  · How does the character feel about the other character in the story? Give an example.

  · How does the character change at the end of the story?

_____

_____

_____

_____

_____

▶ Connect with

J. Discuss the Guiding Question: How can a powerful character inspire a range of reactions?

1. What emotions does the creature inspire in his creator?

_____

_____

2. If you were in the creator's position, how would you feel?

_____

3. How would you react to the creature's request for a companion?

_____

Unit 4 Review

Name _____

Academic Vocabulary Review

Academic Vocabulary

classic	relate
element	specific
identify	structure
locate	theme

A. Circle the Academic Vocabulary word that best fits into each sentence.

1. A poem does not have the same (**structure** / **element**) as a long novel.

2. The play is a (**classic** / **specific**) that has been performed many times.

3. Yooku said the (**theme** / **element**) of the play is "always tell the truth."

4. I could (**relate** / **identify**) each of the actors on stage.

B. Use your own words to define each Academic Vocabulary word. Then write an example for each word.

Word	My Definition	Example
1. **element**		
2. **locate**		
3. **relate**		

C. Answer the questions in complete sentences.

1. Tell three ways the **structure** of a poem is different from a story.

_____

_____

2. What is the **theme** of your favorite book?

_____

_____

3. Think of your two favorite movies. Tell two ways they **relate**.

_____

_____

Name _____

Key Vocabulary Review

A. Read each sentence. Circle the Key Vocabulary word that best fits into each sentence.

1. You can use paint and a paintbrush to (**create** / **destroy**) art.

2. When you (**disappear** / **apply**) for a job, it is a good idea to tell about your skills.

3. The (**character** / **actor**) who played the king was very entertaining.

4. She gave the correct (**response** / **process**) to the teacher's question.

5. (**Experiments** / **Commercials**) may make you want to buy certain products.

6. Before they perform, actors usually prepare (**lonely** / **offstage**).

7. The (**hideous** / **successful**) monster frightened the people.

8. A good (**creature** / **mascot**) helps a crowd cheer for their team.

B. Use your own words to write what each Key Vocabulary word means. Then write a synonym for each word.

Word	My Definition	Synonym
1. **disappear**		
2. **evil**		
3. **amazed**		
4. **classic**		
5. **process**		
6. **terror**		
7. **audience**		
8. **original**		

Unit 4 Key Vocabulary

actor	character	creature	experiment	mascot	response
amazed	classic	destroy	fascinated	offstage	scientist
apply	commercial	disappear	hideous	original	successful
audience	create	evil	lonely	process	terror

C. Answer the questions in complete sentences.

1. Who is your favorite scary movie **creature** ? Why?

   _____

   _____

2. Why is it wrong to **destroy** another person's belongings?

   _____

   _____

3. Why might you perform a science **experiment** ?

   _____

   _____

4. If you were a **scientist** , what would you want to discover?

   _____

   _____

5. What is your favorite kind of **character** in a story?

   _____

   _____

6. What is the last movie you saw that completely **fascinated** you?

   _____

   _____

7. What does it mean to be **successful** ?

   _____

   _____

8. What cheers you up when you are **lonely** ?

   _____

Mind Map

Use the Mind Map to show your ideas about **discovery** . As you read the selections in this unit, add new ideas you learn about **discovery** .

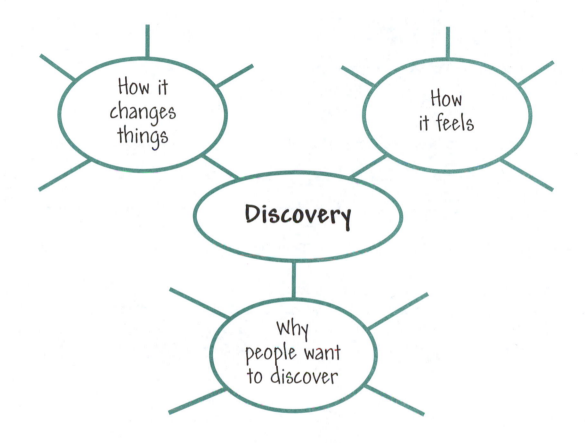

Academic Vocabulary

Think about a **discovery** you want to make. Why is it important to you?
Use the word **discovery** in your answer.

_____

_____

_____

Focus on Reading

Text Structure: Main Idea and Details

A. Read the passage. Underline clues about the theme.

> The Science Fair
> Water-grown plants, salt-water generator,
> Piano-playing robots, solar powered charger.
>
> The sixth grade science fair is this week.
> My perpetual motion machine sprung a leak.
>
> I thought and thought as I stroked my chin.
> Perhaps the yeti I found in my backyard can win?

Is the theme stated in the poem? What parts of the poem give clues about the theme? _____

_____

_____

B. Read the passage. Underline clues about the main idea.

> Students create amazing projects for the science fair at our school. Shauna's science project shows how the Grand Canyon was formed. Minh's project explains why the night sky looks different at different times of the year. Laura's project is my favorite. It shows what type of bubble gum is best for blowing bubbles.

Is the main idea stated? How do you know? _____

_____

_____

Academic Vocabulary

Your teacher has **organized** a science fair. The **theme** is reduce, reuse, recycle. What is your project? Give details to support your main idea.

_____

_____

_____

_____

Focus on Vocabulary

Use Word Parts

Some Word Parts
Prefix: *dis-* means "the opposite of"
Prefix: *un-* means "not"
Suffix: *-ful* means "full of"
Suffix: *-ist* means "one who"

▶ Read the passages. Follow these steps.

1. Look at each underlined word. Cover any prefixes or suffixes.
2. Think about the meaning of the base word.
3. Uncover any prefixes or suffixes and determine their meanings.
4. Put the meanings together to understand the whole word.

A. Follow the directions above. Write the meaning of each underlined word.

> Scientists today can go very deep in the ocean. They discover many strange and unusual life forms. Some creatures have no stomachs or mouths. Others have no eyes. Some fish even glow in the dark! The deep ocean is full of wonderful life forms.

scientists _____

discover _____

unusual _____

wonderful _____

B. Follow the directions above. Write the meaning of each underlined word.

> Scientists often disagree about discoveries. For example, some tree frog specialists think that these colorful frogs sit still to restore energy. Other scientists noticed that these frogs have a special liquid on their skin to keep them cool. They think that the frogs sit still so the liquid doesn't rub off.

disagree _____

specialists _____

colorful _____

Academic Vocabulary

A fish is **similar** to a frog because _____

_____

_____

_____ .

Build Background

Name _____

Critical Viewing Guide

▶ Take Notes

A. View the video. Take notes on at least three things that you learned.

_____

_____

_____

_____

_____

_____

_____

_____

▶ Analyze the Video

B. Review your notes to help answer these questions.

1. Write two sentences to explain what was in the video.

_____

_____

_____

2. What was the most interesting thing you learned?

_____

_____

_____

3. What did the video tell you about **discoveries**? Explain why people take risks to make **discoveries**.

_____

_____

_____

Learn Key Vocabulary

Name _____

Return to *Titanic*: Key Vocabulary

A. Study each word. Circle a number to rate how well you know it. Then complete the chart.

Rating Scale	**1** I have never seen this word before.	**2** I am not sure of the word's meaning.	**3** I know this word and can teach the word's meaning to someone else.

▲ A diver **discovers** the **wreck** of an old ship.

Key Words	Check Understanding	Deepen Understanding
❶ alarm (u-**larm**) *noun* Rating: 1 2 3	An **alarm** should be ignored. Yes No	When does an alarm ring? _____ _____ _____ _____ _____
❷ discover (dis-**ku**-vur) *verb* Rating: 1 2 3	Some scientists **discover** cures for disease. Yes No	What can you discover under a bed? _____ _____ _____ _____ _____
❸ explorer (ik-**splor**-ur) *noun* Rating: 1 2 3	**Explorers** enjoy travel. Yes No	What makes someone a great explorer? _____ _____ _____ _____ _____
❹ famous (fā-mus) *adjective* Rating: 1 2 3	If someone is **famous**, they are well known. Yes No	Would you like to be famous? Tell why. _____ _____ _____ _____ _____

Name _____

Explorers use robots to **search** deep in the **ocean.** ▶

Key Words	Check Understanding	Deepen Understanding
❺ ocean (ō-shun) *noun* **Rating:** 1 2 3	You could easily swim across the **ocean**. **Yes**　　　　**No**	How could you cross the ocean? _____ _____ _____ _____ _____
❻ passenger (pa-sen-jur) *noun* **Rating:** 1 2 3	A **passenger** is the person driving the car. **Yes**　　　　**No**	Share one example of when you have been a passenger. _____ _____ _____ _____
❼ search (surch) *verb, noun* **Rating:** 1 2 3	A person would **search** for a lost wallet. **Yes**　　　　**No**	What tools would you use to search for something underwater? _____ _____ _____ _____
❽ wreck (rek) *noun* **Rating:** 1 2 3	A **wreck** is clean and organized. **Yes**　　　　**No**	What could you find in a shipwreck? _____ _____ _____ _____ _____

B. Use at least two of the Key Vocabulary words. Write about a time you lost something important and had to look for it.

_____

_____

_____

Prepare to Read

Determine Main Idea and Details

A. Complete the Main-Idea and Details Chart as you read "Return to the *Titanic*."

Main Ideas	Details
Titanic was the largest ship in the world.	It was as long as four city blocks.

B. Complete the Main-Idea and Details Chart as you read "Talking with Robert Ballard."

Main Ideas	Details

Return to *Titanic*

Key Vocabulary

alarm	ocean
discovered	passengers
explorer	search
famous	wreck

A. Read the paragraphs.
Write a Key Vocabulary word in each blank.
Reread the paragraphs to make sure the words make sense.

"Return to *Titanic*" is about a _____ ship that sank in the Atlantic _____ in 1912.

It is a very sad story. *Titanic* crashed into an iceberg during the night. A sailor tried to set off an

_____ in time for the ship to turn, but it was too late. Most of the _____ on the ship did

not survive. There were not enough lifeboats to save them.

Titanic sat at the bottom of the ocean for 71 years. No one knew exactly where it was. Then in 1985,

an _____ named Bob Ballard started to _____ for the _____. He and his team

were successful. They _____ *Titanic*!

B. Write complete sentences to answer these questions about "Return to *Titanic*."

1. Many people said it was impossible to **discover** *Titanic*. How did Bob Ballard do it?

_____

_____

_____

_____

_____

_____

2. Imagine you are exploring *Titanic*. What do you hope to see?

_____

_____

_____

_____

_____

Vocabulary Study

Use Word Parts

Prefix	Meaning
dis-	the opposite of
re-	again
un-	not
Suffix	**Meaning**
-able	having the quality of; can be done
-er, -or	one who
-ful	full of
-ist	one who

▶ Follow the steps below to figure out the meaning of each word.

1. Cover the prefix or suffix.
2. Think about the meaning of the base word.
3. Uncover the prefix or suffix. What does it mean?
4. Put the meanings together. Write the definition.
5. Then complete each sentence.

1. **disadvantage** _____

   Arriving late to class is a disadvantage because _____ .

2. **respectful** _____

   I am always respectful when I _____ .

3. **farmer** _____

   A farmer must know how to _____ .

4. **reelect** _____

   I want to reelect our class president because _____ .

5. **artist** _____

   An artist must be good at _____ .

6. **unsteady** _____

   An unsteady ladder is dangerous because _____ .

7. **director** _____

   The director of the school play was very good at _____ .

8. **dependable** _____

   Dogs are dependable pets because _____ .

9. **useful** _____

   A computer is useful becuase _____ .

Academic Vocabulary

Return to *Titanic*: Academic Vocabulary Review

Academic Vocabulary	
discover	similar
organize	theme

A. Use your own words to tell what each Academic Vocabulary word means.

Word	My Definition
1. **discover**	
2. **organize**	
3. **similar**	
4. **theme**	

B. Rewrite each sentence. Replace the underlined words with an Academic Vocabulary word.

1. Dogs and pigs are <u>alike</u> in many ways.

_____

2. Juanita likes to <u>arrange</u> the markers on her desk in a special order.

_____

3. The <u>main message</u> of the story is friendship.

_____

4. Tyreece likes to <u>find</u> new recipes to cook for his family and friends.

_____

Build Background

Critical Viewing Guide

▶ **Take Notes**

A. View the video. Take notes on at least three things that you learned.

_____

_____

_____

_____

_____

_____

_____

▶ **Analyze the Video**

B. Review your notes to help answer these questions.

1. Write two sentences to explain what was in the video.

_____

_____

_____

2. What was the most interesting thing you learned?

_____

_____

_____

3. How can old stories help you **discover** things about your culture and other cultures, too?

_____

_____

_____

_____

Learn Key Vocabulary

Name _____

The Forgotten Treasure: Key Vocabulary

A. Study each word. Circle a number to rate how well you know it. Then complete the chart.

Rating Scale	**1** I have never seen this word before.	**2** I am not sure of the word's meaning.	**3** I know this word and can teach the word's meaning to someone else.

Scientists find many **beautiful treasures** that help us understand ancient cultures. ▶

Key Words	Check Understanding	Deepen Understanding
❶ beautiful (**byū**-ti-ful) *adjective* **Rating:** 1 2 3	Ancient works of art can be very **beautiful**. Yes　　　No	List other words that describe *beautiful*: _____ _____ _____ _____ _____
❷ forest (**for**-ust) *noun* **Rating:** 1 2 3	There are usually different kinds of trees in a **forest**. Yes　　　No	List other words that describe *forest*: _____ _____ _____ _____ _____
❸ forget (**fur**-get) *verb* **Rating:** 1 2 3	It is a good idea to **forget** to study for a test. Yes　　　No	List other words that describe *forget*: _____ _____ _____ _____ _____
❹ locate (**lō**-kāt) *verb* **Rating:** 1 2 3	It is easy to **locate** something that is buried in the ground. Yes　　　No	List other words that describe *locate*: _____ _____ _____ _____ _____

Name _____

Did You Know?

Skeleton comes from a Greek word that means "dried up."

Key Words	Check Understanding	Deepen Understanding
❺ loss (laws) *noun* Rating: 1 2 3	The **loss** of something important can upset a person. Yes No	List other words that describe *loss:* _____ _____ _____ _____ _____
❻ remember (ri-**mem**-bur) *verb* Rating: 1 2 3	If you **remember** where you put something, you can find it. Yes No	List other words that describe *remember:* _____ _____ _____ _____ _____
❼ skeleton (ske-lu-tun) *noun* Rating: 1 2 3	You might see a **skeleton** in a museum. Yes No	List other words that describe *skeleton:* _____ _____ _____ _____ _____
❽ treasure (tre-zhur) *noun* Rating: 1 2 3	A **treasure** does not have any real value. Yes No	List other words that describe *treasure:* _____ _____ _____ _____ _____

B. Use one of the Key Vocabulary words to write about something that is very valuable to you.

_____

_____

_____

Name _____

Determine Theme

A. Complete the Theme Chart with important details from "The Forgotten Treasure." Write what the details make you think. Use the details and your thoughts to determine a theme for the story.

Clues from the Title:	Clues from the Characters:
"The Forgotten Treasure" makes me think that _____.	
Theme:	
Clues from the Setting:	Clues from the Plot:

B. Complete a Theme Chart for "There Is No Word for Goodbye."

Clues from the Title:	Clues from the Characters:
Theme:	
Clues from the Setting:	Clues from the Plot:

The Forgotten Treasure

Key Vocabulary

beautiful	loss
forest	remember
forget	skeleton
located	treasures

A. Read the paragraph.
Write a Key Vocabulary word in each blank.
Reread the paragraph to make sure the words make sense.

A hunter had four sons that he prized above all else. He called them his _____ . He lived with them and their _____ mother. One day the hunter went into the _____ and did not return. The sons felt great sorrow for their _____ . They said they would always _____ their father. But they soon began to _____ about him until their baby brother reminded them of their father. The sons looked until they _____ their father's bones. When they put the bones together to make a _____ , their father came back to life and gave the youngest son a gift.

B. Write complete sentences to answer these questions about "The Forgotten Treasure."

1. Why do you think the sons **forgot** their father?

_____

_____

_____

_____

_____

_____

2. How do you think the youngest son knew that something was missing?

_____

_____

_____

_____

_____

_____

_____

Vocabulary Study

Use Word Parts

Suffix	Meaning
-er, -or	one who
-ful	full of
-ous	full of, having
-y	like, having that quality

▶ Use the chart to add a suffix to each base word. Write the new word. Then write the new word in a sentence. Remember these spelling rules:

1. If the suffix begins with a consonant, make no change to the base word unless it ends in -y.
2. If the suffix begins with a vowel, you may need to make a change.

1. **wonder** _____

   Sentence: _____

2. **invent** _____

   Sentence: _____

3. **marvel** _____

   Sentence: _____

4. **stick** _____

   Sentence: _____

5. **cloud** _____

   Sentence: _____

6. **hope** _____

   Sentence: _____

7. **punish** _____

   Sentence: _____

8. **joy** _____

   Sentence: _____

9. **teach** _____

   Sentence: _____

Academic Vocabulary

The Forgotten Treasure: Academic Vocabulary Review

A. Write each Academic Vocabulary word next to the correct definition.

1. to put something in writing _____

2. the order in which events happen _____

3. main message of a story _____

B. Circle the word that best fits into each sentence.

1. Like a story, a museum exhibit may have a particular (**sequence / theme**) such as dinosaurs, sharks, or space.

2. In what (**record / sequence**) do you want to go to the exhibits?

3. In a museum, workers are careful to (**record / theme**) dates of objects and other useful details.

C. Use at least two Academic Vocabulary words. Write about a time when you visited a museum. Or, write about a museum you would like to visit.

_____

_____

_____

_____

_____

Build Background

Name _____

Critical Viewing Guide

▶ **Take Notes**

A. View the images. Take notes on at least three things that you learned.

_____

_____

_____

_____

_____

_____

_____

_____

▶ **Analyze the Images**

B. Review your notes to help answer these questions.

1. Write two sentences to explain what was in the images.

_____

_____

_____

2. What was the most interesting thing you learned?

_____

_____

_____

3. What did the images tell you about **discovering** treasures? Describe a treasure you would like to **discover**.

_____

_____

_____

_____

Name _____

Mysteries of the Ancient Past: Key Vocabulary

A. Study each word. Circle a number to rate how well you know it. Then complete the chart.

Rating Scale	**1** I have never seen this word before.	**2** I am not sure of the word's meaning.	**3** I know this word and can teach the word's meaning to someone else.

▲ An **artifact** found underground or in the ocean gives us a **clue** about the past.

Key Words	Check Understanding	Deepen Understanding
❶ ancient (ānt-shunt) *adjective* Rating: 1 2 3	☐ very old ☐ very popular	I would expect an ancient piece of pottery to be _____ _____ _____ _____ .
❷ archaeologist (ar-kē-**ah**-lu-jist) *noun* Rating: 1 2 3	☐ a doctor who treats children ☐ a person who studies things from ancient cultures	An archaeologist would be excited to find _____ _____ _____ _____ .
❸ artifact (**ar**-ti-fakt) *noun* Rating: 1 2 3	☐ a product made yesterday ☐ something that people made or used long ago	Years from now, an artifact that scientists will use to learn about our time might be _____ _____ _____ .
❹ bury (**bair**-ē) *verb* Rating: 1 2 3	☐ to put in the ground and cover with dirt ☐ a kind of fruit	A person might bury treasure because _____ _____ _____ .

Name _____

An **archaeologist** tries to learn about **ancient civilizations**. ▶

Key Words	Check Understanding	Deepen Understanding
❺ civilization (si-vu-lu-**zā**-shun)　*noun* **Rating:**　1　2　3	☐ a culture or society from a certain place and time ☐ a group that builds bridges	A good place to learn about an ancient civilization is ____ _____ _____ _____ _____ .
❻ clue (klü)　*noun* **Rating:**　1　2　3	☐ a sickness like a cold or the flu ☐ something that helps you solve a problem	A clue can be helpful when _____ _____ _____ _____ _____ .
❼ pyramid (**pear**-u-mid)　*noun* **Rating:**　1　2　3	☐ a building with a square base and four triangular sides ☐ a large animal found in Africa	The pyramids are amazing because _____ _____ _____ _____ _____ .
❽ tomb (tüm)　*noun* **Rating:**　1　2　3	☐ a library ☐ a grave	Some things that I would expect to find in an ancient Egyptian tomb are _____ _____ _____ _____ .

B. Use one of the Key Vocabulary words. Write about why you think it would be interesting to study the past.

_____

_____

_____

Determine Main Idea and Details

As you read "Mysteries of the Ancient Past," look for the main idea and details of each section. Complete the Main-Idea Chart. Create a new chart for each section of text.

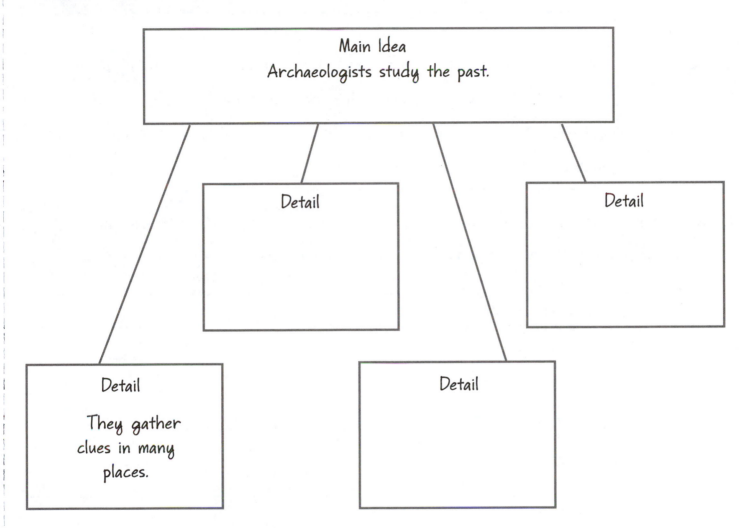

Main Idea
Archaeologists study the past.

Detail

Detail

Detail

Detail
They gather clues in many places.

Mysteries of the Ancient Past

Key Vocabulary

ancient	civilizations
archaeologists	clues
artifacts	pyramids
buried	tombs

A. Read the paragraph.
Write a Key Vocabulary word in each blank.
Reread the paragraph to make sure the words make sense.

Scientists who study old things are called _____ . They gather _____ about the past by looking at objects, or _____ , from long ago. These scientists can tell how people in past _____ lived. They can tell a lot by looking at carvings inside the _____ built in Egypt. For example, items _____ with bodies in _____ show us what life was like in _____ times.

B. Write complete sentences to answer these questions about "Mysteries of the Ancient Past."

1. How do you think Carter felt when he opened King Tut's **tomb**?

_____

_____

_____

_____

2. What can you learn about **ancient** Egyptians by looking at their **artifacts**?

_____

_____

_____

_____

3. What photographs in the selection do you think are the most interesting? Explain.

_____

_____

_____

_____

_____

Vocabulary Study

Use Word Parts

Prefix	Meaning
dis-	opposite
mid-	middle
mis-	wrongly
pre-	before
super-	above

▶ Follow the steps below to complete the activity.

1. Add a prefix from the chart to each base word.
2. Write the new word. Keep the spelling of the prefix and the base word the same.
3. Then write a sentence with the new word.

1. **led** _____

   Sentence: _____

2. **color** _____

   Sentence: _____

3. **summer** _____

   Sentence: _____

4. **connect** _____

   Sentence: _____

5. **human** _____

   Sentence: _____

6. **view** _____

   Sentence: _____

7. **behave** _____

   Sentence: _____

8. **heat** _____

   Sentence: _____

9. **power** _____

   Sentence: _____

Academic Vocabulary

discover	record
fact	sequence
organize	similar

Mysteries of the Ancient Past:
Academic Vocabulary Review

A. Draw a line to match the Academic Vocabulary word with its meaning.

Word	Definition
1. **discover**	almost the same
2. **fact**	to put things in a certain order
3. **organize**	to find out something you did not know before
4. **record**	the order in which events happen
5. **sequence**	to put something in writing
6. **similar**	a piece of information that is true

B. Use each Academic Vocabulary word in a sentence.

1. **discover** _____

_____

2. **fact** _____

_____

3. **organize** _____

_____

4. **record** _____

_____

5. **sequence** _____

_____

6. **similar** _____

_____

The Power of Mysteries

by Alan Lightman

1   I believe in the power of the unknown. I believe that a sense of the unknown **propels us** in all of our creative activities, from science to art.

2   When I was a child, after bedtime I would often get out of my bed in my pajamas, go to the window and stare at the stars. I had so many questions. How far away were those tiny points of light? Did space go on forever and ever, or was there some end to space, some giant edge? And if so, what lay beyond the edge?

3   Another of my childhood questions: Did time go on forever? I looked at pictures of my parents and grandparents and tried to imagine their parents, and so on, back through the generations, back and back through time. Looking out of my bedroom window into the vastness of space, time seemed to stretch forward and backward without end, **engulfing** me, engulfing my parents and great-grandparents, the entire history of earth. Does time go on forever? Or is there some beginning of time? And if so, what came before?

4   When I grew up, I became a professional **astrophysicist**. Although I never answered any of these questions, they continued to challenge me, to haunt me, to drive me in my scientific research, to cause me to live on tuna fish and no sleep for days at a time while I was obsessed with a science problem. These same questions, and questions like them, challenge and haunt the leading scientists of today.

5   Einstein once wrote that "the most **beautiful** experience we can have is the mysterious. It is the fundamental emotion which **stands at the cradle of** true art and true science." What did Einstein mean by "the mysterious?" I don't think he meant that science is full of unpredictable or unknowable or supernatural forces. I think that he meant a sense of awe, a sense that there are things larger than us, that we do not have all the answers at this moment. A sense that we can stand right at the boundary between known and unknown and gaze into that cavern and be exhilarated rather than frightened.

Key Vocabulary
- **beautiful** *adj.*, very pretty; amazing

In Other Words
propels us pushes us forward
engulfing surrounding
astrophysicist person who studies the way objects move in space
stands at the cradle of is the starting point for learning about

Historical Background
Albert Einstein was a famous and award-winning physicist.

6   Scientists are happy, of course, when they find answers to questions. But scientists are also happy when they become stuck, when they **discover** interesting questions that they cannot answer. Because that is when their imaginations and creativity are **set on fire**. That is when the greatest progress occurs.

7   One of the **Holy Grails** in physics is to find the so-called "theory of everything," the final theory that will **encompass all the fundamental laws of nature**. I, for one, hope that we never find that final theory. I hope that there are always things that we don't know—about the physical world as well as about ourselves. I believe in the creative power of the unknown. I believe in the exhilaration of standing at the boundary between the known and the unknown. I believe in the unanswered questions of children.

> "... the most beautiful experience we can have is the mysterious."

Key Vocabulary
- **discover** *v.*, to find something that is lost or hidden

In Other Words
set on fire truly inspired
Holy Grails greatest quests, or searches
encompass all the fundamental laws of nature answer all of our questions about the universe

▲ The Horsehead Nebula is a dark nebula, or interstellar cloud. Its swirling gases are in the form of a horse head. It is about 1500 light years from Earth.

▶ Read for Understanding

A. What kind of text is this? How do you know?

_____

B. Write a sentence that tells the topic of the selection.

_____

▶ Reread and Summarize

C. On **Practice Book** pages 170–171, circle the 3–5 most important words in each section. Make notes about why you chose each word. Why is the word important?

1. Section 1: (paragraphs 1–4)

_____

_____

2. Section 2: (paragraph 5)

_____

_____

3. Section 3: (paragraphs 6–7)

_____

_____

D. Use your topic sentence from above and your notes to write a summary of the selection.

_____

_____

_____

▶ Reread and Analyze

E. Analyze how the writer conveys the main idea of "The Power of Mysteries."

1. Reread paragraphs 1 and 2 on **Practice Book** page 170. What is the main idea of the passage? Underline the sentence that states the main idea.

   _____

   _____

2. Underline another sentence on **Practice Book** pages 170–171 that states an important idea that supports the main idea. Explain how you determined it was the main idea.

   _____

   _____

F. Analyze how the writer explains the main idea of "The Power of Mysteries."

1. Read the second sentence in paragraph 4 on **Practice Book** page 170. What does it explain about the main idea? Use evidence from the text to support your answer.

   _____

   _____

   _____

2. On **Practice Book** pages 170–171, underline other details that explain the main idea of the text. Describe what these details tell about the main idea.

   _____

   _____

▶ **Discuss and Write**

G. Synthesize your ideas about main idea and details.

1. With the class, discuss how the writer developed the main idea through details. List the details you discuss.

_____

_____

_____

2. Choose one of the details that you listed. Write a paragraph about how the writer conveyed the main idea of the text through this detail. Use the questions below to organize your thoughts.

   · What is the main idea of the passage?

   · What is a detail that supports the main idea?

   · What more does this detail tell about the main idea?

_____

_____

_____

_____

_____

▶ **Connect with**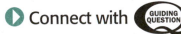

H. Discuss the Guiding Question: How do discoveries change us and the world?

1. How does <u>not</u> discovering something change the way scientists think?

_____

2. How do you think the discovery of the theory of everything would change the way people think?

_____

3. What do you think the writer would say about how discoveries change us and the world?

_____

Academic Vocabulary Review

A. Circle the Academic Vocabulary word that best fits into each sentence.

1. The (**sequence** / **discover**) of events is the order in which things happen.

2. When you (**record** / **discover**) something, you find out something you didn't know before.

3. Hanging your clothes in the closet is one way to (**organize** / **record**) your room.

4. When things are almost the same, they are (**similar** / **theme**).

B. Read each statement. Circle **Yes** or **No** to answer.

1. You make a messy room messier when you **organize** it.   **Yes**   **No**

2. You are sharing **facts** when you describe information that is true.   **Yes**   **No**

3. The **theme** of a story is its main message.   **Yes**   **No**

4. Baseball, swimming, and golf are **similar** sports.   **Yes**   **No**

C. Answer the questions in complete sentences.

1. If you were an explorer, what would you like to **discover**? Explain why.

   _____

   _____

2. Describe how you and someone you know are **similar**.

   _____

   _____

3. How would you **organize** the classroom differently? Explain.

   _____

   _____

4. **Record** a **fact** about your favorite season. Tell why it is important.

   _____

Name _____

Key Vocabulary Review

A. Read each sentence. Circle the Key Vocabulary word that best fits into each sentence.

1. A person who studies cultures from the past is called an (**artifact** / **archaeologist**).

2. If someone makes a good impression on you, you are likely to (**remember** / **forget**) them.

3. A scientist who studies shipwrecks spends time in the (**ocean** / **forest**).

4. A (**wreck** / **tomb**) is a special burial place for a dead person.

5. The sound of an (**explorer** / **alarm**) alerts people to danger.

6. If you want to solve a mystery, a (**clue** / **loss**) is helpful.

7. A group of people from a certain place and time is called a (**passenger** / **civilization**).

8. A scientist may find the remains, or (**pyramid** / **skeleton**), of a person.

B. Use your own words to write what each Key Vocabulary word means.
   Then write a synonym for each word.

Word	My Definition	Synonym
1. **ancient**		
2. **beautiful**		
3. **bury**		
4. **discover**		
5. **explorer**		
6. **famous**		
7. **locate**		
8. **search**		

Unit 5 Key Vocabulary

alarm	beautiful	discover	forget	passenger	skeleton
ancient	bury	explorer	locate	pyramid	tomb
archaeologist	civilization	famous	loss	remember	treasure
artifact	clue	forest	ocean	search	wreck

C. Answer the questions in complete sentences.

1. Give an example of an **artifact**.

   _____

   _____

2. Describe a **forest**.

   _____

   _____

3. Tell about something you can **forget**. Give an example.

   _____

   _____

4. Tell about a time when you experienced a **loss**.

   _____

   _____

5. Describe a time when you were a **passenger**.

   _____

   _____

6. Describe a **pyramid**.

   _____

   _____

7. What kind of **treasure** would you like to find?

   _____

   _____

8. Why is it important to study **civilizations** from the past?

   _____

   _____

Name _____

Mind Map

Use the mind map to show your ideas about **freedom**. As you read the selections in this unit, add new ideas you learn about why people value their **freedom**.

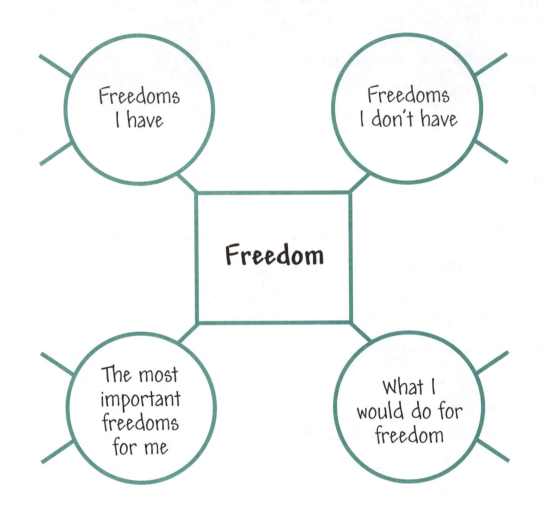

Academic Vocabulary

Think about what it means to have **freedom**. Why is it important to people? Use the word **freedom** in your answer.

_____

_____

_____

_____

Name _____

Text Structure: Cause and Effect

Read the passage. Notice how the writer uses cause and effect as a text structure. Use the list of clue words below to help you find causes and effects. Underline clue words that help you.

> Hiro and his brother Jun crept through the brush. They were quiet so they would not get caught. If the guards found them trying to leave, then they would lock up the boys. The emperor was cruel to anyone who did not obey him. As a result, people were not free to do what they wanted, so Hiro and Jun planned to leave. The brothers were determined to get free.

What are the causes and effects in the passage?

Causes _____

_____

_____

Effects _____

_____

_____

Tell how you know. _____

_____

_____

_____

_____

Cause and Effect Clue Words
as a result
because
because of
caused
consequently
if/then
led to
since
so
therefore

Academic Vocabulary

Write about how someone might **arrange** an escape to freedom.

_____

_____

_____

_____

Focus on Vocabulary

Name _____

Use Context Clues for Unfamiliar Words

▶ Read the passages. When you read, you may come to a word you do not know. Follow these steps.

1. Read the words nearby, and look for signal words.
2. Predict what the word means.
3. Try out your predicted meaning to see if it makes sense.
4. Check the word's meaning in a dictionary.

A. Follow the directions above. Write the meaning of each underlined word.

> Many people in England came to America during the 1600s. One group was called Pilgrims. The Pilgrims came to America because they were <u>forbidden</u> to practice their religion in England. They did not have religious freedom. This made them feel <u>oppressed</u> and helpless. The Pilgrims made the journey to America so they could <u>establish</u> their own churches.

forbidden _____

oppressed _____

establish _____

B. Follow the directions above. Write the meaning of each underlined word.

> Emilia's father decided that their family must <u>depart</u> from their homeland. The family had to leave because they could not <u>earn</u>, or make, money. There were no jobs for Emilia's mother and father. They knew they could <u>obtain</u> jobs in another country. Emilia's parents wanted to make a better life for their family.

depart _____

earn _____

obtain _____

Academic Vocabulary

My little brother did not know what the word *gymnasium* meant. I had to give him **context**

to help him, so I _____

_____

_____ .

Build Background

Critical Viewing Guide

▶ Take Notes

A. View the video. Take notes on at least three things that you learned.

_____

_____

_____

_____

_____

_____

_____

▶ Analyze the Video

B. Review your notes to help answer these questions.

1. Write two sentences to explain what was in the video.

_____

_____

_____

2. What was the most interesting thing you learned?

_____

_____

_____

3. What did the video tell about the dangerous journeys slaves took to gain **freedom**? Explain why people risked their safety to help slaves to **freedom**.

_____

_____

_____

_____

Learn Key Vocabulary

Name _____

Escaping to Freedom: Key Vocabulary

A. Study each word. Circle a number to rate how well you know it. Then complete the chart.

Rating Scale	**1** I have never seen this word before.	**2** I am not sure of the word's meaning.	**3** I know this word and can teach the word's meaning to someone else.

▲ Many Africans were **captured** from their homes and forced to work in Colonial America. These people were robbed of their **freedom**.

Key Words	Check Understanding	Deepen Understanding
❶ assist (u-sist) *verb* Rating: 1 2 3	Circle the synonym for **assist**. help heal	When I assist a friend or family member, I feel _____ _____ _____ _____ _____ .
❷ capture (kap-chur) *noun, verb* Rating: 1 2 3	Circle the synonym for **capture**. catch release	To capture a rabbit, you must be _____ _____ _____ _____ _____ .
❸ escape (is-kāp) *verb, noun* Rating: 1 2 3	Circle the synonym for **escape**. walk flee	One place I have wanted to escape from is _____ _____ _____ _____ _____ .
❹ freedom (frē-dum) *noun* Rating: 1 2 3	Circle the synonym for **freedom**. deal liberty	A freedom that I enjoy is _____ _____ _____ _____ _____ .

Key Vocabulary, continued

> ### Did You Know?
> The word **slave** comes from the Latin word for a person of Slavic origin. Many Slavic people were made slaves by the Roman Empire.

Key Words	Check Understanding	Deepen Understanding
❺ reward (ri-**word**) *noun* **Rating:** 1 2 3	Circle the synonym for **reward**. rewind prize	Something for which you might get a reward is _____ _____ _____ _____ _____ .
❻ right (rīt) *noun* **Rating:** 1 2 3	Circle the synonym for **right**. privilege left	I think it is important to have the right to _____ _____ _____ _____ _____ .
❼ slave (slāv) *noun* **Rating:** 1 2 3	Circle the synonym for **slave**. servant sled	It is against the law for anyone in the United States to own a slave because _____ _____ _____ _____ .
❽ travel (tra-vul) *verb* **Rating:** 1 2 3	Circle the synonym for **travel**. switch move	A place I would like to travel to is _____ _____ _____ _____ _____ .

B. Use at least two of the Key Vocabulary words. Write about the benefits of living in the United States today.

_____

_____

_____

Text Structure: Cause and Effect

As you read "Escaping to Freedom," look for cause-and-effect relationships.
Complete these Cause-and-Effect Diagrams.

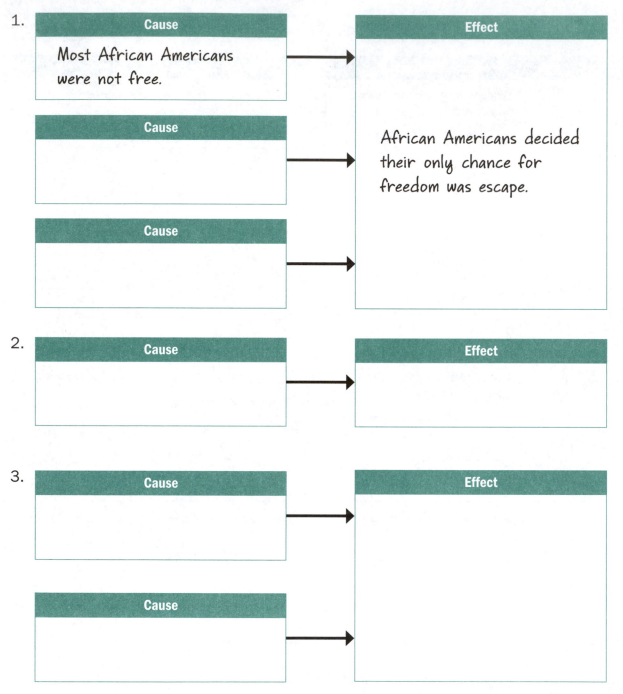

1.

Cause	Effect
Most African Americans were not free.	

Cause

Cause

Effect: African Americans decided their only chance for freedom was escape.

2.

Cause	Effect

3.

Cause	Effect

Cause

Escaping to Freedom

A. Read the paragraph.
Write a Key Vocabulary word in each blank.
Reread the paragraph to make sure the words make sense.

I, Amos Riley, offer a $200 _____ for the _____ of Josiah Henson and his family.

The family _____ and ran away from my farm two weeks ago. The six _____ may be

_____ at night.

I know my _____ as Henson's owner. Henson cannot leave until he buys his _____ .

Anyone who helps or _____ Henson in any way will be arrested.

B. Write complete sentences to answer these questions about "Escaping to Freedom."

1. What experiences gave Josiah Henson the courage to "follow the drinking gourd"?

_____

_____

_____

_____

_____

_____

_____

2. What would make a person risk being a part of the Underground Railroad?

_____

_____

_____

_____

_____

_____

Vocabulary Study

Use Context Clues

▶ Follow the steps below to figure out the meaning of each underlined word.

1. Read the sentence. Identify which words are context clues.
2. Use the context clues to figure out the meaning of the underlined word.
3. Write the meaning of the underlined word.

1. The teacher looked around the classroom and <u>witnessed</u> the student cheating on a test.

   witnessed _____

2. The <u>aggressive</u> dog was snarling and showing its teeth.

   aggressive _____

3. My grandmother owns a cat named Fluffy that she <u>grooms</u> daily by combing its fur.

   grooms _____

4. Sara's mom <u>allotted</u> ten dollars to entertainment, so Sara could buy a movie ticket.

   allotted _____

5. An <u>anonymous</u>, or unknown, person gave money to the animal shelter.

   anonymous _____

6. He <u>located</u> the exit door near the front of the building.

   located _____

7. She <u>dismissed</u> her brother's bad idea and did not think about it again.

   dismissed _____

8. The waiter held the glass <u>steady</u>, because he did not want to spill the water.

   steady _____

9. The teacher <u>verified</u>, or checked, that the answer was correct.

   verified _____

Academic Vocabulary

Academic Vocabulary

arrange	freedom
context	interpret

Escaping to Freedom: Academic Vocabulary Review

A. Draw a line to match each Academic Vocabulary word with its meaning.

Word	Definition
1. **arrange**	the parts near a word that help explain its meaning
2. **context**	to explain or tell what something means
3. **freedom**	not limited in what you do
4. **interpret**	to put things in a certain order

B. Read each statement. Circle **Yes** or **No** to answer.

1. A teacher may **interpret** a poem so students understand it.   **Yes   No**

2. You should put a bird inside a cage to give it **freedom**.   **Yes   No**

3. If you look at the **context** of a new word, it will help you understand the meaning.   **Yes   No**

4. One way to **arrange** flowers is to throw them away.   **Yes   No**

C. Answer the questions in complete sentences.

1. If you had the **freedom** to **arrange** your classroom differently, how would you do it?

_____

_____

2. Who would you ask to help **interpret** the meaning of a painting or other work of art?

_____

_____

3. What resource can you use to find the meaning of a word when the **context** is not given?

_____

_____

Build Background

Name _____

Critical Viewing Guide

▶ **Take Notes**

A. View the video. Take notes on at least three things that you learned.

_____

_____

_____

_____

_____

_____

_____

_____

▶ **Analyze the Video**

B. Review your notes to help answer these questions.

1. Write two sentences to explain what was in the video.

_____

_____

_____

2. What was the most interesting thing you learned?

_____

_____

_____

3. What did the video tell about living without **freedom**?

_____

_____

_____

_____

Learn Key Vocabulary

Name _____

Brave Butterflies: Key Vocabulary

A. Study each word. Circle a number to rate how well you know it. Then complete the chart.

Rating Scale	**1** I have never seen this word before.	**2** I am not sure of the word's meaning.	**3** I know this word and can teach the word's meaning to someone else.

▲ In some countries, people who **organize** protests are **arrested**. Peaceful people sometimes have to deal with **violent** punishment from their government.

Key Words	Check Understanding	Deepen Understanding
❶ arrest (u-**rest**) *verb* Rating: 1 2 3	☐ to agree with someone ☐ to put someone in jail	List other words that describe *arrest:* _____ _____ _____ _____ _____
❷ dictator (**dik**-tā-tur) *noun* Rating: 1 2 3	☐ a leader who doesn't share power ☐ a president in a democracy	List other words that describe *dictator:* _____ _____ _____ _____ _____
❸ journal (**jur**-nul) *noun* Rating: 1 2 3	☐ a record of someone's thoughts, feelings, and actions ☐ a model that shows a scene from a book	List other words that describe *journal:* _____ _____ _____ _____ _____
❹ hopeful (**hōp**-ful) *adjective* Rating: 1 2 3	☐ full of good thoughts about what will happen ☐ carefree or happy	List other words that describe *hopeful:* _____ _____ _____ _____ _____

Name _____

Did You Know?

The word **politics** comes from the Greek word *politikos*, which means "of, for, or relating to citizens."

Key Words	Check Understanding	Deepen Understanding
5 organize (**or**-gu-nīz) *verb* **Rating:** 1 2 3	☐ to plan and set up ☐ to grow or tend to something	List other words that describe *organize:* _____ _____ _____ _____ _____
6 politics (**pah**-lu-tiks) *noun* **Rating:** 1 2 3	☐ the science of motion ☐ the business of government	List other words that describe *politics:* _____ _____ _____ _____ _____
7 rescue (**res**-kyū) *noun* **Rating:** 1 2 3	☐ when something is stopped ☐ when someone is saved	List other words that describe *rescue:* _____ _____ _____ _____ _____
8 violent (**vī**-u-lunt) *adjective* **Rating:** 1 2 3	☐ using force ☐ a purplish color	List other words that describe *violent:* _____ _____ _____ _____ _____

B. Use at least two of the Key Vocabulary words. Write about what you think is the best way to make a change in government.

_____

_____

_____

Text Structure: **Cause and Effect**

As you read "Brave Butterflies," note causes and effects in the Cause-and-Effect Chains.

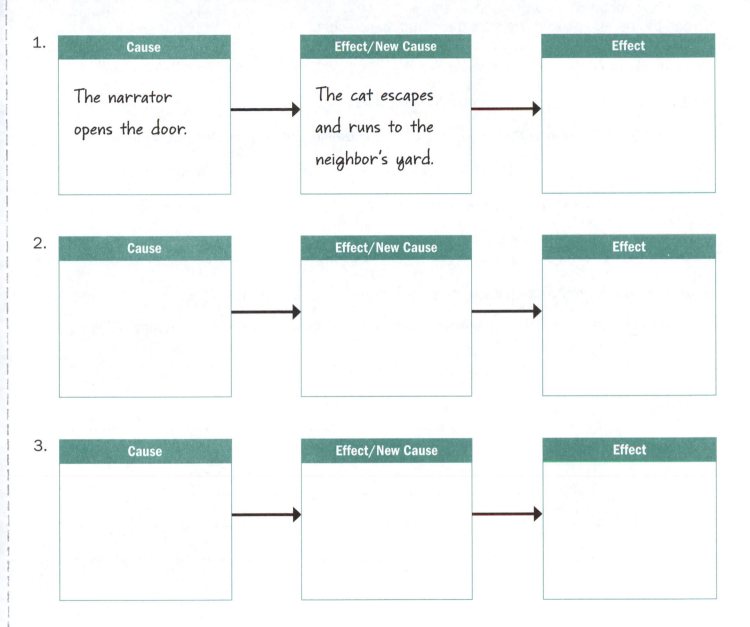

1.

Cause	Effect/New Cause	Effect
The narrator opens the door.	The cat escapes and runs to the neighbor's yard.	

2.

Cause	Effect/New Cause	Effect

3.

Cause	Effect/New Cause	Effect

Selection Review

Name _____

Brave Butterflies

Key Vocabulary

arrest	organize
dictator	politics
hopeful	rescue
journal	violent

A. Read the paragraph.
Write a Key Vocabulary word in each blank.
Reread the paragraph to make sure the words make sense.

We were all scared that the police would _____ Papi. He and other people held secret

meetings to talk about _____ and the government. He wrote in his _____ about his

group's activities. They were trying to _____ a movement against the Dominican Republic's

strict and cruel _____ . The group wanted everyone to be able to enjoy freedom. Papi felt

_____ that working for freedom would _____ everyone in the country from this

dangerous and _____ man.

B. Write complete sentences to answer these questions about "Brave Butterflies."

1. If you were Ana, do you think you would have told your parents what you overheard? Explain.

_____

_____

_____

_____

_____

_____

_____

2. What makes people willing to take risks in the name of freedom?

_____

_____

_____

_____

_____

_____

_____

Vocabulary Study

Use Context Clues

▶ Follow the steps below to figure out the meaning of each underlined word.

1. Read the sentences. Identify which words are context clues. Look for both synonym clues and antonym clues.
2. Use the context clues to figure out the meaning of the underlined word.
3. Write the meaning of the underlined word.

1. He was positive that he left his keys on the table. He was <u>doubtful</u> that they could be found anywhere else.

   doubtful _____

2. Michael drives his car in city traffic. It is so <u>time consuming</u> that he leaves an hour before his friend, who uses a bike to get from one place to another quickly.

   time consuming _____

3. Daren used such an <u>abundant</u> amount of paint that there was hardly any left for his sister to use.

   abundant _____

4. Akeem was <u>horrified</u> when he entered the haunted house, but he calmed down when he realized the monsters were fake.

   horrified _____

5. Violet was such a friendly person that it was <u>absurd</u> when her friend called her rude.

   absurd _____

6. Melinda's teacher <u>complimented</u> her artwork and praised her effort.

   complimented _____

7. Lionel thought the horror movie was so <u>repulsive</u> that he felt sick after he saw it.

   repulsive _____

8. The girl did not want to go home yet, so she walked slowly and <u>meandered</u> through the neighborhood streets.

   meandered _____

Academic Vocabulary

Academic Vocabulary

demonstrate   topic
explain

Brave Butterflies: Academic Vocabulary Review

A. Write the Academic Vocabulary word next to its definition.

Definition	Word
1. the subject of a piece of writing or of a discussion	
2. to make an idea clear so people understand it	
3. to prove something or to make it clear	

B. Circle the Academic Vocabulary word that best fits into each sentence.

1. Henry will (**explain** / **topic**) the writing project to our team.

2. We will look for articles about the (**demonstrate** / **topic**) to get information.

3. Keisha will (**demonstrate** / **topic**) how to do a science activity.

C. Use these two Academic Vocabulary words in a sentence.

explain   **topic**

_____

_____

Build Background

Critical Viewing Guide

▶ **Take Notes**

A. View the images. Take notes on at least three things that you learned.

_____

_____

_____

_____

_____

_____

_____

▶ **Analyze the Images**

B. Review your notes to help answer these questions.

1. Write two sentences to explain what was in the images.

_____

_____

_____

2. What was the most interesting thing you learned?

_____

_____

_____

3. Why did people choose to take risks for their **freedom**?

_____

_____

_____

_____

Learn Key Vocabulary

Seeking Freedom: Key Vocabulary

A. Study each word. Circle a number to rate how well you know it. Then complete the chart.

Rating Scale	**1** I have never seen this word before.	**2** I am not sure of the word's meaning.	**3** I know this word and can teach the word's meaning to someone else.

▲ Sometimes, people organize a **protest** in **public** to try to make a change in **government**.

Key Words	Check Understanding	Deepen Understanding
❶ government (gu-vurn-munt) *noun* **Rating:** 1 2 3	The **government** can make laws that affect the people of our country. Yes No	In the United States, the government _____ _____ _____ _____ _____ .
❷ law (law) *noun* **Rating:** 1 2 3	It is not important to obey traffic **laws**. Yes No	An example of a law that helps people is _____ _____ _____ _____ _____ .
❸ leader (lē-dur) *noun* **Rating:** 1 2 3	A **leader** is a person who is in charge of others. Yes No	A good leader is a person who _____ _____ _____ _____ _____ .
❹ opinion (u-pin-yun) *noun* **Rating:** 1 2 3	In the United States, you are not allowed to express your **opinion** about the government. Yes No	An opinion I have about my government is that _____ _____ _____ _____ _____ .

Name _____

Key Words	Check Understanding	Deepen Understanding
❺ protest (**prō**-test) *verb* Rating: 1 2 3	When you **protest**, you make a statement against an idea. Yes No	If you want to protest something, it is important to ___ _____ _____ _____ _____ .
❻ public (**pu**-blik) *noun* Rating: 1 2 3	If you do something in **public**, you do it in front of others. Yes No	An example of a fun event that happens in public is _____ _____ _____ .
❼ responsibility (ri-spont-su-**bi**-lu-tē) *noun* Rating: 1 2 3	Most people have no **responsibilities**. Yes No	As a pet owner, you have the responsibility to _____ _____ _____ _____ _____ .
❽ system (**sis**-tum) *noun* Rating: 1 2 3	A **system** can help people to stay organized. Yes No	A system I use when I study is _____ _____ _____ _____ .

B. Use at least two of the Key Vocabulary words. Write about something you would like to change about the United States and how you would try to change it.

_____

_____

_____

Text Structure: Cause and Effect

As you read "Seeking Freedom," look for cause-and-effect relationships in
each section. Complete a Cause-and-Effect Chart for each section.

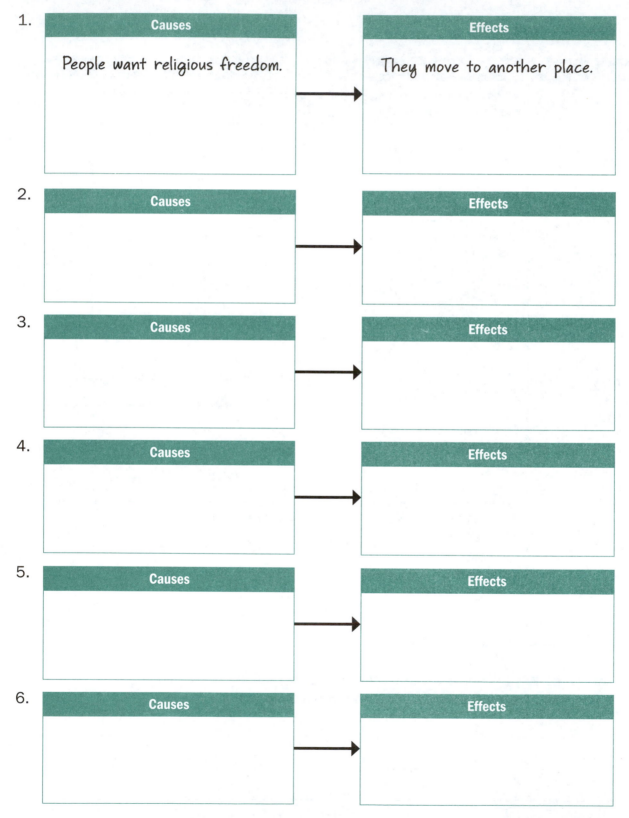

1.
Causes	Effects
People want religious freedom.	They move to another place.

2.
Causes	Effects

3.
Causes	Effects

4.
Causes	Effects

5.
Causes	Effects

6.
Causes	Effects

Selection Review

Seeking Freedom

Key Vocabulary

government	protest
laws	public
leaders	responsibility
opinions	system

A. Read the paragraph.
Write a Key Vocabulary word in each blank.
Reread the paragraph to make sure the words make sense.

In the United States, the _____ , or organization, of _____ protects people's freedom.

It depends on help from people, or the _____ . They vote to elect their _____ .

Everyone who enjoys freedom must take _____ for it and respect everyone's rights. There are

countries where people cannot express their _____ about the way things are run. People there

can be punished if they _____ unfair _____ .

B. Write complete sentences to answer these questions about "Seeking Freedom."

1. How have **laws** in the United States changed to bring freedom to more people?

_____

_____

_____

_____

_____

_____

2. Why might people in another country speak out against their **government** ?

_____

_____

_____

_____

_____

_____

Vocabulary Study

Name _____

Use Context Clues

▶ Follow the steps below to figure out the meaning of each underlined word.

1. Read the sentence. Identify which words are context clues.
   Look for example clues.
2. Use the context clues to figure out the meaning of the underlined word.
3. Write the meaning of the underlined word.

1. Melinda was upset because her friend told <u>confidential</u> information about her. Now everyone knows Melinda's fears, hopes, and dreams.

   confidential _____

2. The strong winds caused a lot of <u>destruction</u>, including fallen trees and broken windows.

   destruction _____

3. The new school principal started many new <u>procedures</u>, such as a rule that students had to stay indoors during lunch.

   procedures _____

4. <u>Perishable</u> foods, such as fresh fruits and vegetables, will stay fresh in the refrigerator for only a week.

   perishable _____

5. Some people use <u>extreme</u> measures to get concert tickets to see their favorite band. For example, they may sit outside all night long and wait for the ticket booth to open!

   extreme _____

6. I want to sign up for <u>extracurricular</u> activities, such as the volleyball team, the debate team, and the homecoming committee.

   extracurricular _____

7. Many parents have very busy <u>professions</u>, so they are not always home for dinner.

   professions _____

© National Geographic Learning, a part of Cengage Learning, Inc.

Seeking Freedom: Academic Vocabulary Review

Academic Vocabulary	
arrange	fact
context	freedom
demonstate	

A. Use your own words to tell what each Academic Vocabulary word means.

Word	My Definition
1. **arrange**	
2. **context**	
3. **demonstrate**	
4. **fact**	
5. **freedom**	

B. Write an Academic Vocabulary word to complete each sentence.

1. Watch Matt _____ how to do the math problem.

2. Erin will _____ books in order so she can find them again easily.

3. It is a _____ that our school won the championship in swimming.

4. When I finish my work, I have the _____ to do what I want.

5. I used a dictionary to find the meaning of the word because the _____ did not help me.

C. Use each Academic Vocabulary word in a sentence.

1. **context** _____

   _____

2. **demonstrate** _____

   _____

From
HARRIET TUBMAN
CONDUCTOR
on the
UNDERGROUND RAILROAD

BY ANN PETRY

1   In December 1851, when Harriet Tubman started out with the **band of fugitives** that she planned to take to Canada, she had been in the **vicinity** of the plantation for days, planning the trip, carefully selecting the **slaves** that she would take with her.

2   She had announced her arrival in the slave quarter by singing the forbidden spiritual—"Go down, Moses, 'way down to Egypt Land"—singing it softly outside the door of a slave cabin, late at night. The husky voice was beautiful even when it was barely more than a **murmur** borne on the wind.

3   Once she had made her presence known, word of her coming spread from cabin to cabin. The slaves whispered to each other, ear to mouth, mouth to ear, "Moses is here." "Moses has come." "Get ready. Moses is back again." The ones who had agreed to go North with her put ashcake and salt herring in an old bandanna, hastily tied it into a bundle, and then waited patiently for the signal that meant it was time to start.

4   There were eleven in this party, including one of her brothers and his wife. It was the largest group that she had ever conducted, but she was determined that more and more slaves should know what **freedom** was like.

5   She had to take them all the way to Canada. The Fugitive Slave **Law** was no longer a great many **incomprehensible words** written down on the country's law books. The new law had become a reality. It was Thomas Sims, a boy, picked up on the streets of Boston at night and shipped back to Georgia. It was Jerry and Shadrach, **arrested** and jailed with no warning.

Key Vocabulary

- **slave** *n.*, someone who belongs to another and works without pay
- **freedom** *n.*, the power a person has because of the rules of a country
- **law** *n.*, a country's rules
- **arrest** *v.*, to put someone in jail

In Other Words

band of fugitives group of escaping slaves
vicinity area
murmur whisper
incomprehensible words words you can't understand

"... she was determined that more and more slaves should know what FREEDOM was like."

6 She had never been in Canada. The route beyond Philadelphia was strange to her. But she could not let the runaways who accompanied her know this. As they walked along she told them stories of her own first flight, she kept painting **vivid** word pictures of what it would be like to be free.

7 But there were so many of them this time. She knew moments of doubt when she was half afraid, and kept looking back over her shoulder, imagining that she heard **the sound of pursuit**. They would certainly be **pursued**. Eleven of them. Eleven thousand dollars' worth of flesh and bone and muscle that belonged to Maryland planters. If they were caught, the eleven runaways would be whipped and sold South, but she—she would probably be hanged.

◀ "Step On Board," by Fern Cunningham in 1999 is a sculpture in Harriet Tubman Park, Boston, MA.

Historical Background
Moses was a Hebrew prophet whose story is told in the Old Testament book of the Bible. Moses led Hebrew slaves to freedom.

In Other Words
vivid detailed
the sound of pursuit people chasing them
pursued chased after

▶ Read for Understanding

A. What kind of text is this? How do you know?

_____

_____

B. Write a sentence that tells the topic of the selection.

_____

_____

▶ Reread and Summarize

C. On **Practice Book** pages 203–203, circle the 3–5 most important words in each section. Make notes about why you chose each word. Why is the word important?

1. Section 1: (paragraphs 1–3)

_____

_____

2. Section 2: (paragraphs 4–7)

_____

_____

D. Use your topic sentence from above and your notes to write a summary of the selection.

_____

_____

_____

▶ Reread and Analyze

E. Analyze how the author uses cause-effect to connect events in the text.

1. Reread paragraph 5 on **Practice Book** page 202. What happened to the Fugitive Slave Law? How did this affect slaves? Underline words and phrases to support your answers. Use evidence from the text to support your answer.

_____

_____

_____

2. Underline another example of cause and effect in the text on **Practice Book** pages 202–203. Explain how the author uses cause-effect to connect events in the text.

_____

_____

F. Analyze how the author uses cause-effect to show how a situation leads someone to take action.

1. Reread paragraph 4 on **Practice Book** page 202. What leads Harriet Tubman to take action? What is the result? Underline the words and phrases that support your answer. Use evidence from the text to support your answer.

_____

_____

_____

2. In the **Practice Book**, underline another example of how a situation leads a person to take action. Explain what the cause is and what the effect is.

_____

_____

Name _____

▶ **Discuss and Write**

G. Synthesize your ideas about how the writer used cause-effect.

1. With the class, discuss how the writer used cause-effect to develop ideas. List the causes and effects you discuss.

_____

_____

_____

_____

2. Choose one of the cause-effect relationships that you listed. Write a paragraph about how the writer used cause-effect. Use the questions below to organize your thoughts.

   • What is the cause?

   • What is the effect?

   • Did a situation lead someone to take action? Explain.

   • How does this cause-effect relationship contribute to your understanding of the text?

_____

_____

_____

_____

_____

▶ **Connect with** ⬭ GUIDING QUESTION

H. Discuss the Guiding Question: How far should people go for the sake of freedom?

1. What was Harriet Tubman risking for the sake of freedom?

_____

2. What would happen if these runaway slaves were caught?

_____

3. Do you think Harriet Tubam was going too far for the sake of freedom? Explain.

_____

Academic Vocabulary Review

Academic Vocabulary	
arrange	fact
context	freedom
demonstrate	interpret
explain	topic

A. Choose the best Academic Vocabulary word to write in each blank. Reread the paragraph to make sure the words make sense.

One of the most famous speeches on the _____ of freedom is
topic / fact

"I Have a Dream." Dr. Martin Luther King, Jr., made the speech in Washington, D.C., in 1963.

The speech was broadcast on television. People around the United States listened to Dr. King

_____ the importance of civil rights.
explain / interpret

B. Write a definition for each word. Then write whether it is a thing or an action.

Word	Definition	Action or Thing
1. **arrange**		
2. **context**		
3. **demonstrate**		

C. Rewrite each sentence. Replace the underlined words with an Academic Vocabulary word.

1. My teacher explained the difference between <u>information that is true</u> and opinion.

_____

2. The article explains the importance of <u>not being limited in what you do</u>.

_____

3. The museum guide will <u>explain about</u> the old scrolls for the visitors.

_____

Name _____

Key Vocabulary Review

A. Read each sentence. Circle the Key Vocabulary word that best fits into each sentence.

1. The police officer will (**assist / arrest**) the criminal.

2. The workers saved the girl from the flood, and the (**rescue / reward**) was a success.

3. A (**slave / leader**) belongs to another person.

4. A country is controlled by its (**freedom / government**).

5. It is important to be able to express your (**opinion / law**).

6. The organization's members are unhappy with the new law, so they will (**protest / travel**) against it.

7. The new president made his first speech in (**journal / public**).

8. A (**system / dictator**) does not share power with anyone else.

B. Use your own words to write what each Key Vocabulary word means. Then write a synonym for each word.

Word	My Definition	Synonym
1. **assist**		
2. **capture**		
3. **escape**		
4. **freedom**		
5. **organize**		
6. **reward**		
7. **system**		
8. **violent**		

Name _____

Unit 6 Key Vocabulary

arrest	escape	journal	organize	rescue	slave
assist	freedom	law	politics	responsibility	system
capture	government	leader	protest	reward	travel
dictator	hopeful	opinion	public	right	violent

C. Answer the questions in complete sentences.

1. Where would you like to **travel**?

   _____

   _____

2. What is something that makes you **hopeful** about the rest of the school year?

   _____

   _____

3. Think of a **law** that helps people. How does it help people?

   _____

   _____

4. What is one **responsibility** that you have at home?

   _____

   _____

5. What makes a good **leader**?

   _____

   _____

6. Do you think **politics** is interesting? Why or why not?

   _____

   _____

7. What, in your opinion, is a **right** that everyone should have?

   _____

   _____

8. Why do you think a person would write in a **journal**?

   _____

   _____

Name _____

Mind Map

Use the mind map to show what we can learn from the stars and **space**. As you read the selections in this unit, add new ideas about what we can learn from the stars and **space**.

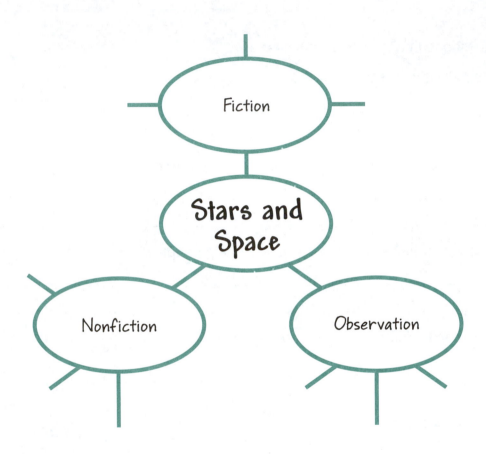

Academic Vocabulary

Think about what it might be like to live in **space**. How would your life be different? Use the word **space** in your answer.

_____

_____

_____

_____

Name _____

Analyze Argument

Read the passage. Consider the argument and evidence.

> **Near-Earth Objects**
>
> Near-Earth Objects (NEOs) are asteroids, meteoroids, and comets that orbit, or circle around, our solar system. They are called NEOs because they pass near Earth. Some of these objects have actually hit Earth. Earth is full of deep holes that prove it. People should support scientists' important efforts to study NEOs. NEOs are a threat to our safety. We can also learn a lot about our universe by studying them. NASA's Near-Earth Object Program supports efforts to find at least 90% of NEOs by the year 2020. Programs like this need our support. It is important that we help. We need to find these Near-Earth Objects now!

1. What is the author's argument in this passage?

   _____

   _____

   _____

2. What evidence does the author use to support the argument?

   _____

   _____

   _____

3. Analyze the argument and the evidence. Is the evidence valid?
   Why or why not?

   _____

Academic Vocabulary

If you were a scientist, how would you **evaluate** a Near-Earth Object?

_____

_____

_____

_____

Focus on Vocabulary

Name _____

Use Context Clues for Multiple-Meaning Words

▶ Read the passages. Follow these steps to figure out the correct meaning of the multiple-meaning words.

1. Look at each underlined word. Look at the other words in the sentence.
2. Read the sentences that come before and after to find more clues.
3. Use the clues to determine a meaning that makes sense.
4. As you read the sentence, think about the word's meaning. If it does not make sense, look in a dictionary for more meanings.

A. Follow the directions above. Write the meaning of each underlined word.

> Did you know that the sun is a star? It is the star closest to Earth. The sun projects solar energy. Solar energy is Earth's main form of energy. Earth would be dark and the oceans would be frozen without the sun. The sun is much bigger than Earth. More than one million Earths could fit inside the sun!

projects _____

form _____

fit _____

B. Follow the directions above. Write the meaning of each underlined word.

> For many years, scientists thought that there were nine planets in the solar system. Pluto was the smallest of these planets. In 2006, scientists gave us a new report. They said that Pluto was too small to be a planet. Instead, they used the term "dwarf planet" to describe Pluto. Now scientists have found only eight planets in the solar system.

report _____

term _____

found _____

Academic Vocabulary

When it is cold outside, we need to wear **appropriate** clothing, such as _____

_____

_____ .

Critical Viewing Guide

▶ Take Notes

A. View the images. Take notes on at least three things that you learned.

_____

_____

_____

_____

_____

_____

_____

▶ Analyze the Images

B. Review your notes to help answer these questions.

1. Write two sentences to explain what was in the images.

_____

_____

2. What was the most interesting thing you learned?

_____

_____

_____

3. What did the images show about **space**? Why do you think people look for patterns in the stars?

_____

_____

_____

Learn Key Vocabulary

Name _____

The Earth Under Sky Bear's Feet: Key Vocabulary

A. Study each word. Circle a number to rate how well you know it. Then complete the chart.

Rating Scale	**1** I have never seen this word before.	**2** I am not sure of the word's meaning.	**3** I know this word and can teach the word's meaning to someone else.

▲ Even when they are not used, satellites **remain** in orbit and **roam** the space above Earth.

Key Words	Check Understanding	Deepen Understanding
❶ advice (ud-**vīs**) *noun* Rating: 1 2 3	Circle the synonym for **advice**. help commercial	When you need advice about school, whom do you ask? _____ _____ _____ _____
❷ continue (kun-**tin**-yū) *verb* Rating: 1 2 3	Circle the synonym for **continue**. last ponder	What topics would you like to continue to study at school? _____ _____ _____ _____
❸ hunter (**hun**-tur) *noun* Rating: 1 2 3	Circle the synonym for **hunter**. prey predator	What animal do you think is a good hunter? Explain why. _____ _____ _____ _____
❹ remain (ri-**mān**) *verb* Rating: 1 2 3	Circle the synonym for **remain**. reread stay	If you are lost, why is it a good idea to remain in one place? _____ _____ _____ _____

Key Vocabulary, continued

Name _____

For centuries, people told **tales** about outer space. Writers **continue** to tell stories about what may be out there. ▶

Key Words	Check Understanding	Deepen Understanding
❺ roam (rōm) *verb* Rating: 1 2 3	Circle the synonym for **roam**. groan wander	What place do you like to roam? _____ _____ _____ _____ _____
❻ scatter (ska-tur) *verb* Rating: 1 2 3	Circle the synonym for **scatter**. spread sparkle	What might scatter when the wind blows? _____ _____ _____ _____ _____
❼ tale (tāl) *noun* Rating: 1 2 3	Circle the synonym for **tale**. story tail	What are some characteristics of a good tale? _____ _____ _____ _____ _____
❽ track (trak) *noun* Rating: 1 2 3	Circle the synonym for **track**. area footprint	Where might animals or people leave tracks? _____ _____ _____ _____ _____

B. Use at least two of the Key Vocabulary words. Write about your thoughts when you look up at the night sky.

_____

_____

_____

Name _____

Analyze Characters' Viewpoints

As you read each myth, analyze the characters' viewpoints and complete the chart.

Character	What the Character Says, Does, or Thinks	Character's Viewpoint
Grandmother	says she will share some stories their old people tell about Sky Bear	The stories are important to her.
Three Hunters		
Ko–tci–man–yo		
Seven Wise Men		

Selection Review

Name _____

The Earth Under Sky Bear's Feet

Key Vocabulary

advice	roams
continues	scatter
hunters	tale
remain	tracks

A. Read the paragraph.
Write a Key Vocabulary word in each blank.
Reread the paragraph to make sure the words make sense.

In "The Earth Under Sky Bear's Feet," each story, or _____, tells how star patterns were

formed. In one story, three _____ follow a bear's _____ all day and even into the night.

The bear does not stop when it gets to the hilltop. It _____ right into the sky. Sky Bear

_____ the sky every night. In another story, a girl opens a sack of stars and they _____

in every direction. The stars that _____ become patterns in the sky. In the final story, seven

wise men get tired of giving _____ and help. They try to hide in the night sky.

B. Write complete sentences to answer these questions about "The Earth Under Sky Bear's Feet."

1. What might Sky Bear and the wise men see when they look down at night?

_____

_____

_____

_____

_____

_____

2. Imagine you can place the stars into patterns in the sky. What animals would you make?

_____

_____

_____

_____

_____

_____

Vocabulary Study

Use Context Clues

▶ Follow the steps below to figure out the meaning of each word.

1. Look at the underlined word. Think about the meanings you know for that word.
2. Look at other words in the sentence. Use context clues to determine which meaning makes sense.
3. Replace the word with the meaning and say the sentence. If it does not make sense, look in a dictionary for more meanings.
4. Write the meaning of the word.

1. I used my umbrella to <u>block</u> the rain from hitting my head.

   _____

2. He <u>marked</u> the page in the book where he stopped reading.

   _____

3. The animals run around inside a <u>pen</u> all day.

   _____

4. The brother and sister had a <u>race</u> to see who could get to the car first.

   _____

5. The little boy tried to <u>snap</u> the buttons on his pants together.

   _____

6. I try to float in the pool, but I always <u>sink</u> to the bottom.

   _____

7. Sarah sewed a colorful <u>patch</u> on her jeans.

   _____

8. Tyrone missed a quiz yesterday because he was not <u>present</u>.

   _____

9. Penny would not climb the ladder because it was not <u>stable</u>.

   _____

The Earth Under Sky Bear's Feet:
Academic Vocabulary Review

A. Draw a line to match the Academic Vocabulary word with its meaning.

Word	Definition
1. **appropriate**	to judge something's value or worth
2. **discuss**	the area beyond Earth
3. **evaluate**	correct for the situation
4. **space**	to talk about something

B. Read each statement. Circle **Yes** or **No** to answer.

1. To **discuss** an important idea, you must be silent.   **Yes**   **No**

2. Stars and other planets are in **space** beyond Earth.   **Yes**   **No**

3. The **appropriate** action is the right thing to do.   **Yes**   **No**

4. When you **evaluate** an object, you wrap it carefully.   **Yes**   **No**

C. Answer the questions in complete sentences.

1. If you could find a new star in **space** , what name would you give it?

_____

_____

2. Think of two different sports teams and **evaluate** their uniforms. Which do you like and why?

_____

_____

Build Background

Critical Viewing Guide

▶ Take Notes

A. View the video. Take notes on at least three things that you learned.

_____

_____

_____

_____

_____

_____

_____

_____

▶ Analyze the Video

B. Review your notes to help answer these questions.

1. Write two sentences to explain what was in the video.

_____

_____

_____

2. What was the most interesting thing you learned?

_____

_____

_____

3. Why do you think it is important to learn about **space**?

_____

_____

_____

_____

Learn Key Vocabulary

Name _____

A Universe of Stars: Key Vocabulary

A. Study each word. Circle a number to rate how well you know it. Then complete the chart.

Rating Scale	**1** I have never seen this word before.	**2** I am not sure of the word's meaning.	**3** I know this word and can teach the word's meaning to someone else.

Outer **space** is full of stars. The planets in our solar system **orbit** a star we call the sun. ▶

Key Words	Check Understanding	Deepen Understanding
① distance (**dis**-tunts) *noun* Rating: 1 2 3	**Distance** can be measured in miles. Yes No	List other words that relate to *distance*: _____ _____ _____ _____ _____
② orbit (**or**-but) *verb* Rating: 1 2 3	Earth **orbits** the moon. Yes No	List other words that relate to *orbit*: _____ _____ _____ _____ _____
③ space (spās) *noun* Rating: 1 2 3	You can travel into **space** on an airplane. Yes No	List other words that relate to *space*: _____ _____ _____ _____ _____
④ telescope (**te**-lu-skōp) *noun* Rating: 1 2 3	You can use a **telescope** to see things that are very far away. Yes No	List other words that relate to *telescope*: _____ _____ _____ _____ _____

Name _____

This spacecraft travels an incredible **distance**. It will help scientists to learn more about the **universe**. ▶

Key Words	Check Understanding	Deepen Understanding
❺ **temperature** (**tem**-pur-chur) *noun* **Rating:** 1 2 3	If something is cold, it has a high **temperature**. **Yes**　　**No**	List other words that relate to *temperature*: _____ _____ _____ _____ _____
❻ **unit** (**yū**-nit) *noun* **Rating:** 1 2 3	An inch is a **unit** used to measure distance. **Yes**　　**No**	List other words that relate to *unit*: _____ _____ _____ _____ _____
❼ **universe** (**yū**-nu-vurs) *noun* **Rating:** 1 2 3	The **universe** is a small section of outer space. **Yes**　　**No**	List other words that relate to *universe*: _____ _____ _____ _____ _____
❽ **vary** (**vair**-ē) *verb* **Rating:** 1 2 3	If hats **vary** in color, there are many different colored hats. **Yes**　　**No**	List other words that relate to *vary*: _____ _____ _____ _____ _____

B. Use at least two of the Key Vocabulary words. Write about whether or not you would like to explore other planets.

_____

_____

_____

Analyze Author's Purpose

As you read each selection, make a list of the elements or details that show the author's purpose. Then write what the author's purpose is.

"A Universe of Stars"	"The Astronomer"
Purpose: to inform and explain explanations	Purpose:

Name _____

Key Vocabulary

distances	temperatures
orbit	unit
space	universe
telescopes	vary

A Universe of Stars

A. Read the paragraph.
Write a Key Vocabulary word in each blank.
Reread the paragraph to make sure the words make sense.

People use _____ to look at and study objects in _____ . Earth and other nearby

planets _____ the sun, which is our nearest star. The stars seen in the night sky are great

_____ away from Earth. The stars are so far away that their distances from Earth are

measured in a _____ called a light year. From studying stars we know that some burn at higher

_____ than others. Their sizes _____ , too. Studying the stars helps us understand

the entire _____ .

B. Write complete sentences to answer these questions about "A Universe of Stars."

1. What do you think is the most exciting thing about exploring **space** ?

_____

_____

_____

_____

_____

_____

2. How would you describe our sun?

_____

_____

_____

_____

_____

_____

Vocabulary Study

Use Context Clues

▶ Follow the steps below to figure out the meaning of each word.

1. Look at each underlined word. Use context clues and a dictionary to help you find the appropriate meaning.
2. Write the meaning of each underlined word.
3. Write the context clues that helped you determine the meaning.

1. At the <u>fork</u> in the road, the driver had to decide whether to go left or right.

   Meaning: _____

   Context Clues: _____

2. The boy <u>coasts</u> down the hill on his bicycle.

   Meaning: _____

   Context Clues: _____

3. The athlete needed to <u>train</u> for six weeks before competing in the game.

   Meaning: _____

   Context Clues: _____

4. She was <u>short</u> with him because she was angry and unhappy.

   Meaning: _____

   Context Clues: _____

5. I applied a thick <u>coat</u> of red paint on the bench.

   Meaning: _____

   Context Clues: _____

6. The inner <u>core</u>, or center, of Earth is very hot.

   Meaning: _____

   Context Clues: _____

7. He softly <u>tipped</u> the basketball over the rim with his fingers.

   Meaning: _____

   Context Clues: _____

Analyze Style

A. Read the passage.

> July 20, 1969, was a great day for the world. The world would never be the same. Human beings made a technological accomplishment when Neil Armstrong took the "small step" onto the moon from the lunar module, *The Eagle*. Buzz Aldrin followed him onto the moon. What a feeling to look out and see Earth like no one else ever had! They could see Earth much like we look up at the moon. In the short time the men were on the moon, they planted the American flag and collected lots of moon rocks. When they were done, they docked with the spaceship *Columbia* and headed for home.

B. Reread the passage. What types of words does the author use? What effect do they have?

_____

_____

_____

_____

_____

_____

_____

C. Choose a book from your library in class. Read a few pages and analyze the author's style. Describe the author's style using examples from the passage you read.

_____

_____

_____

_____

_____

_____

_____

_____

_____

Academic Vocabulary

Name _____

A Universe of Stars: Academic Vocabulary Review

A. Write each Academic Vocabulary word next to the correct definition.

Definition	Word
1. to judge something's value or worth	
2. correct for the situation	
3. a certain way of expressing an idea	
4. area beyond Earth	

B. Answer the questions in complete sentences.

1. At what age is it **appropriate** for children to begin playing soccer?

   _____

   _____

2. The **style** you use to write a text message on your phone is probably different from the **style** you use to write a paper for school. Explain how each **style** is different.

   _____

   _____

3. **Evaluate** the weather where you are today.

   _____

   _____

4. What do people see in **space**? Name three objects in **space**.

   _____

   _____

Build Background

Critical Viewing Guide

▶ **Take Notes**

A. View the video. Take notes on at least three things that you learned.

_____

_____

_____

_____

_____

_____

_____

_____

▶ **Analyze the Video**

B. Review your notes to help answer these questions.

1. Write two sentences to explain what was in the video.

_____

_____

_____

2. What was the most interesting thing you learned?

_____

_____

_____

3. It is difficult to see the stars in **space** because of Earth's lights. What are some things you can do to reduce light pollution?

_____

_____

_____

Learn Key Vocabulary

Name _____

Not-So-Starry Nights: Key Vocabulary

A. Study each word. Circle a number to rate how well you know it. Then complete the chart.

Rating Scale	**1** I have never seen this word before.	**2** I am not sure of the word's meaning.	**3** I know this word and can teach the word's meaning to someone else.

▲ **Pollution** can **reduce** the number of stars we can see in the night sky.

Key Words	Check Understanding	Deepen Understanding
❶ benefit (**be**-nu-fit) *noun* Rating: 1 2 3	☐ something that is helpful ☐ something that is harmful	List examples for the word *benefit*: _____ _____ _____ _____
❷ environment (in-**vī**-run-munt) *noun* Rating: 1 2 3	☐ a jealous feeling ☐ the area where plants and animals live and grow	List examples for the word *environment*: _____ _____ _____ _____ _____
❸ migrate (**mī**-grāt) *verb* Rating: 1 2 3	☐ to move from one place to another ☐ to split up into groups	List examples for the word *migrate*: _____ _____ _____ _____
❹ pollution (pu-**lü**-shun) *noun* Rating: 1 2 3	☐ a type of perfume ☐ waste that harms nature	List examples for the word *pollution*: _____ _____ _____ _____

Name _____

Key Words	Check Understanding	Deepen Understanding
⑤ protect (pru-**tekt**) *verb* **Rating:** 1 2 3	☐ to keep safe ☐ to use a computer	List examples for the word *protect*: _____ _____ _____ _____ _____
⑥ reduce (ri-**düs**) *verb* **Rating:** 1 2 3	☐ to make smaller ☐ to repeat	List examples for the word *reduce*: _____ _____ _____ _____ _____
⑦ release (ri-**lēs**) *verb* **Rating:** 1 2 3	☐ to understand ☐ to let out	List examples for the word *release*: _____ _____ _____ _____ _____
⑧ wasted (**wāst**-ud) *adjective* **Rating:** 1 2 3	☐ wanted ☐ not used	List examples for the word *wasted*: _____ _____ _____ _____ _____

B. Use at least two of the Key Vocabulary words. Explain why you think keeping Earth clean is important.

_____

_____

_____

Analyze Argument and Evidence

As you read "Not-So-Starry Nights," identify arguments the author makes. Then decide if the author supports that argument and what reasons or evidence are used for support. Complete the Argument Chart.

Argument	Support (Yes/No)	Evidence
A star-filled sky is an important part of our lives.		

Selection Review

Name _____

Not-So-Starry Nights

Key Vocabulary

benefit	protect
environment	reduce
migrate	released
pollution	wasted

A. Read the paragraph.
Write a Key Vocabulary word in each blank.
Reread the paragraph to make sure the words make sense.

Light _____ is a growing problem. It is true that light can _____ people who need it for safety or to see in the dark. However, a lot of night light fades into the clouds as it is _____ into the sky. It needs to be aimed at the ground so that it isn't _____. Many animals are sensitive to light. Darkness helps _____ some animals from being eaten. The moon and stars guide animals that _____. If we _____ light in the _____, we do everyone a favor.

B. Write complete sentences to answer these questions about "Not-So-Starry Nights."

1. What are some ways that you and your family can **reduce** your use of light?

_____

_____

_____

_____

_____

_____

2. What are some ways that light **pollution** is as bad as other kinds of **pollution**?

_____

_____

_____

_____

_____

_____

Vocabulary Study

Name _____

Use Context Clues

▶ Follow the steps below to figure out the meaning of each underlined word.

1. **1.** Look at each underlined word. Use context clues to help you write the meaning of each underlined word.
2. **2.** Write the context clues that helped you determine the meaning.
3. **3.** Check your meaning in a dictionary.

1. The computer instructor told his students to get on the <u>web</u> to research an interesting topic.

   Meaning: _____

   Context Clues: _____

2. The baseball player was finished batting after he hit the ball and was <u>out</u>.

   Meaning: _____

   Context Clues: _____

3. The play shown at the theater had ten members in the <u>cast</u>.

   Meaning: _____

   Context Clues: _____

4. I need to <u>book</u> a room at the hotel for a week.

   Meaning: _____

   Context Clues: _____

5. Use the computer <u>mouse</u> to click on an object.

   Meaning: _____

   Context Clues: _____

6. The political <u>party</u> chose a candidate for president after a group vote.

   Meaning: _____

   Context Clues: _____

7. I am attending a job <u>fair</u> this weekend to try to find a good job.

   Meaning: _____

   Context Clues: _____

© National Geographic Learning, a part of Cengage Learning, Inc.

Unit 7 Star Power **233**

Academic Vocabulary

Not-So-Starry Nights: Academic Vocabulary Review

Academic Vocabulary	
analyze	fact
compare	locate
evaluate	

A. Use your own words to tell what each Academic Vocabulary word means.

Word	My Definition
1. **analyze**	
2. **compare**	
3. **evaluate**	
4. **fact**	
5. **locate**	

B. Rewrite each sentence. Replace each underlined word or phrase with an Academic Vocabulary word.

1. The students think about the similarities and differences between the two planets.

    _____

2. Shirley provided the piece of information they needed to make a decision.

    _____

3. Tom and Carmen can examine all of the parts of the plan.

    _____

4. After they grade the plan and suggest changes, we can begin work.

    _____

5. The new lights will let the science club find more objects in space.

    _____

John F. Kennedy's Speech on Going to the Moon

BY JOHN F. KENNEDY

1   If we are to win the battle that is now going on around the world between freedom and **tyranny**, the dramatic achievements in **space** which occurred in recent weeks should have made clear to us all, as did the **Sputnik** in 1957, the impact of this adventure on the minds of men everywhere, who are attempting to make a determination of which road they should take. Since early in my term, our efforts in space have been under review. With the advice of the Vice President, who is Chairman of the National Space Council, we have examined where we are strong and where we are not, where we may succeed and where we may not. Now it is time to take longer strides—time for a great new American **enterprise**—time for this nation to take a clearly leading role in space achievement, which in many ways may hold the key to our future on earth.

2   I believe we possess all the resources and talents necessary. But the facts of the matter are that we have never made the national decisions or **marshaled** the national resources required for such leadership. We have never specified long-range goals on an urgent time schedule, or managed our resources and our time so as to insure their fulfillment.

3   Recognizing the head start obtained by the Soviets with their large rocket engines, which gives them many months of lead time, and recognizing the likelihood that they will exploit this lead for some time to come in still more impressive successes, we nevertheless are required to make new efforts on our own. For while we cannot guarantee that we shall one day be first, we can guarantee that any failure to make this effort will make us last. We take an additional risk by making it in full view of the world, but as shown by the **feat of astronaut Shepard**, this very risk enhances our stature when we are successful. But this is not merely a race. Space is open to us now; and our eagerness to share its meaning is not governed by the efforts of others. We go into space because whatever mankind must undertake, free men must fully share.

Key Vocabulary
- **space** *n.*, the area beyond Earth

In Other Words
tyranny unjust government
Sputnik Soviet space satellite
enterprise project
marshaled arranged properly
feat of astronaut Shepard fact that astronaut Alan Shepard was the first American to travel into space

4   I therefore ask the Congress, above and beyond the increases I have earlier requested for space activities, to provide the funds, which are needed to meet the following national goal[s]:

5   First, I believe that this nation should commit itself to achieving the goal, before this decade is out, of landing a man on the moon and returning him safely to the earth. No single space project in this period will be more impressive to mankind, or more important for the long-range exploration of space; and none will be so difficult or expensive to accomplish. We propose to accelerate the development of the appropriate lunar spacecraft. We propose to develop **alternate liquid and solid fuel boosters**, much larger than any now being developed, until certain, which is superior. We propose additional funds for other engine development and for **unmanned explorations**—explorations which are particularly important for one purpose which this nation will never overlook: the survival of the man who first makes this daring flight. But in a very real sense, it will not be one man going to the moon—if we **make this judgment affirmatively**, it will be an entire nation. For

"I believe we should go to the moon."

all of us must work to put him there.

6   It is a most important decision that we make as a nation. But all of you have lived through the last four years and have seen the significance of space and the adventures in space, and no one can predict with certainty what the ultimate meaning will be of mastery of space.

7   I believe we should go to the moon. But I think every citizen of this country as well as the Members of the Congress should consider the matter carefully in making their judgment, to which we have given attention over many weeks and months, because it is a **heavy burden**, and there is no sense in agreeing or desiring that the United States take an affirmative position in outer space, unless we are prepared to do the work and bear the burdens to make it successful. If we are not, we should decide today and this year.

8   New objectives and new money cannot solve these problems. They could in fact, **aggravate them further**—unless every scientist, every engineer, every serviceman, every technician, contractor, and civil servant gives his personal pledge that this nation will move forward, with the full speed of freedom, in the exciting adventure of space.

In Other Words

alternate liquid and solid fuel boosters other ways to power spacecraft

unmanned explorations space exploration without human astronauts

make this judgment affirmatively decide to explore space

heavy burden important decision

aggravate them further make them worse

▶ Read for Understanding

A. What kind of text is this? How do you know?

_____

_____

B. Write a sentence that tells the topic of the selection.

_____

_____

▶ Reread and Summarize

C. On **Practice Book** pages 236–237, circle the 3–5 most important words in each section. Make notes about why you chose each word. Why is the word important in the section?

1. Section 1: (paragraphs 1–3)

_____

_____

2. Section 2: (paragraphs 4–7)

_____

_____

3. Section 3: (paragraph 8)

_____

_____

D. Use your topic sentence from above and your notes to write a summary of the selection.

_____

_____

_____

_____

▶ Reread and Analyze

E. Analyze the position in this text.

1. Reread paragraphs 4–5 on **Practice Book** page 237. What is the speech's topic? What is John F. Kennedy's position on the issue? What reasons and evidence does he use to support his position? Underline words and phrases that support your answers.

_____

_____

_____

2. Underline phrases and sentences on **Practice Book** pages 236–237 that support the writer's argument. Explain how these reasons and evidence support the argument.

_____

_____

F. Analyze the facts and emotions used to support an argument.

1. Reread paragraph 3 on **Practice Book** page 236. What are some facts presented by John F. Kennedy? Underline those facts.

_____

_____

_____

2. How does Kennedy use language to appeal to people's emotions? Give one example.

_____

_____

▶ **Discuss and Write**

G. Synthesize your ideas about analyzing an argument.

1. With the class, discuss how the writer used reasons and evidence to support his argument. List reasons, facts, or other pieces of evidence used by the writer.

_____

_____

_____

2. Using the reasons and evidence that you listed, write a paragraph about how Kennedy supported his argument. Use the questions below to organize your thoughts.

· What is the topic? What is Kennedy's argument about the topic?

· What reasons, facts, and other pieces of evidence does Kennedy use?

· What language does Kennedy use to convince the reader?

· Do you think Kennedy's argument is convincing? Explain.

_____

_____

_____

_____

_____

▶ **Connect with**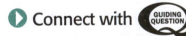

H. Discuss the Guiding Question: What can we learn from the stars?

1. According to John F. Kennedy, why is it important for the United States to participate in space exploration?

_____

2. What do you think John F. Kennedy thinks we can learn from space exploration?

_____

_____

_____

Academic Vocabulary Review

Academic Vocabulary

analyze	evaluate
appropriate	fact
compare	locate
discuss	space
element	style

A. Circle the Academic Vocabulary word that best fits into each sentence.

1. Scientists like to (**discuss** / **locate**) star facts with each other.

2. The (**fact** / **style**) of Dr. Suarez's long report was very formal.

3. The contest judges will (**appropriate** / **evaluate**) each entry for its strengths.

4. Flour is the basic (**element** / **fact**) needed to bake a cake.

B. Use your own words to tell what each Academic Vocabulary word means. Then write a synonym.

Word	My Definition	Synonym
1. **analyze**		
2. **appropriate**		
3. **fact**		
4. **locate**		

C. Complete each sentence.

1. If I could travel in **space**, I would _____

_____

_____ .

2. To **compare** a winter day and a summer day, I would tell about _____

_____

_____ .

3. My **style** of expression is different when I write than when I speak because _____

_____

_____ .

Key Vocabulary Review

A. Read each sentence. Circle the Key Vocabulary word that best fits into each sentence.

1. Fresh air is a great (**benefit** / **advice**) of keeping the planet clean.

2. If you kick a pile of leaves, the leaves will (**continue** / **scatter**) all over the yard.

3. It is important to (**reduce** / **protect**) our planet.

4. The boy will (**release** / **remain**) the fish back into the pond.

5. The (**distance** / **temperature**) is very low, so we know that it is cold outside.

6. Birds (**vary** / **migrate**) in the winter.

7. There are so many stars in the (**universe** / **telescope**).

8. A foot is a (**unit** / **orbit**) that we use to measure length.

B. Use your own words to write what each Key Vocabulary word means.
Then write an example for each word.

Word	My Definition	Example
1. **distance**		
2. **environment**		
3. **hunter**		
4. **orbit**		
5. **pollution**		
6. **reduce**		
7. **track**		
8. **vary**		

Unit 7 Key Vocabulary

advice	environment	pollution	remain	tale	unit
benefit	hunter	protect	roam	telescope	universe
continue	migrate	reduce	scatter	temperature	vary
distance	orbit	release	space	track	wasted

C. Answer the questions in complete sentences.

1. Share an example of a way that you can prevent water from being **wasted** .

   _____

   _____

2. Whom do you count on for **advice** ?

   _____

   _____

3. What is something that you will **continue** to do for as long as possible?

   _____

   _____

4. Share an example of a place in which you would like to **roam** .

   _____

   _____

5. Where would you like to **remain** for a month?

   _____

   _____

6. What would you hope to find if you were to explore outer **space** ?

   _____

   _____

7. What is your favorite **tale** ?

   _____

   _____

8. What is something that you would like to see through a **telescope** ?

   _____

   _____

Mind Map

Use the mind map to show your ideas about how people express feelings and **beliefs** through art. As you read the selections in this unit, add new ideas you learn about art and expression.

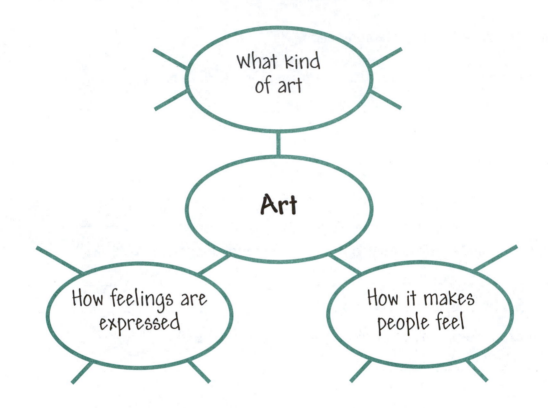

Academic Vocabulary

Think about how people express a **belief**. Why do you think people have different **beliefs**? Use the word **belief** in your answer.

_____

_____

_____

_____

Name _____

Text Features: In Fiction and in Nonfiction

Read the passage. Look for text features that help make the text more understandable by organizing information and showing information visually. Then answer the questions.

Making Scrapbooks with Grandma

Grandma started making scrapbooks before I was born. She helped me with my first scrapbook last year. I used photos of my family playing ball. Now I have many themes in my scrapbooks. I have fun making scrapbooks.

Steps We Take

When Grandma and I work on our scrapbooks, we first decide which pictures we want to use. Then we select patterned paper to put the pictures on. After that, we arrange the pictures and stick them on the pages.

My favorite part of the project is adding stickers and captions to the pages. We can work for hours on a scrapbook. When we are finished, my whole family enjoys looking at our scrapbooks.

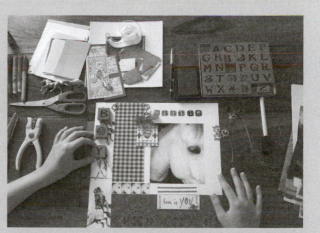

▲ A scrapbook can be made using a wide variety of materials, such as ribbons, stickers, and rubber stamps.

1. What text features help you understand the passage?

_____

_____

2. Write how the text features help guide you through the text by organizing information and showing information visually.

_____

_____

Academic Vocabulary

What images would you **select** to make your own scrapbook page? Explain why.

_____

_____

_____

_____

Go Beyond the Literal Meaning

▶ Read the passages. Follow these steps to figure out the meanings
of the underlined phrases.

1. Look at the sentences nearby. See if they give clues to the meaning.
2. Predict a literal meaning that might fit in the context.
3. Reread the sentence to see if your definition makes sense. If it does
   not, ask someone to explain the phrase.

A. Follow the directions above. Write the meaning of each underlined phrase.

> People who are <u>excellent</u> at drawing might <u>try their hand at</u> painting. You must
> know how colors work together when painting. You must also learn how to hold
> the brush correctly. This can <u>make a world of difference</u>.

try their hand at _____

make a world of difference _____

Which word means almost the same as <u>excellent</u>? How does the author's
use of <u>excellent</u> change the sentence?

_____

B. Follow the directions above. Write the meaning of each underlined phrase.

> Many ice skaters <u>believe</u> skating is an art form. An ice skater's movements are
> <u>a brush stroke across a painter's canvas</u>. Ice skaters perform many tricky jumps,
> spins, and dance moves. Skaters must <u>put their mind on</u> their skating.

a brush stroke across a painter's canvas _____

put their mind on _____

What word means almost the same as <u>believe</u>? How does the author's use
of <u>believe</u> change the sentence?

_____

Academic Vocabulary

If a new student comes to our class, he or she will not know about our school or our class.
There are many things I will **communicate** to the new student, such as _____

_____

Critical Viewing Guide

▶ Take Notes

A. View the video. Take notes on at least three things that you learned.

_____

_____

_____

_____

_____

_____

_____

_____

▶ Analyze the Video

B. Review your notes to help answer these questions.

1. Write two sentences to explain what was in the video.

_____

_____

_____

2. What was the most interesting thing you learned?

_____

_____

_____

3. What did the video tell about different **beliefs**? Tell how some cultures express their **beliefs**.

_____

_____

_____

_____

Learn Key Vocabulary

Name _____

Old Music Finds New Voices: Key Vocabulary

A. Study each word. Circle a number to rate how well you know it. Then complete the chart.

Do you dream of a **career** in music? If you practice playing your **instrument**, you can be a musician! ▶

Rating Scale	**1** I have never seen this word before.	**2** I am not sure of the word's meaning.	**3** I know this word and can teach the word's meaning to someone else.

Key Words	Check Understanding	Deepen Understanding
❶ approve (u-**prüv**) *verb* **Rating:** 1 2 3	☐ to think something is right or good ☐ to argue with someone	If my teacher approves, I will _____ _____ _____ _____ _____ .
❷ career (ku-**rear**) *noun* **Rating:** 1 2 3	☐ a job someone trains for and does full-time ☐ a container for cards	A career I would enjoy is _____ _____ _____ _____ _____ .
❸ competition (kom-pu-**ti**-shun) *noun* **Rating:** 1 2 3	☐ a project done by a team ☐ a contest	To win a spelling competition, you must _____ _____ _____ _____ _____ .
❹ concert (**kont**-surt) *noun* **Rating:** 1 2 3	☐ an event where people play music for an audience ☐ an event where teams play against each other	If I went to a concert, I might see _____ _____ _____ _____ _____ .

When these dancers perform the dances of their ancestors, they **preserve** their **roots.** ▶

Key Words	Check Understanding	Deepen Understanding
❺ **instrument** (**int**-stru-munt) *noun* Rating: 1 2 3	☐ an imaginary device ☐ something that you play to make music	If I could play any instrument, I would play _____ _____ _____ _____ _____ .
❻ **preserve** (pri-**zurv**) *verb* Rating: 1 2 3	☐ to save or keep ☐ to throw away	A family tradition that I would like to preserve is_____ _____ _____ _____ .
❼ **roots** (rüts) *noun* Rating: 1 2 3	☐ a person's tradition or culture ☐ what you eat for breakfast	My family's roots are in _____ _____ _____ _____ .
❽ **support** (su-**port**) *verb* Rating: 1 2 3	☐ to suspect ☐ to help	My friends support me when _____ _____ _____ _____ .

B. Use at least two of the Key Vocabulary words. Write about what you think it would be like to perform in front of a large audience.

_____

_____

_____

Analyze News Media

As you read "Old Music Finds New Voices," look for facts and opinions.
Complete the Fact and Opinion Chart.

What I Read	Fact or Opinion	What It Makes Me Think
Schools offer courses in mariachi music.	fact	I will learn more about how important mariachi music is.

Old Music Finds New Voices

A. Read the paragraph.
Write a Key Vocabulary word in each blank.
Reread the paragraph to make sure the words make sense.

Mexican-American teens are getting in touch with their _____ . They are exploring mariachi music by singing and playing _____ . Some teens perform in parades and _____ . Some, like singer Virginia Stille, win prizes in _____ . Their families _____ of their interest. They _____ their teens' talents. Some teens may choose musical _____ . All of them use music to _____ their links to their culture.

B. Write complete sentences to answer these questions about "Old Music Finds New Voices."

1. What are some of the ways that people can **support** mariachi?

_____

_____

_____

_____

_____

_____

2. How can singing provide a strong connection to family **roots**?

_____

_____

_____

_____

_____

_____

Interpret Metaphors

▶ Follow the steps below to figure out the meaning of each metaphor.
   1. Read the sentence. Find the metaphor and underline it.
   2. Think about the two things that are compared in the metaphor.
   3. Explain the meaning of the metaphor.

1. The inside of the car was a raging fire in the hot sunshine.

   _____

2. The biker's motorcycle is the sunshine of his life.

   _____

3. My dad boiled over like a pot of water.

   _____

4. Her legs were jelly when she stood up to make a speech.

   _____

5. The athlete's heart was a beating drum before the race began.

   _____

6. My job is an anchor weighing me down when I want to rise up.

   _____

7. His mind is a machine that constantly turns out ideas.

   _____

8. The ants are an army waiting to conquer the food left out on the kitchen counter.

   _____

9. The dancer's graceful moves were a breath of fresh air after watching the previous
   dancers fall down.

   _____

Academic Vocabulary

Name _____

Academic Vocabulary

belief	report
communicate	select
interpret	

Old Music Finds New Voices:
Academic Vocabulary Review

A. Draw a line to match each Academic Vocabulary word with its meaning.

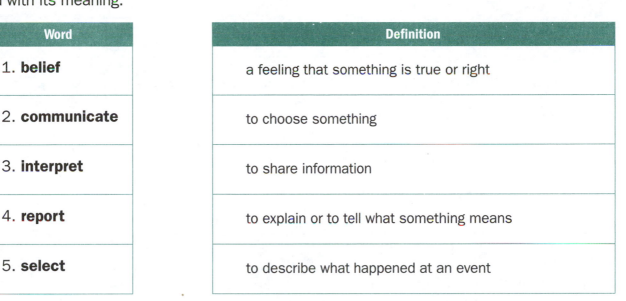

Word	Definition
1. **belief**	a feeling that something is true or right
2. **communicate**	to choose something
3. **interpret**	to share information
4. **report**	to explain or to tell what something means
5. **select**	to describe what happened at an event

B. Write the Academic Vocabulary word that best completes each sentence.

1. Our _____ is that our school choir can win the state competition.

2. Brandon will _____ on the competition in the school newspaper.

3. We asked the radio station to _____ the information.

4. Abigail and Kent will _____ music to listen to in class.

5. Mr. Levy will help them _____ the meaning of the lyrics.

C. Answer the questions in complete sentences.

1. What kind of music would you like to **report** about for a writing assignment? Why?

_____

_____

2. If you had a friend who lived in another country, how would you **communicate** with that friend?

_____

_____

Build Background

Critical Viewing Guide

▶ **Take Notes**

A. View the images. Take notes on at least three things that you learned.

_____

_____

_____

_____

_____

_____

_____

_____

▶ **Analyze the Images**

B. Review your notes to help answer these questions.

1. Write two sentences to explain what was in the images.

_____

_____

_____

2. What was the most interesting thing you learned?

_____

_____

_____

3. What did the images show about expressing **beliefs**? Why is it important to express a **belief**?

_____

_____

_____

_____

Learn Key Vocabulary

Name _____

Making Faces: Key Vocabulary

A. Study each word. Circle a number to rate how well you know it. Then complete the chart.

Rating Scale	**1** I have never seen this word before.	**2** I am not sure of the word's meaning.	**3** I know this word and can teach the word's meaning to someone else.

▲ This Japanese actor will **perform** in a **costume**.

Key Words	Check Understanding	Deepen Understanding
❶ **belief** (bu-**lēf**) *noun* **Rating:** 1 2 3	A **belief** is a feeling that you are wrong. **Yes** **No**	List other words that describe *belief*:_____ _____ _____ _____ _____
❷ **carve** (**karv**) *verb* **Rating:** 1 2 3	A woodworker uses a saw to **carve** wood. **Yes** **No**	List other words that describe *carve*:_____ _____ _____ _____ _____
❸ **collect** (ku-**lekt**) *verb* **Rating:** 1 2 3	Someone who **collects** baseball cards does not have any baseball cards. **Yes** **No**	List other words that describe *collect*:_____ _____ _____ _____ _____
❹ **costume** (**kos**-tüm) *noun* **Rating:** 1 2 3	A **costume** can make you look like somebody else. **Yes** **No**	List other words that describe *costume*:_____ _____ _____ _____ _____

Name _____

For celebrations in some countries, people **design** and **decorate** their own **masks**. ▶

Key Words	Check Understanding	Deepen Understanding
5 decorate (**de**-ku-rāt) *verb* **Rating:** 1 2 3	You can **decorate** your room to make it look nicer. **Yes** **No**	List other words that describe *decorate*:_____ _____ _____ _____ _____
6 design (di-**zīn**) *noun* **Rating:** 1 2 3	The **design** of a costume does not affect the way it looks. **Yes** **No**	List other words that describe *design*:_____ _____ _____ _____ _____
7 mask (mask) *noun* **Rating:** 1 2 3	You usually wear a **mask** on your feet. **Yes** **No**	List other words that describe *mask*:_____ _____ _____ _____ _____
8 perform (pur-**form**) *verb* **Rating:** 1 2 3	When you **perform**, you do something in front of an audience. **Yes** **No**	List other words that describe *perform*:_____ _____ _____ _____ _____

B. Use at least two of the Key Vocabulary words. Write about how you like to celebrate a tradition.

_____

_____

_____

Analyze Author's Purpose and Tone

A. As you read "Making Faces," look at the author's word choice to analyze the author's purpose. Think about the connotation of the words to help you identify the author's tone. Complete the Author's Purpose Chart.

Word Choice	Tone	Purpose
shocked; strange face	friendly	to entertain

B. What is the author's purpose? Use details from the text to support your answer.

_____

_____

_____

_____

Making Faces

Key Vocabulary

beliefs	decorated
carve	designs
collects	masks
costumes	perform

A. Read the paragraph.
Write a Key Vocabulary word in each blank.
Reread the paragraph to make sure the words make sense.

Dear Grandpa,

I went to visit my neighbor. His name is Ronald, and he _____ things from his travels.

He has many face _____ from all over the world. Artists _____ beautiful

_____ from wood to make masks. Some of the masks are _____ with beads and

feathers. People wear them to _____ traditional dances. Ronald also told me about

_____ people wear in the dances. He can tell you all about the customs and

_____ behind the things he collects. Ronald is the most interesting person I know!

Love,

Janet

B. Write complete sentences to answer these questions about "Making Faces."

1. What animal **design** would you choose to make a **mask** that shows your personality? Why?

_____

_____

_____

_____

_____

2. How can **masks** make people feel fear or courage or joy?

_____

_____

_____

_____

_____

Vocabulary Study

Name _____

Analyze Idioms

▶ Follow the steps below to figure out the meaning of each idiom.
1. Read the sentence. Look for context clues that help you figure out the meaning of the underlined phrase.
2. Write the meaning of the underlined idiom.
3. Then use the idiom in a sentence to express your own ideas.

1. I forgot to study because it slipped my mind that I had a math test.

   Meaning: _____

   Sentence: _____

2. My mother told me I was trying her patience when I asked her again for a new pair of jeans.

   Meaning: _____

   Sentence: _____

3. When I spilled my lunch on my lap, I wished the ground would swallow me.

   Meaning: _____

   Sentence: _____

4. My sister pulled a fast one on me when she did not return my money.

   Meaning: _____

   Sentence: _____

5. I gave my teacher the answers, but he said I was on the wrong track.

   Meaning: _____

   Sentence: _____

6. The college student knew how to write an essay inside and out.

   Meaning: _____

   Sentence: _____

7. I went into the store to buy some crackers, but one thing led to another, and I ended up buying a bottle of juice and some apples, too.

   Meaning: _____

   Sentence: _____

Academic Vocabulary

Making Faces: Academic Vocabulary Review

Academic Vocabulary

belief	element
communicate	identify
create	select

A. Write the Academic Vocabulary word next to the correct definition.

Definition	Word
1. to find out or to show what something is	
2. to choose something	
3. to share information	
4. a feeling that something is true or right	
5. to make something new	
6. a basic part of a whole	

B. Respond to each item with a complete sentence.

1. Describe a face mask you would like to **create**.

_____

2. What is one way to **identify** the most popular music among your friends?

_____

3. Think about your favorite movie. Which **element** do you like best, characters or setting? Why?

_____

4. Is it your **belief** that more students like soccer or basketball? Support your opinion.

_____

5. **Select** three colors to paint your classroom. Tell why you chose those colors.

_____

6. If you had to tell friends about an event, how would you **communicate** the information?

_____

© National Geographic Learning, a part of Cengage Learning, Inc.

Name _____

Critical Viewing Guide

▶ **Take Notes**

A. View the images. Take notes on at least three things that you learned.

_____

_____

_____

_____

_____

_____

_____

_____

▶ **Analyze the Images**

B. Review your notes to help answer these questions.

1. Write two sentences to explain what was in the images.

_____

_____

_____

2. What was the most interesting thing you learned?

_____

_____

_____

3. What did the images show about the **belief** that human flight is possible?

_____

_____

_____

_____

Learn Key Vocabulary

Name _____

Wings: Key Vocabulary

A. Study each word. Circle a number to rate how well you know it. Then complete the chart.

Rating Scale	**1** I have never seen this word before.	**2** I am not sure of the word's meaning.	**3** I know this word and can teach the word's meaning to someone else.

▲ The people who invented early flying machines **struggled** to get off the ground. Imagine how **proud** you would have felt to be the first person in flight!

Key Words	Check Understanding	Deepen Understanding
❶ **complain** (kum-**plān**) *verb* **Rating:** 1 2 3	Circle the synonym for **complain**. grumble praise	Sometimes I complain because _____ _____ _____ _____ _____ .
❷ **drift** (**drift**) *verb* **Rating:** 1 2 3	Circle the synonym for **drift**. swim float	You could drift down the river in a _____ _____ _____ _____ _____ .
❸ **droop** (**drüp**) *verb* **Rating:** 1 2 3	Circle the synonym for **droop**. drip bend	If a flower droops, it probably needs _____ _____ _____ _____ _____ .
❹ **impressed** (im-**prest**) *adjective* **Rating:** 1 2 3	Circle the synonym for **impressed**. enclosed affected	I am impressed by _____ _____ _____ _____ _____ .

Name _____

Key Words	Check Understanding	Deepen Understanding
❺ proud (**prowd**) *adjective* Rating: 1 2 3	Circle the synonym for **proud.** **pleased** **slow**	Something that makes me proud is _____ _____ _____ _____ _____ .
❻ struggle (**stru**-gul) *verb* Rating: 1 2 3	Circle the synonym for **struggle.** **mess up** **work hard**	Something I struggle with is _____ _____ _____ _____ _____ .
❼ useless (**yūs**-lus) *adjective* Rating: 1 2 3	Circle the synonym for **useless.** **worthless** **useful**	An example of something that is useless is _____ _____ _____ _____ _____ .
❽ whisper (**whis**-pur) *verb* Rating: 1 2 3	Circle the synonym for **whisper.** **shout** **mumble**	I have to whisper when _____ _____ _____ _____ _____ .

B. Use at least two of the Key Vocabulary words. Write about a time when you achieved one of your goals.

_____

_____

_____

Analyze Plot

As you read "Wings," look for story details that tell how the plot unfolds and how the characters respond to plot events. Complete the Plot Diagram as you read.

Climax: _____
_____

Event 4: _____
_____

Event 3: _____
_____

Event 2: _____
_____

Event 1: _____
_____

Rising Action

Falling Action

Resolution: _____
_____

Problem: _____
_____

Exposition: Ikarus Jackson is a flying boy.

Selection Review

Wings

Key Vocabulary

complains	proud
drifts	struggles
droop	useless
impressed	whispers

A. Read the paragraph.
Write a Key Vocabulary word in each blank.
Reread the paragraph to make sure the words make sense.

I am _____ with my new classmate, Ikarus. He floats and _____ above the crowd.

When he isn't flying, his wings _____ . They just hang like _____ feathery flaps.

He _____ to keep them under control during school. Everyone stands in small groups and

_____ about him. Ikarus never _____ about it to anyone, but I know it must hurt.

Ikarus is _____ of his amazing talent. I think that Ikarus and I are going to be great friends.

B. Write complete sentences to answer these questions about "Wings."

1. What do Ikarus and the narrator have in common?

_____

_____

_____

_____

_____

_____

2. What special power, talent, or skill would you like to have? How do you think
   other people would respond to you?

_____

_____

_____

_____

_____

_____

_____

Vocabulary Study

Name _____

Similes

▶ Follow the steps below to figure out the meaning of each simile.
1. Read the sentence and find the simile.
2. Write what the simile compares.
3. Explain how the two things are alike.

1. The forest is like an endless maze.

   The simile compares _____.

   Explanation: _____

2. The elderly woman seems as weak as a broken chair.

   The simile compares _____.

   Explanation: _____

3. Her family is like a warm, fuzzy blanket.

   The simile compares _____.

   Explanation: _____

4. The surface of the water was like a mirror.

   The simile compares _____.

   Explanation: _____

5. The food tasted like cardboard.

   The simile compares _____.

   Explanation: _____

6. He laughed as loud as the roar of an airplane's engine.

   The simile compares _____.

   Explanation: _____

7. Michael's new car goes as fast as a rocket.

   The simile compares _____.

   Explanation: _____

Compare Characters

A. Read the passage. Think about what the allusion means.

> Kylie's paintings are well known by most students. Her work has been featured in art shows at school. The announcements always say, "Come see the paintings of our own Vincent van Gogh!" Kylie has entered art contests, too. However, unlike van Gogh, Kylie is a quiet and happy person. She would never dream of cutting off her ear. She paints great sunflowers though!

B. Reread the passage to answer the questions.

1. Vincent van Gogh's art appears in museums and includes famous pictures of sunflowers. What does the allusion to Vincent van Gogh tell you about Kylie?

   _____

   _____

2. Vincent van Gogh cut off part of his ear in an angry moment. How does this allusion help you understand Kylie as a person?

   _____

   _____

C. Think of a famous artist, musician, or other well-known person or character. Write a passage about two people who meet in class. Use at least one allusion to the famous person in your writing.

_____

_____

_____

_____

_____

_____

_____

_____

Academic Vocabulary

Name _____

Academic Vocabulary

| communicate | interpret |
| compare | series |

Wings: Academic Vocabulary Review

A. Use your own words to tell what each Academic Vocabulary word means.

Word	My Definition
1. **communicate**	
2. **compare**	
3. **interpret**	
4. **series**	

B. Write each Academic Vocabulary word in a sentence.

1. **communicate** _____

_____

2. **compare** _____

_____

3. **interpret** _____

_____

4. **series** _____

_____

Pas de Trois

by Sandy Asher

"You cannot,"
it's been said,
"separate the dancer
from the dance."

5 Sculptors
step away,
poets
put down their pens;
their work **endures**.

10 Hands
that pluck the strings
of a harp
are neither instrument
nor **celestial song**.

15 But no dance exists
without its dancer.

To my eye, this line
choreographs:
glissade,
20 arabesque,
tombé,
pirouette…
Strength, balance,
energy and rhythm
25 draw me in.
A dance is clearly **intended**.

Between us
appears
the dancer.

In Other Words
endures lives on
celestial song song of the heavens
choreographs designs a dance
intended meant to be

▲ **Critical Viewing** How is the painting like dance? According to the poem, how is it not like dance?

Cultural Background

Ballet is a type of dance that includes specific positions and movements.

arabesque   glissade   tombé   pirourette

▶ **Read for Understanding**

A. What kind of text is this? How do you know?

_____

_____

B. Write a sentence that tells the topic of the selection.

_____

_____

▶ **Reread and Summarize**

C. On **Practice Book** page 270, circle the 3–5 most important words in each section. Make notes about why you chose each word. Why is the word important?

1. Section 1: (lines 1–14)

_____

_____

2. Section 2: (lines 15–22)

_____

_____

3. Section 3: (lines 23–29)

_____

_____

D. Use your topic sentence from above and your notes to write a summary of the selection.

_____

_____

_____

◗ Reread and Analyze

E. Analyze how the author's word choice has figurative, or symbolic, meanings.

    1. Reread lines 5–9 on **Practice Book** page 270. What do the words in these lines mean? Use evidence from the text to support your answer.

    _____

    _____

    _____

    2. Underline another word or phrase on **Practice Book** page 270 that has a figurative meaning and explain its meaning. Use evidence from the text to support your answer.

    _____

    _____

F. Analyze how each stanza helps develop the theme.

    1. Reread lines 10–16 on **Practice Book** page 270. How do these stanzas develop the theme that dance is a special art, unlike others? Use evidence from the text to support your answer.

    _____

    _____

    _____

    2. On **Practice Book** page 270, circle other stanzas and explain how they develop the theme.

    _____

    _____

▶ **Discuss and Write**

G. Synthesize your ideas about how the writer used figurative language and how the stanzas develop the theme.

1. With the class, discuss the writer's word choice. List examples from the poem as you discuss.

_____   _____   _____

_____   _____   _____

_____   _____   _____

2. Choose one stanza from the poem. Write a paragraph about the writer's word choice. Use the questions below to organize your thoughts.

· What is the stanza about?

· What are the meanings of the words and phrases used?

· How does this stanza fit into the rest of the poem?

_____

_____

_____

_____

_____

▶ **Connect with**

H. Discuss the Guiding Question: What do we learn about people from their artful expressions?

1. What do we learn about dancers through their artful expression?

_____

2. How are dancers different from poets, sculptors, and musicians?

_____

_____

3. What is the writer's message about artful expressions?

_____

Name _____

Academic Vocabulary Review

Academic Vocabulary

belief	interpret
communicate	report
compare	select
element	series
identify	

A. Circle the Academic Vocabulary word that best fits into each sentence.

1. To (**compare** / **select**), you look at how two things are alike.

2. A (**series** / **belief**) is a feeling that something is true.

3. To (**compare** / **communicate**) is to share information.

4. A group of related things that are put in order is a (**series** / **report**).

B. Write a synonym for each Academic Vocabulary word.
Choose from the words in the chart below.

Word	Choose from these words:			Synonym
1. **series**	box	group	design	
2. **element**	feature	grade	category	
3. **interpret**	share	speak	explain	
4. **select**	build	advise	choose	
5. **report**	tell	clear	smooth	

C. Complete each sentence.

1. To **identify** the favorite book of students in your class, you could _____

_____.

2. To **select** a movie for the class to watch, you could _____

_____.

3. To do a **report** on a famous opera, you could _____

_____.

4. To **compare** two sculptures made out of found objects, you might _____

_____.

Key Vocabulary Review

A. Read each sentence. Circle the Key Vocabulary word that best fits into each sentence.

1. I heard some wonderful music at the (**concert** / **costume**).

2. Before we could eat, Dad had to (**perform** / **carve**) the turkey.

3. The soup was cold, so he (**collected** / **complained**) to the waiter.

4. The branches of the tree (**droop** / **drift**) so far down that they almost touch the ground.

5. You have to (**struggle** / **whisper**) at the library.

6. The guitar is my favorite (**instrument** / **career**).

7. The broken doorbell is (**useless** / **proud**).

8. Sue (**supports** / **collects**) stamps in a scrapbook.

B. Use your own words to write what each Key Vocabulary word means. Then write an example for each word.

Word	My Definition	Example
1. **approve**		
2. **belief**		
3. **competition**		
4. **costume**		
5. **drift**		
6. **mask**		
7. **perform**		
8. **struggle**		

Name _____

Unit 8 Key Vocabulary

approve	collect	costume	droop	perform	struggle
belief	competition	decorate	impressed	preserve	support
career	complain	design	instrument	proud	useless
carve	concert	drift	mask	roots	whisper

C. Answer the questions in complete sentences.

1. If you could **decorate** your desk with something you like, what would you use?

   _____

   _____

2. What is something that **impressed** you?

   _____

   _____

3. Why is it important to **preserve** your family traditions?

   _____

   _____

4. What is something you have done that made you **proud**?

   _____

   _____

5. Why do you think people like to know about their **roots**?

   _____

   _____

6. What is your favorite **design**?

   _____

   _____

7. How do you **support** your friends?

   _____

   _____

8. What would you like to do for a **career**?

   _____

   _____

Grammar Practice

1 How Do You Make a Statement?

Capitalize the First Word, and Use a Period at the End.

A **statement** is one kind of sentence.
A statement tells something.

- A statement begins with a **capital letter**.

   Some people are animal lovers.

   Animal lovers are people who really like animals.

- A statement ends with a **period** (.).

   I am an animal lover**.**

   My mom is an animal lover, too**.**

Try It

A. Write the statements correctly. Add capital letters.

1. my dogs are loyal pets. _My dogs are loyal pets._____

2. one of my dogs is Rosie. _____

3. she is part lab and part golden retriever. _____

   _____

4. both those breeds are friendly, happy dogs. _____

   _____

B. Write the statements correctly. Add capital letters and periods.

5. my mother is a vet _My mother is a vet._____

6. her patients are animals _____

7. her biggest patient is a horse _____

8. her smallest patient is a mouse _____

Write It

C. Complete the statements about animals. Use a period at the end.

9. My favorite animal is _____

_____

10. Some animals in my neighborhood are _____

_____

11. Pets are _____

_____

D. (12–15) Are you an animal lover? Write at least four statements about animals that you see or know.

_____

_____

_____

_____

_____

Edit It

E. (16–20) Edit the journal entry. Fix the five mistakes in the statements. The first is done for you.

May 12

today I am at my mom's office. A new litter
of puppies is here The mother is a big black
dog with long, silky hair. her puppies are not
black, though. One of them is all white One
puppy is tan with white and black spots. he is
my favorite puppy. I want to take him home.

Proofreader's Marks

Capitalize:

dogs are animals.

Add period:

Cats are animals, too

See all Proofreader's Marks on page xi.

2 What Are the Forms of *Be*?

Am, Is, and *Are*

- Use **I** with **am**.

  I am on the soccer team.

- Use **he**, **she**, or **it** with **is**.

  It is a good team.

  Mr. Ruiz is the coach. **He is** a great coach.

  Sara is the goalie. **She is** a good goalie.

- Use **we**, **you**, or **they** with **are**.

  We are in the championship game.

  You are ready to play.

  The other team is good. **They are** ready to play, too.

Forms of *Be*
I **am**
he, she, or it **is**
we, you, or they **are**

Try It

A. (1–6) Complete each sentence in the paragraph. Use **am**, **is**, or **are**.

  I _____*am*_____ hopeful about the game. We _____ a
hard-working team. Ana is our captain. She _____ a good leader.
The players like Ana. They _____ glad Ana is captain. "You
_____ a winning team," Ana says. I _____ sure she is right.

B. Complete each sentence. Use the verb **am**, **is**, or **are**. Match the verb to
the subject.

7. You _____ ready to score.

8. They _____ in front of the goal.

9. It _____ a goal.

10. We _____ ahead.

11. I _____ ready to take charge.

12. We _____ the winners.

C. Answer the questions. Use am, is, and are in your answers.

13. What is the role of a good team player? It _____

_____.

14. What are team captains? They _____

_____.

15. Are you a player on a sports team? I _____

_____.

D. (16–19) Pretend you are a team captain. Write at least four sentences that you would say to your team to help them reach their goals. Use **am**, **is**, and **are** in your sentences.

_____

_____

_____

_____

Edit It

E. (20–25) Edit the letter. Fix the six incorrect verbs. Make sure to use **am**, **is**, and **are** correctly.

Coach,

    I is happy to be team captain. The players are my friends. They am all great soccer players. Sara is so good. She are an awesome goalie. We is capable of great things. You am a wonderful role model.

    It is time for a winning season. We is ready to play!

                        Ana

Proofreader's Marks

Change text:
We ~~is~~ soccer players. *are*

See all Proofreader's Marks on page xi.

❸ What Are the Forms of *Be*?

Am, Is, and *Are*

- Use the correct form of the verb **be**.
  Study these examples.

  I **am** from the United States.
  My mom **is** from Vietnam.
  She **is** Vietnamese and American.
  The two cultures **are** different.
  We **are** part of both cultures.

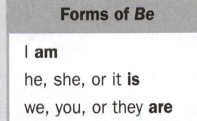

Forms of *Be*

I **am**
he, she, or it **is**
we, you, or they **are**

- Use **not** after the verbs **am**, **is**, and **are** to make a sentence negative.
  The short form of **is not** is **isn't**. The short form of **are not** is **aren't**.

  1. Dad **is not** from Vietnam.

  Dad **isn't** from Vietnam.

  2. My parents **are not** from the U.S.

  My parents **aren't** from the U.S.

Try It

A. Write the correct verb form to complete each sentence.

1. I _____ from a multicultural neighborhood.
　　　　　　　am / are

2. We _____ all alike in many ways.
　　　　　　is / are

3. The parents _____ all from the United States.
　　　　　　isn't / aren't

4. Each background culture _____ different.
　　　　　　　is / are

B. (5–10) Complete the paragraph. Use the correct form of **be**.

Julio's parents _____ from Colombia. They _____ speakers of both Spanish and English. Julio _____, too. I _____ able to speak Vietnamese, but my father can't. He _____ a speaker of Vietnamese. French _____ his native language.

C. Complete sentences that tell about neighbors in a multicultural neighborhood. Use a form of **be** in each sentence.

11. My next-door neighbors come from Italy. They _____.

12. Their son learns their customs from them. He _____.

13. I learn from my parents, too. I _____.

14. All children learn a lot from parents. Customs _____.

D. (15–18) Write at least four sentences about how your family's culture influences you. Use the correct form of **be** at least four times.

_____

_____

_____

_____

_____

Edit It

E. (19–25) Edit the interview. Use proofreader's marks to fix the seven mistakes with verbs.

Q: Your parents aren't from Canada, are they?

A: No, they is from Greece. We live in New York.

Q: How does their culture affect you?

A: Mom are a great cook. She makes Greek food. I are excited about learning how to cook Greek food. Dad aren't such a good cook, but he am a great Greek folk dancer. He are my teacher. I is glad my parents are Greek.

Proofreader's Marks

Change text:

Greek ~~am~~ is Dad's native language.

See all Proofreader's Marks on page xi.

Can You Start a Question with *Am, Is,* or *Are*?

Yes, When You're Looking for a Yes or No Answer

A **question** is one kind of sentence. A question asks something.

- A question begins with a **capital letter** and ends with a **question mark**.
  Am I in New York**?**

- If you want a "yes" or "no" answer, you can start a question with **am**, **is**, or **are**.

Question	Answer
Am I in New York?	No, you are not.
Is our city big?	Yes, our city is big.
Are you from the United States?	Yes, I am from the United States.

Try It

A. Write the questions correctly. Add capital letters and question marks.

1. is your family big _____Is your family big?_____

2. are you a student in this school _____

3. am I a teacher _____

4. is our school in New Mexico _____

5. are people in our community friendly_____

6. is the United States a country _____

B. Write **am**, **is**, or **are** to complete each question.
Add the correct end punctuation mark.

7. _____Is_____ the library close to our neighborhood __?___

8. _____ we in France _____

9. _____ I a middle school student _____

10. _____ there 50 states in the United States _____

11. _____ the United States a small country _____

12. _____ our state in the United States _____

Write It

C. Complete each question. Ask about our neighborhood.
Add the correct end punctuation mark.

13. Am _____

14. Is _____

15. Is _____

16. Are _____

17. Are _____

D. (18–20) What questions might you ask a new student? Write three
questions. Start each question with **am**, **is**, or **are**.

_____

_____

_____

_____

How Else Can You Start a Question?

With the Words *Who*, *What*, *When*, *Where*, *Why*, and *How*

If you want specific information, start a question with a question word such as **Who**, **What**, **When**, **Where**, **Why**, or **How**. Here are some examples.

Question Word	Asks About	Question	Answer
Who?	A person	Who are you?	I am a teacher.
What?	A thing	What do you teach?	I teach art.
When?	A time	When is art class?	It is at 11 a.m.
Where?	A place	Where is art class?	It is in Room 12.
Why?	A reason	Why are you here?	I am here to teach.
How?	In what way	How do you teach?	I show examples.

Try It

A. Write a question word from the chart to complete each question. We will use the question word that goes with the word in parentheses.

1. _____What_____ are your favorite school subjects? **(thing)**

2. _____ is your math teacher? **(person)**

3. _____ is homework helpful? **(in what way)**

4. _____ is your science class? **(place)**

5. _____ is lunch? **(time)**

6. _____ are your classes different every day? **(reason)**

B. Read each answer. Then write the question word that completes each question.

7. The principal is Mrs. Kelley. _____Who_____ is the principal?

8. The cafeteria is on the second floor. _____ is the cafeteria?

9. I take the bus to school. _____ are you on the bus?

10. Basketball practice is after school. _____ is basketball practice?

11. I have math, Spanish, and English homework. _____ is your homework?

12. I put on my alarm clock. _____ are you up in time for school?

Write It

C. Read each answer. Write a question that it answers.

13. Mr. Ruiz is a wonderful teacher. _____

14. Science is the best subject. _____

15. The science lab is next to the gym. _____

16. School is over at 2:30. _____

D. (17–20) Make believe you are a new student. What questions would you ask to learn about your new school? Write four questions. Start each question with a question word.

_____

_____

_____

_____

6 How Can You Change a Statement Into a Question?

Change the Order of the Words and the End Mark.

- A statement tells something. A statement ends with a period.
  Spring is Mom's favorite season**.**

- A question asks something. A question ends with a question mark.
  Is spring Mom's favorite season**?**

- You can change a statement into a question. First change the **word order**.
  Then change the **end mark**.

Statement	Question
Summer is a season.	Is summer a season?
The seasons are different.	Are the seasons different?

Try It

A. Change each statement into a question. Change the order of the underlined words.

1. <u>July is</u> in summer. _____ in summer?

2. <u>Leaves are</u> colorful in fall. _____ colorful in fall?

3. <u>Snowstorms are</u> common in winter. _____ common in winter?

4. <u>Spring is</u> rainy. _____ rainy?

B. Change the statement into a question. Complete the question.

5. Summer is hot. _____ hot?

6. Days are long in summer. _____ long in summer?

7. Skiing is a winter sport. _____ a winter sport?

8. The ski slopes are busy in winter. _____ busy in winter?

C. Read each statement. Then change it into a question. Write the question.

9. Summer is the best season. _____

10. The weather is hot and steamy. _____

11. The beaches are full of swimmers. _____

12. The kids are happy to be out of school. _____

D. (13–15) What is your favorite season? Write three statements about that season. Use **is** or **are** in each statement. Then change each statement into a question.

_____

_____

_____

_____

_____

Edit It

E. (16–20) Edit the letter. Fix the five mistakes in end marks.

Dear Grandma,

Today is the first day of summer? I am so happy about that. Summer is my favorite season? Is summer your favorite season, too. You are coming to visit in July this year. I cannot wait to see you. Are you ready for the long trip We are going to take you to the beach this year? We will have fun.

Love,

Carlos

Proofreader's Marks
Add a period: Winter is a season ⊙
Add a question mark: Is winter a season⌄
Change text: Winter is a season?⊙
See all Proofreader's Marks on page xi.

7 How Do You Give a Command?

Start with the Verb.

- A **statement** is one kind of sentence. A statement tells something. It begins with a **capital letter** and ends with a **period**.

  Mom has chores for me to do at home.

- A **command** is another kind of sentence. A command tells someone to do something. A command begins with a **capital letter** and ends with a **period**.

  Clean your room. **S**et the table.

- A polite command starts with the word *please*.

  Please wash the floors.

Try It

A. Write a word from the box to complete each command.

mow	get	please	put

1. _____Please_____ help Mom with the chores.

2. _____ the lawn mower from the garage.

3. _____ the grass in the backyard.

4. _____ the mowed grass in a bag.

B. Think of a word to complete each command. Write the word.

5. _____Take_____ the dog for a walk.

6. _____ the leash on first.

7. _____ to the dog park.

8. _____ be careful when you cross the streets.

C. Read each statement. Change it into a command. Write the command.

9. Dad needs help with the chores. _____

10. We can start with the indoor chores. _____

11. Someone has to wash the floors. _____

12. You have to dust the bookshelves. _____

D. (13–15) What chores do you have to do at home? Write three commands. Tell someone what chores to do for you.

_____

_____

_____

_____

_____

Edit It

E. (16–20) Edit the list of chores to do. Fix the five mistakes in the commands.

List of Afterschool Chores

1. Bring in the mail and the newspaper

2. go to the grocery store.

3. Buy some milk and some bread?

4. the cat its dinner.

5. Please your homework.

Proofreader's Marks
Add a period:
Clean your room
Add text:
help
Please me.
Change text:
Walk the dog
See all Proofreader's Marks on page xi.

8 When Do You Use Exclamations?

When You Want to Show Strong Feeling

- An **exclamation** is a sentence that shows strong feeling. An exclamation begins with a **capital letter** and ends with an **exclamation point**.

  This mountain is fantastic**!**

  The view from the top is outstanding**!**

- A **strong command** shows strong feeling, too. It begins with a **capital letter** and ends with an **exclamation point**.

  Watch out**! D**on't fall off the edge of the cliff**!**

- Not every sentence shows strong feeling. Do not use exclamations all the time. Only use them to show strong feeling.

  We are at the top of the mountain. Come and look. I can see for miles**!**

Try It

A. Write the exclamations and strong commands correctly.

1. that deer is so fast _That deer is so fast!_

   _____

2. watch out for that root _____

   _____

3. the leaves are the most colorful ever _____

   _____

4. that is the biggest squirrel _____

   _____

5. be careful not to trip on that tree stump _____

   _____

6. the woods are so pretty _____

   _____

B. Which three sentences do you think show strong feeling?
Write those as exclamations. Write the other sentences as statements.

7. i like to walk in the park in fall _I like to walk in the park in fall._ _____

_____

8. wow, that squirrel has huge cheeks _____

_____

9. the squirrel collects its winter food _____

_____

10. these leaves are the most amazing colors _____

_____

11. the trees are absolutely gorgeous this fall _____

_____

Write It

C. Answer each question. In at least two of your answers, use exclamations.

12. What is the most amazing animal you have ever seen?_____

_____

13. What do autumn leaves look like in your neighborhood? _____

_____

14. What is your favorite outdoor activity? _____

_____

15. What do you watch out for when you are outside? _____

_____

D. (16–20) Write at least five sentences about something you do outside.
Use three exclamations to show strong feeling. Remember to use the correct
punctuation marks for all of your sentences.

_____

_____

_____

9 Are All Sentences the Same?

No, They Have Different Purposes.

Four Kinds of Sentences

1. Make a **statement** to tell something. End with a period.

> You are at the park. Someone left trash.
> The trash can is nearby.

2. Ask a **question** to find out something. End with a question mark.

> Are you at the park? Who left trash? Is the trash can nearby?

3. Give a **command** to tell someone what to do. End with a period.

> Pick up the trash. Put it in the trash can. Do not litter.

4. Use an **exclamation** to express a strong feeling. End with an exclamation point.

> Trash is all over the park! This trash is awful!

Start every sentence with a capital letter.

Try It

A. Write whether each sentence is a statement, a question, an exclamation, or a command.

1. I hate litter! __exclamation__

2. Where is the trash can? _____

3. Please use the trash can. _____

4. The trash can is for trash. _____

5. Help me pick up this trash. _____

6. Is the park clean now? _____

7. Clean parks are so beautiful! _____

B. Change each sentence and write it on the line. Punctuate your sentences correctly.

8. Are trash cans outside our school? (Change to a statement.)

   Trash cans are outside our school.

9. You should put your garbage in the can. (Change to a command.)

   _____

10. It is time to take action! (Change to a question.)

    _____

11. Is our schoolyard clean? (Change to a statement.)

    _____

Write It

C. Complete the sentences about trash that people throw outside. Write at least one of each kind of sentence. Punctuate your sentences correctly.

12. Trash is _____

13. Please put _____

14. Are you _____

15. The outdoors are _____

16. Never throw _____

17. Is the park _____

D. (18–20) Why shouldn't people throw trash on the ground outside? Write at least three different kinds of sentences.

_____

_____

_____

_____

_____

10 Vary Your Sentences

Remember: You can make your writing more interesting when you use different kinds of sentences.

> To vary your sentences, you can include a question or an exclamation in a group of sentences.
>
> Laura wants to hike with her mom. She must clean her room first. Her room is a real mess. Look at her room now. ~~The room is clean.~~
>
> Is the room clean?

Try It

A. Write each sentence in another way. More than one answer is possible.

1. Laura and Mom are on their way. _Are Laura and Mom on their way?_

2. The drive is really long. _____

3. The scenery is pretty. _____

4. Two deer are on the road right in front of them. _____

5. The deer are huge. _____

B. Write words to complete each sentence.

6. _____Where_____ are Laura and Mom now?

7. _____ see trash on the ground in the parking lot.

8. _____ is really messy!

9. _____ a trash can nearby?

Write It

C. Laura and Mom hike up a mountain trail. Complete the statement, the exclamation, and the two questions to tell about their hike. Remember to use the correct end marks.

10. Laura and Mom _____

_____

11. What animals _____

_____

12. The view from the top _____

_____

13. Is _____

_____

D. (14–16) What are some activities you do with your family? Write a statement, a question, and an exclamation to tell what you like to do with your family.

_____

_____

_____

Grammar at Work

E. (17–20) Vary the four underlined sentences to make this writing more interesting.

Families are important. We learn from our families. I learn about chores. I hate chores. I finish my chores, though. Chores help me learn about responsibility. I learn about the environment. Trash is a big problem. It pollutes the earth. I also learn about fun from my family. My family and I have super times together.

Proofreader's Marks

Change text:

Is your family trip fun?

~~Your family trip is fun.~~

See all Proofreader's Marks on page xi.

© National Geographic Learning, a part of Cengage Learning, Inc.

11 What's a Plural Noun?

A Word That Names More Than One Thing

One	More Than One
A **singular noun** names one thing.	A **plural noun** names more than one thing.

Use these spelling rules to form plural nouns.

1. To make most nouns plural, just add **-s**.

2. If the noun ends in **s**, **z**, **sh**, **ch**, or **x**, add **-es**.

One	More Than One
goal	goals
slice	slices
ax	axes
sketch	sketches
kiss	kisses

Try It

A. (1–10) Complete the chart. Write the plural form of each noun.

Singular Nouns (one)	Plural Nouns (more than one)
friend	
box	
student	
rash	
space	
desire	
bench	
ring	
bus	
patch	

B. Complete each sentence. Write the plural of the noun in parentheses.

11. Most ___*students*___ have goals, or things they want to do. **(student)**

12. They may want to get good _____. **(grade)**

13. Some want to do well in _____ like soccer or softball. **(sport)**

14. Others want to hear new _____ and information. **(idea)**

15. We all have different desires and _____. **(wish)**

16. Our dreams are as different as our _____. **(face)**

17. We can lead better lives if we set _____. **(goal)**

Write It

C. Use at least one plural noun to write about your goals, wishes, and dreams.

18. Write about some of your goals in school this year. _____

_____

19. Write about one of your wishes. _____

_____

20. Write about one of your dreams for the future. _____

_____

D. (21–25) Write at least five sentences to tell why it is important to have goals in life. Use at least four plural nouns in your writing. Remember to use the correct form of plural nouns.

_____

_____

_____

_____

_____

12 Can You Just Add -s or -es to Make a Noun Plural?

Not Always

One	More Than One
A **singular noun** names one thing.	A **plural noun** names more than one thing.

Use these spelling rules to form plural nouns.

1. If a noun ends in **y** after a consonant, change the **y** to **i** and add **-es**.

2. If the noun ends in **y** after a vowel, add **-s** after the **y**.

One	More Than One
kitty	kitt**ies**
fly	fl**ies**
penny	penn**ies**
turkey	turkey**s**
tray	tray**s**

Try It

A. (1–6) Complete the chart. Write the plural form of each noun.

Singular Nouns (one)	Plural Nouns (more than one)
lady	
city	
puppy	
valley	
key	
pony	

B. Complete each sentence. Write the plural of the noun in parentheses.

7. Most _____families_____ want a happy home life. **(family)**

8. Family members look for _____ to help each other. **(way)**

9. Both girls and _____ can do any chore around the house. **(boy)**

10. Children can help take care of pets like goldfish or _____. **(puppy)**

11. One parent can answer a baby's _____ while the other sleeps. **(cry)**

12. Everyone can try to give kind _____ to others' questions. **(reply)**

13. Most of us want to make our _____ at home pleasant. **(day)**

Write It

C. Use at least one plural noun to write about families.

14. Write about a favorite family member. _____

_____

15. Write about a happy or sad family memory. _____

_____

16. Write about someone else's family. _____

_____

D. (17–20) Write at least four sentences about how you could be a kind parent. Use at least four plural nouns in your writing. Remember to use the correct form of plural nouns.

_____

_____

_____

_____

_____

13 Can You Just Add -s or -es to Make a Noun Plural?

Not Always

One	More Than One
A **singular noun** names one thing.	A **plural noun** names more than one thing.

1. Some nouns have special plural forms.
   A **person** who loves animals can be a vet.
   People who love kids can be teachers.

2. Other nouns do not change to form the plural.
   An adult **moose** has large antlers.
   I saw many **moose** on a trip to Maine.

One	More Than One
man	men
woman	women
child	children
tooth	teeth
person	people
aircraft	aircraft
foot	feet

Try It

A. (1–7) Complete the chart. Write the plural form of each noun.

Singular Nouns (one)	Plural Nouns (more than one)
woman	
child	
foot	
person	
tooth	
man	
moose	

B. Complete each sentence. Write the plural of the noun in parentheses.

8. Most _____*people*_____ want useful jobs. **(person)**

9. Some like to work with planes and other _____. **(aircraft)**

10. Others like to work with _____ . **(child)**

11. Zoo workers take care of _____ and other animals. **(moose)**

12. Dentists are happy to work on _____. **(tooth)**

13. Foot doctors like to keep your _____ healthy. **(foot)**

14. Men and _____ can enjoy all kinds of jobs. **(woman)**

Write It

C. Use at least one plural noun to write about jobs.

15. Write about a job that someone in your family has. _____

_____

16. Write about a job that someone in your family wants to have. _____

_____

17. Write about a job that you want to have some day. _____

_____

D. (18–20) Write at least three sentences about jobs that both boys and girls might like. Use at least three plural nouns in your writing. Remember to use the correct form of plural nouns.

_____

_____

_____

_____

_____

14 What Do You Need for a Sentence?

A Subject and a Predicate

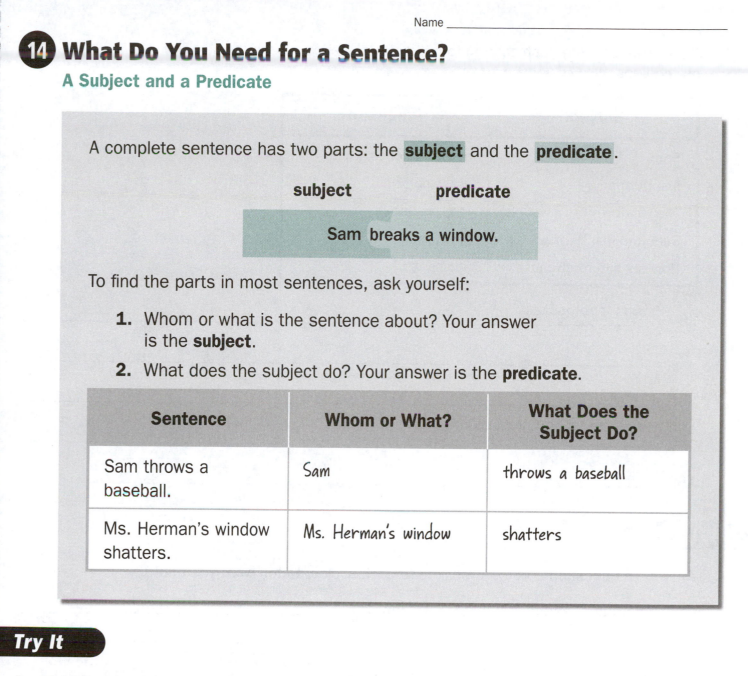

A complete sentence has two parts: the **subject** and the **predicate**.

| subject | predicate |

Sam **breaks a window.**

To find the parts in most sentences, ask yourself:

1. Whom or what is the sentence about? Your answer is the **subject**.

2. What does the subject do? Your answer is the **predicate**.

Sentence	Whom or What?	What Does the Subject Do?
Sam throws a baseball.	Sam	throws a baseball
Ms. Herman's window shatters.	Ms. Herman's window	shatters

Try It

A. Match each subject to a predicate.

1. The window   believes Sam.

2. Glass   went too far.

3. Sam   calls it an accident.

4. The ball   is broken.

5. Ms. Herman   covers the ground.

B. Choose words from each column to make five sentences. Write the sentences on the lines.

Subject	Predicate
Sam	become friends.
Ms. Herman	are important.
The window	forgives Sam.
Sam and Ms. Herman	gets fixed.
Honesty and forgiveness	apologizes.

6. Sam apologizes. _____

7. _____

8. _____

9. _____

10. _____

Write It

C. Answer the questions. Add a predicate to each subject to tell what you think.

11. What does honesty mean to you? Honesty _____
_____.

12. What does forgiveness mean to you? Forgiveness _____
_____.

D. (13–15) Write at least three sentences that tell why it is important to apologize and to forgive. Remember to include a subject and a predicate in each sentence.

_____

_____

_____

_____

_____

15 What Is a Sentence About?

The Subject

The **complete subject** can be one word or several words. The noun is the most important word in the subject. A **noun** is the name of a person, place, or thing.

1. This **shop** sells clothes.
2. **Workers** sew the clothes in factories.
3. Many of the **factories** are old.
4. **Conditions** are very poor.
5. The **shopkeeper** knows about this.

Nouns in the Subject	
Person	workers shopkeeper
Place	shop factories
Thing	conditions

Try It

A. Complete the subject of the sentence. Add a noun from the chart above.

1. The ___shopkeeper___ buys from factories.

2. The _____ are hot and crowded.

3. _____ are not well paid.

4. _____ are getting worse.

5. This _____ does not deserve our business!

B. Complete each subject. Add a noun from the box.

family	people	sign	woman

6. A tall ___woman___ carries a sign.

7. The _____ shows the workers' wages.

8. Many _____ protest the low wages.

9. My _____ won't shop at the store.

Write It

C. Answer each question with a sentence. Be sure your subject includes a noun.

10. Who deserves fair wages? All _____ deserve fair wages.

11. What should be clean and safe? All _____ should be clean and safe.

12. Who should be treated with respect? All _____

_____.

D. (13–15) When you boycott someone or something, you refuse to deal with that person, place, or thing. Write at least three sentences telling about something that should be boycotted. Remember to include a noun in each subject.

_____

_____

_____

_____

_____

Edit It

E. (16–20) Edit the journal entry below. Fix five subjects.

> May 15
>
> My older sister joined a protest march today.
> The was held to make people aware of a new
> store. The sells sports shoes from another
> country. Many were paid low wages to make the
> shoes. The should be boycotted! All should be
> paid fairly.

Proofreader's Marks

Add text:
Their ^wages are low.

See all Proofreader's Marks on page xi.

16 What's the Most Important Word in the Predicate?

The Verb

- The **complete predicate** in a sentence often tells what the subject does. The **verb** shows the action.

    A new student **comes** to school.

    Some of my friends **ignore** him.

- Sometimes the predicate tells what the subject has. It uses these **verbs**:

    The new student **has** a great smile.

    My friends **have** no reason to dislike him.

- Other times, the predicate tells what the subject is or is like. The **verb** is a form of **be**.

    The new student **is** a friendly person.

    My friends **are** unkind to him.

    I **am** unhappy about this.

Try It

A. Complete each sentence with a verb from the box.

ask	has	have	is	sits

1. The new student _____ alone.

2. I _____ an idea.

3. I _____ the new student to join us.

4. The new student's name _____ Eric.

5. Eric _____ a good sense of humor.

B. Complete each sentence with a verb.

6. Eric _____ an older brother.

7. Eric and his brother _____ athletes.

8. My friends _____ to Eric's football stories.

9. Eric _____ the center of attention!

Write It

C. A new student comes to your school. What do you do? Answer the questions. Use a verb in each sentence.

10. What do you say to your friends? I _____

   _____.

11. How do you show you are a kind person? I _____

   _____.

D. (12–14) Now write at least three sentences about how you would make a new student feel welcome at your school. Remember to use a verb in each predicate.

   _____

   _____

   _____

   _____

Edit It

E. (15–20) Edit the letter below. Fix six predicates. Use the verbs **has**, **have**, **is**, and **are**.

Dear Granddad,

   I am happy at my new school. I some new friends. I sit with them at lunch. They easy to talk to. I talk to them about playing football. One boy friendlier than the others. He a brother, too. They both athletes. Please come visit soon! I so much to tell you.

                                             Your grandson,

                                             Eric

Proofreader's Marks

Add text:

                    is
   Your brother ⌃ friendly.

See all Proofreader's Marks on page xi.

17 How Do You Know What Action Verb to Use?

Match It to the Subject.

- **Action verbs** tell when a subject does something, like **strum**, **tap**, or **wait**.

- Action verbs do not change form when the subject is **I** or **you**.

  1. I **strum** my guitar.   **2.** You **strum** your banjo.

  3. I **tap** my right foot.   **4.** You **tap** your left foot.

  5. I **wait** for you to join in.   **6.** You **wait** for me to begin.

  7. I **sing** the melody.   **8.** You **sing** harmony.

- Some sentences have more than one action verb. All the verbs must match the subject.

  I **hear** the song, **memorize** it, and **sing**.

Try It

A. Complete each sentence. Write the correct form of the verb.

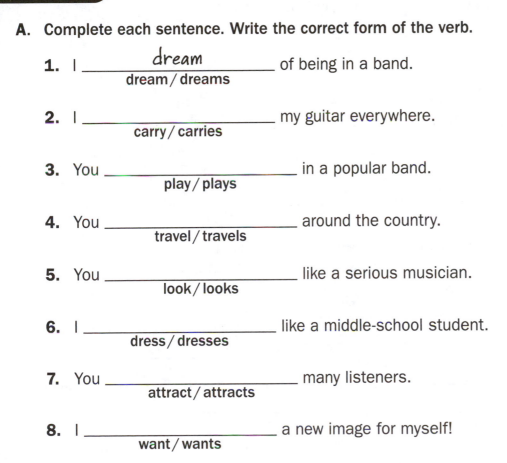

1. I _____ *dream* _____ of being in a band.
       dream / dreams

2. I _____ my guitar everywhere.
       carry / carries

3. You _____ in a popular band.
       play / plays

4. You _____ around the country.
       travel / travels

5. You _____ like a serious musician.
       look / looks

6. I _____ like a middle-school student.
       dress / dresses

7. You _____ many listeners.
       attract / attracts

8. I _____ a new image for myself!
       want / wants

B. Complete each sentence with a verb from the box. Use each verb twice.

listen	practice	say	share	think

9. I _____ music is important.

10. You _____ a good education is also important.

11. You _____ your music on the road.

12. I _____ my music at school.

13. I _____ ideas with my friends.

14. You _____ ideas with other musicians.

15. I _____ to music on the radio.

16. You _____ to live musicians.

17. I _____ that being a good musician is my goal.

18. You _____ that being a good musician is rewarding.

Write It

C. Imagine that you are talking to a friend who inspires you. Complete each sentence with two action verbs. Make sure the verbs match the subject.

19–20. I _____ and _____.

21–22. You _____ and _____.

D. (23–25) What else would you say to your friend about reaching your goals? Write at least three more sentences. Use **I** and **you** as the subjects. Make sure each verb matches the subject.

_____

_____

_____

_____

18 How Do You Know What Action Verb to Use?

Match It to the Subject.

- **Action verbs** tell when a subject does something.
- If the sentence is about one other person, place, or thing, add **-s** to the action verb.

   1. Marta **walks** down the hall.   **2.** Her friends **walk** down the hall, too.

   3. Marta **wears** a beautiful shirt.   **4.** Her friends **wear** baggy sweaters.

   5. Marta **pays** very little for clothes.   **6.** Many girls **pay** a lot for clothing.

   7. Marta **shows** her creativity.   **8.** Her friends **show** their admiration.

- Some sentences have more than one action verb. All the verbs must agree with the subject:

   Marta **looks** at clothing and **knows** what to buy.
   Her friends **watch** Marta and **learn** from her.

Try It

A. Complete each sentence. Write the correct form of the verb.

   1. Tim _____ draws _____ funny cartoons.
   draw/draws

   2. His brother _____ in a photo shop.
   work/works

   3. John _____ Tim's drawings to work.
   bring/brings

   4. The cartoons _____ attention.
   attract/attracts

B. Write the correct form of the verb in parentheses.

   5. John _____ asks _____ his boss a question. **(ask)**

   6. Workers _____ Tim's designs to T-shirts. **(transfer)**

   7. People _____ T-shirts with Tim's cartoons. **(wear)**

C. Answer these questions about a talented friend. Use the correct form of action verbs in your sentences.

8. What does your friend do? My talented friend _____

   _____.

9. How do other people inspire your friend? Other people _____

   _____.

D. (10–13) Now write about the talents you have. Who inspires you? Write at least four sentences. Remember to use the correct form of action verbs.

   _____

   _____

   _____

   _____

   _____

Edit It

E. (14–20) Edit the article. Fix seven action verbs. Use the correct form.

Marta and Tim

Marta and Tim attend Cabot Middle School. They are like their classmates. Marta laugh in the hall. Tim talk in class. Both students fascinates people. Marta shop in all her spare time. People wears T-shirts with Tim's cartoons on them. Teachers asks Marta for shopping advice. Little children seeks Tim's help with cartoons. Both Marta and Tim share their talents happily!

> **Proofreader's Marks**
>
> Change text:
>   makes
> What ~~make~~ them special?
>
> See all Proofreader's Marks on page xi.

19 How Do You Know What Verb to Use?

Match It to the Subject.

Use the form of the verb **have** that matches the subject.

- I **have** healthy parents.
- She **has** healthy parents, too.
- They **have** great ideas about how to stay healthy.
- We **have** healthy habits.
- Do you **have** time to go for a walk now?

Forms of *Have*
I **have**
he, she, or it **has**
we, you, or they **have**

Try It

A. Write the correct form of have in each sentence.

1. My mom _____ a bicycle.
have / has

2. I _____ one, too.
have / has

3. We _____ fun when we ride our bikes together.
have / has

4. Today, my mom _____ the day off from work.
have / has

5. Our family _____ a plan.
have / has

B. (6–10) Complete the paragraph about the plan. Use the correct form of have.

Our plan _____ something to do with bicycles. It _____ something to do with exercise, too. Do you _____ an idea what it is? That's right! My family and I _____ a plan for a bicycle trip! The tires _____ air in them, and we are ready to go.

C. Complete the sentences to tell how family members might stay fit and healthy. Use the correct form of **have** to tell about their interests.

11. The parents _____.

12. One son _____.

13. The daughter _____.

14. We all _____.

D. (15–18) Write at least four sentences to tell what you or your family does to stay fit and healthy. Use a form of **have** at least four times.

_____

_____

_____

_____

_____

Edit It

E. (19–25) **Have** and **has** are missing from this list of things Felix needs to do. Edit the list to make seven corrections by adding **have** or **has**.

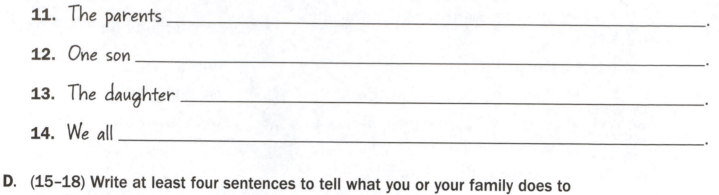

To-Do List

1. Rena has a track meet. I free time, so I will go to her meet.

2. My brother's bike a flat tire. It a leak. I need to fix it.

3. My basketball team a game tomorrow. We a practice at 4 o'clock.

4. I math homework. I need to finish 25 exercises. I to work fast.

Proofreader's Marks

Add text:
My family ~has~ a busy schedule. ∧

See all Proofreader's Marks on page xi.

20 How Do You Know What Verb to Use?

Match It to the Subject.

- Use the form of **do** that matches the subject.
  You can use **do** as a **main verb** or as a
  helping verb.

  Mom **does** a lot of socializing.
  Mom and I **do** things together sometimes.
  I **do** enjoy chatting with people.
  Mom **does** most of the talking.
  She **does** talk too much at times.
  We **do** try to visit friends and neighbors often.

Forms of *Do*
I **do**
he, she, or it **does**
we, you, or they **do**

Try It

A. Write **do** or **does** to complete each sentence.

1. Dad _____ have a quiet personality.
   do / does

2. My sisters _____, too.
   do / does

3. Mom and I are loud. We _____ not have quiet personalities.
   do / does

4. She _____ talk loudly.
   do / does

5. I _____ some loud cheering at sports games.
   do / does

6. My brother Ben _____ some quiet groaning.
   do / does

7. He _____ act more like Dad.
   do / does

B. Choose words from each column to build five sentences about character traits.

I	does	like busy cities.
Mom		enjoy big crowds.
You	do	work hard most of the time.
Dad		laugh a lot.
He		like to hang out with friends.

8. _____

9. _____

10. _____

11. _____

12. _____

Write It

C. Complete the sentences about your personality.
Use **do** or **does** in each sentence.

13. I am like my _____. I _____.

14. I am not like my _____. She _____.

15. I take after my _____. They _____.

16. I do not take after my _____. He _____.

D. (17–20) Imagine you just returned from a family gathering. Write a journal entry to tell what members of your family do and don't like. Use forms of **do** in at least four sentences.

_____

_____

_____

_____

_____

Name _____

21 Write Complete Sentences

Remember: You need a **subject** and a **predicate** to make a complete sentence. Often, the most important word in the subject is a **noun**. Every predicate needs a **verb**.

The **noun** is the most important word in the **subject**.
The **verb** is the most important word in the **predicate**.

Subject	Predicate
Julia	has strong beliefs.
Her beliefs	affect her actions.
Julia's brother	is blind.
The young boy	uses a guide dog.

Try It

A. Add a subject or a predicate to complete each sentence.

1. Julia _____ a favorite cause.

2. _____ tells people about the importance of guide dogs.

3. Guide dog puppies _____ in foster homes.

4. Kind and patient _____ raise them.

5. The _____ just need the right care!

B. Draw a line from each subject to the correct predicate.

6. Julia's brother   is very well trained.

7. The dog   raised the dog as a puppy.

8. A foster family   has a guide dog.

9. Then a trainer   are partners.

10. The boy and the dog   worked with the dog.

C. Write sentences about a cause you support. Be sure each sentence has a
    subject and a predicate.

   11. What cause do you support? I _____ the cause of_____.

   12. Who or what is helped by this cause? _____

   _____

   13. Why do you support this cause? _____

   _____

   14. Do other people you know support this cause? _____

   _____

D. (15–18) Now write at least four sentences about why other people should support your
    cause. Remember, you need a subject and a predicate to make a complete sentence.

   _____

   _____

   _____

   _____

   _____

Grammar at Work

E. (19–25) Fix <u>six</u> incomplete sentences. Then change the last sentence into a
    different kind of sentence.

Guide Dog Volunteers

Tanya Jackson raises guide dog puppies. The puppies in her
home for 18 months. Then go to guide dog school. Tanya like a
foster parent to the pups.

Tanya learned about this work from Julia Brown. Julia the
importance of guide dogs. has a guide dog. The dog everywhere
with him. Do the dog and he love each other?

Proofreader's Marks
Add text:
Guide dogs ^are^ helpful.
See all Proofreader's Marks on page xi.

22 Make Subjects and Verbs Agree

Remember: The verb you use depends on your subject.
These subjects and verbs go together.

Forms of *Be*
I **am** special.
You **are** special.
He, she, or it **is** special.
We, you, or they **are** special.

Action Verbs
I **need** my friends.
You **need** your family.
He, she, or it **needs** care.
We, you, or they **need** each other.

Try It

A. Complete each sentence. Write the correct form of the verb.

1. I _____ one of many siblings.
   am / are

2. We _____ members of a large family.
   is / are

3. My parents _____ hard to inspire us.
   work / works

4. I _____ to accomplish many things.
   plan / plans

5. My mom _____ me she's proud.
   tell / tells

B. Complete each sentence with a verb from the box.

admire	is	inspires	try

6. I greatly _____ Uncle Jack.

7. I always _____ to follow his example.

8. Uncle Jack _____ my inspiration.

9. He _____ me to do my best.

Write It

C. Answer the questions about yourself and people you admire. Be sure each verb agrees with the subject.

10. Whom do you admire? I _____ .

11. Why is this person an inspiration to you? _____

12. What talents do you have? _____

13. Whom do you want to inspire? _____

D. (14–17) Now write at least four more sentences about people you admire and how they influence you. Remember to make subjects and verbs agree.

_____

_____

_____

_____

_____

Grammar at Work

E. (18–24) Fix <u>six</u> mistakes in subject-verb agreement. Fix <u>one</u> incomplete sentence.

> June 22
>
> I always enjoy my visits with Uncle Jack.
>
> He tell me about his years as a baseball player.
>
> His old jersey and cap is in the attic.
>
> They reminds me of what Uncle Jack accomplished.
>
> He played for a major league team. He remain a
>
> part of baseball history today. People admires him.
>
> I wants to stand out like Uncle Jack. I talented,
>
> too!

Proofreader's Marks

Change text:

They ~~is~~ *are* in great condition.

See all Proofreader's Marks on page xi.

23 Is the Subject of a Sentence Always a Noun?

No, It Can Be a Pronoun.

- Use **I** when you talk about yourself.
  I have some family photos.

- Use **you** when you talk to another person.
  Do **you** want to see my photos?

- Use **he** when you talk about one man or one boy.
  Grandpa is in this photo. **He** is a boy in the photo.

- Use **she** when you talk about one woman or one girl.
  Mom is in this photo. **She** looks like Grandpa.

- Use **it** when you talk about one place or thing.
  This photo is my favorite. **It** shows Mom and Grandpa together.

Subject Pronouns
Singular
I
you
he, she, it

Try It

A. Complete each sentence. Use a subject pronoun from the chart above.

1. My name is Henry. _____ have a brother and a sister.

2. Zac is my brother. _____ looks like my dad.

3. Sara is my sister. _____ looks like my mom.

4. Do _____ think I look like my mom or my dad?

B. (5–11) Complete the paragraph. Use subject pronouns from the chart.

   Henry works on a school project. _____ is a collection of family photos. _____ uses his favorite photos. Henry asks his mom, "Will _____ help with the collection?"

   "Yes, _____ will," _____ answers.

   Henry finishes. _____ looks at the photos. "_____ look a little like everyone," he says.

Write It

C. Answer these questions about Henry. Use the correct subject pronouns.

12. Does Henry have a brother? _____

13. Whom does Henry's sister look like? _____

14. What does Henry's collection show? _____

15. Whom do you think Henry looks like? _____

_____

D. (16–20) Write five sentences about whom people in your family look like. Use at least four subject pronouns.

_____

_____

_____

_____

_____

Edit It

E. (21–25) Edit the letter. Fix the five mistakes with subject pronouns.

Dear Grandma,

I made a photo album. He shows pictures of the whole family. Grandma, it would love my album. Grandpa is in one photo. She is a little boy on a bike. Mom is in another photo. I is on a horse. You are in a picture, too, Grandma. It am in the same picture. I look a lot like my grandma in that picture!

Love,

Henry

Proofreader's Marks

Change text:

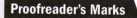

Dad has blue eyes. She looks like Grandma.

See all Proofreader's Marks on page xi.

24 Can a Pronoun Show "More Than One"?

Yes, It Can.

- Use **we** to talk about yourself and another person.

    My sister and I are going to England with Mom.
    We will visit our grandparents there.

- Use **you** to talk to one or more persons.

    "Elaine, do **you** like to travel with your sister?" my friend asked.

    "Elaine and Anna, are **you** ready to go?" Mom asks.

- Use **they** to talk about more than one person or thing.

    My cousins will be in England, too. **They** live there.

Subject Pronouns	
Singular	Plural
I	we
you	you
he, she, it	they

Try It

A. Complete the sentences. Use the correct plural subject pronouns.

1. Anna, Mom, and I get off the plane. _____ are in England now.

2. Our grandparents see us. _____ wave.

3. "_____ both have grown," says Grandma to Anna and me.

4. "_____ are both so tall," adds Grandpa.

5. We take after Dad's parents. _____ are tall, too.

B. (6–10) Complete the paragraph about the girls. Use the correct plural subject pronouns.

Anna and I are surprised. _____ just met our cousins.

_____ look a lot like us. "_____ both look like me!" I say to my cousins.

Anna and I have brown hair. _____ have blue eyes. I look at my cousins' eyes. _____ are blue, too.

C. Answer these questions that Elaine might ask you. Use correct plural subject pronouns.

11. Where do Mom's parents live? _____

12. Where do Anna and I get our height? _____

13. What color are your eyes? _____

D. (14–17) Write four sentences about your extended family. How are you all alike and different? Use at least four plural subject pronouns.

_____

_____

_____

_____

_____

Edit It

E. (18–25) Edit the paragraph. Fix the eight mistakes with subject pronouns.

My cousins and I are alike in some ways. You are all athletic. My cousins are runners. You got their ability from Grandpa. My sister and I aren't runners. They are basketball players. They got that skill from Grandma. "Are he good soccer players, too?" I ask my cousins. "It are," they answer. "Grandpa and Grandma are, too. You love soccer." My cousins and I have the same grandparents. I are alike in that way, too!

Proofreader's Marks
Change text:
We My sister and I are tall. They get that trait from Grandpa.
See all Proofreader's Marks on page xi.

25 Are There Different Subject Pronouns for Men and Women?

Yes, There Are.

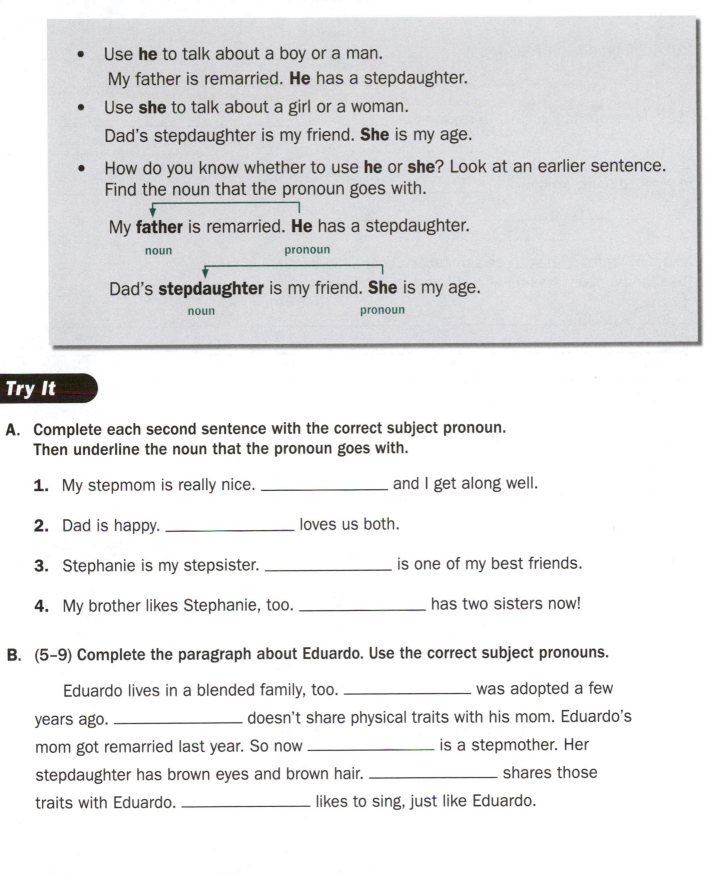

- Use **he** to talk about a boy or a man.
  My father is remarried. **He** has a stepdaughter.

- Use **she** to talk about a girl or a woman.
  Dad's stepdaughter is my friend. **She** is my age.

- How do you know whether to use **he** or **she**? Look at an earlier sentence.
  Find the noun that the pronoun goes with.

  My **father** is remarried. **He** has a stepdaughter.
     noun   pronoun

  Dad's **stepdaughter** is my friend. **She** is my age.
       noun   pronoun

Try It

A. Complete each second sentence with the correct subject pronoun.
Then underline the noun that the pronoun goes with.

1. My stepmom is really nice. _____ and I get along well.

2. Dad is happy. _____ loves us both.

3. Stephanie is my stepsister. _____ is one of my best friends.

4. My brother likes Stephanie, too. _____ has two sisters now!

B. (5–9) Complete the paragraph about Eduardo. Use the correct subject pronouns.

Eduardo lives in a blended family, too. _____ was adopted a few

years ago. _____ doesn't share physical traits with his mom. Eduardo's

mom got remarried last year. So now _____ is a stepmother. Her

stepdaughter has brown eyes and brown hair. _____ shares those

traits with Eduardo. _____ likes to sing, just like Eduardo.

C. Read the sentence. Then write a second sentence that uses the pronoun
he or **she**.

10. Eduardo is my friend. _____

_____

11. My stepsister is part of my family. _____

_____

12. Kyle is my brother. _____

_____

D. (13–15) Write at least three sentences about Eduardo and his family.
Use the pronouns **he** and **she** at least one time each.

_____

_____

_____

_____

Edit It

E. (16–20) Edit the journal entry. Fix five subject pronouns.

June 19

Today, I met my baby cousin Ben for the
first time. She is Aunt Sophia's first baby.
She adopted Ben. It is a very cute baby.
When Ben smiles, they reminds me of Aunt
Sophia. Aunt Sophia smiles all the time. He
is so happy with her new baby. I am looking
forward to babysitting for Ben. She is a
great baby boy!

Proofreader's Marks

Change text:

He
~~It~~ is part of my
extended family.

See all Proofreader's Marks
on page xi.

26 How Do You Avoid Confusion with Pronouns?

Match the Pronoun to the Noun.

- To make your sentences clear, match the pronouns to the nouns.

  Unclear: Diego is curious. **It** makes a family tree.

  Clear: Diego is curious. **He** makes a family tree.

- First, find the noun the pronoun goes with. Then ask yourself:

  Is the noun plural or singular? If plural, use **they**.

  If singular, ask: Is the noun a man, a woman, or a thing?

  Use **he** for a man, **she** for a woman, and **it** for a place or thing.

- Make it easy to tell which noun your pronoun goes with. Ask yourself: What makes a sentence clear or confusing?

  Clear: Diego's sister Carmen visited Acapulco. **She** loved it.

  Unclear: Grandmother picked up Carmen at the airport. **She** was late.

  Clear: Grandmother picked up Carmen at the airport. Carmen was late.

Try It

A. Write the correct pronoun to complete the second sentence.

1. Diego's great-grandparents grew up in Mexico. _____ moved to California.
   He / They

2. Diego's grandmother was born there. _____ grew up in Los Angeles.
   It / She

3. Diego's father went to college in Boston. _____ met Diego's mother there.
   He / She

4. Diego and his sisters live in the U.S. _____ have never been to Mexico.
   It / They

5. This summer, Diego's grandmother will take Diego to Mexico. _____ will introduce him to his Mexican relatives.
   She / They

B. (6–13) Write the correct subject pronouns to complete the paragraph about Diego.

Before Diego goes to Mexico, _____ wants to study his family tree. _____ shows his relatives in Mexico. _____ all live in different parts of the country. Maria is his grandmother's cousin. _____ lives in Mexico City. Her son, Miguel, lives in Acapulco. _____ works in a hotel on the beach there.

Diego feels very lucky. _____ will travel all over Mexico and meet his whole family. Will his relatives look like him? Will _____ have the same interests? The trip will be fun. _____ will be a learning experience, too.

Write It

C. Complete the first sentence about your family. Write a second sentence that uses the pronoun **he**, **she**, or **they**.

14. My family members _____.

_____

_____

15. My grandfather _____.

_____

_____

16. _____ is my cousin. _____

_____

_____

D. (17–20) Write four sentences about other relatives in your family. Use each of the pronouns **he**, **she**, and **they** at least once. Be sure your sentences are clear.

_____

_____

_____

_____

27 Can a Pronoun and a Verb Join Hands?
Yes, in a Contraction

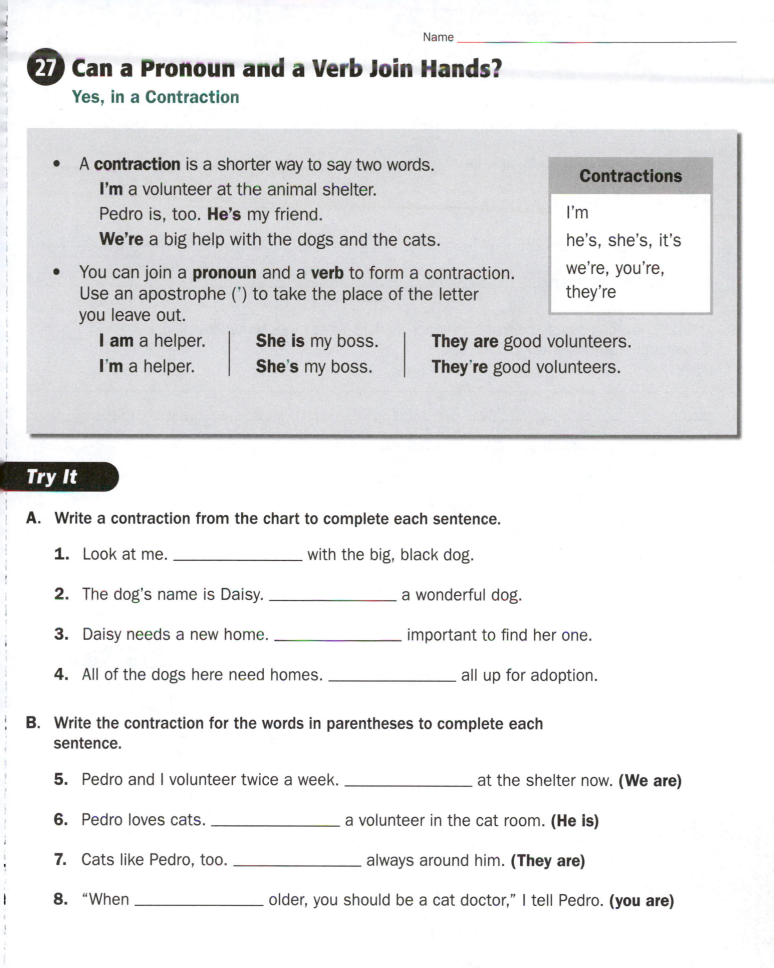

- A **contraction** is a shorter way to say two words.
  I'm a volunteer at the animal shelter.
  Pedro is, too. **He's** my friend.
  We're a big help with the dogs and the cats.

- You can join a **pronoun** and a **verb** to form a contraction. Use an apostrophe (') to take the place of the letter you leave out.

Contractions
I'm
he's, she's, it's
we're, you're, they're

I am a helper.	**She is** my boss.	**They are** good volunteers.
I'm a helper.	**She's** my boss.	**They're** good volunteers.

Try It

A. Write a contraction from the chart to complete each sentence.

1. Look at me. _____ with the big, black dog.

2. The dog's name is Daisy. _____ a wonderful dog.

3. Daisy needs a new home. _____ important to find her one.

4. All of the dogs here need homes. _____ all up for adoption.

B. Write the contraction for the words in parentheses to complete each sentence.

5. Pedro and I volunteer twice a week. _____ at the shelter now. **(We are)**

6. Pedro loves cats. _____ a volunteer in the cat room. **(He is)**

7. Cats like Pedro, too. _____ always around him. **(They are)**

8. "When _____ older, you should be a cat doctor," I tell Pedro. **(you are)**

Write It

C. Read each sentence. Then write another sentence to tell more about helping animals. Use a contraction from the chart in each sentence.

9. The dogs and cats are lonely. _____

10. Pedro is busy. _____

11. I am about to adopt a pet. _____

12. You are a big help. _____

D. (13–15) How can people help at an animal shelter? Write three sentences. Use a contraction from the chart in each one.

_____

_____

_____

_____

_____

Edit It

E. (16–20) Edit the journal entry. Join pronouns and verbs to form five contractions.

I am at the animal shelter. I volunteer here on Tuesdays and Thursdays. I work hard here. One of my jobs is to feed the dogs. It is a fun job. Other jobs are not fun. They are harder to do. The big white cat is Jake. He is a great cat. My favorite dog is Lucy. She is the one I want to adopt. Mom says I can adopt a dog one day. Maybe that dog will be Lucy!

Proofreader's Marks

Change text:

We're
~~We are~~ busy.

See all Proofreader's Marks on page xi.

28 Can a Verb and the Word *Not* Join Hands?

Yes, in a Contraction

- A **contraction** is a shorter way to say two words.

  I **don't** like this movie.

  The characters **aren't** realistic.

  The movie **hasn't** got a plot.

- You can join a **verb** and **not** to form a **contraction**. Use an apostrophe (') to take the place of the letter you leave out.

Contractions	
isn't	aren't
hasn't	haven't
doesn't	don't

The movie **is not** good.	It **does not** interest me.	I **have not** enjoyed it.
The movie **isn't** good.	It **doesn't** interest me.	I **haven't** enjoyed it.

Try It

A. Write a contraction from the chart to complete each sentence.

1. I _____ like this video game.

2. The pictures _____ good.

3. The game _____ fun to play.

4. You _____ bought it yet, have you?

B. Write the contraction for the words in parentheses to complete each sentence.

5. Movies _____ as much fun as video games. **(are not)**

6. This game _____ end! It goes on and on. **(does not)**

7. It _____ bored me, though. **(has not)**

8. My friends _____ want to end the game, either. **(do not)**

Write It

C. Answer each question. Use a contraction from the chart in your answer.

9. What movie don't you want to see? I _____.

10. What movie haven't you seen that you want to see? _____

_____

11. What game doesn't interest you? _____

12. Why isn't it a good game? _____

D. (13–15) What don't you like to do? Write three sentences about what you don't like and why. Use three contractions from the chart.

_____

_____

_____

_____

_____

Edit It

E. (16–20) Edit the list and title. Join verbs and **not** to form five contractions.

What I Have Not Done Yet

- My clothes are not picked up.
- The cat does not have supper yet.
- My homework is not done.
- My dog has not gone on a walk.

Proofreader's Marks

Change text:
       aren't
We ~~are not~~ busy.

See all Proofreader's Marks on page xi.

29 What Kinds of Verbs Are *Can*, *Could*, *May*, and *Might*?

They Are Helping Verbs.

- An action verb can have two parts: a **helping verb** and a **main verb**. The main verb shows the action.

    I buy groceries for Mom. I **can buy** groceries for Mom.

- Some helping verbs change the meaning of the action verb.

    1. Use **can** or **could** to tell about an ability.

    Dad **can drive** me to the market. He **could drive** you, too.

    2. Use **may**, **might**, or **could** to tell about a possibility.

    My sister **may shop** for food with me. My brother **might come**, too. We **could go** to the store together.

- **Can**, **could**, **may**, and **might** stay the same with all subjects. Do not add -**s**.

    Mom **likes** our help. She **can rest** now. She **might take** a nap.

Try It

A. Write **can**, **could**, **may**, or **might** to complete each sentence. More than one answer is possible.

1. Aunt Rosita works full time, so she _____ use a lot of help.

2. Oscar _____ help Aunt Rosita a little every day.

3. On one day, he _____ make lunch for her children.

4. On another day, he _____ prepare dinner.

5. His cousins _____ like the dinner.

6. They _____ ask for more food.

B. Rewrite each sentence. Add **can**, **could**, **may**, or **might**. More than one answer is possible.

7. Oscar cleans the kitchen for Aunt Rosita. _____

_____

8. His cousins help him. _____

_____

9. Then Oscar reads them a story. _____

_____

10. They fall asleep. _____

_____

Write It

C. Complete the sentences about what other things Oscar and his family could do to help Aunt Rosita. Use **can**, **could**, **may**, or **might** in each sentence.

11. Oscar _____.

12. Oscar's parents _____.

13. Oscar's grandmother _____.

14. Oscar's siblings _____.

15. How might Aunt Rosita show her thanks? She _____

_____.

D. (16–20) How could you help your family members? How might they show their thanks for your help? Write at least five sentences. Use **can**, **could**, **may**, or **might**.

_____

_____

_____

_____

_____

30 Where Do You Place the Word *Not* in a Sentence?

Near the Verb

- The word **not** is a **negative word**. A sentence with the word **not** is a negative sentence.

  Mom is **not** at work. She might **not** go in today.

- The word **not** comes after **am**, **is**, or **are**.

  I **am not** at school. The driveway **is not** shoveled.

  The streets **are not** plowed.

- The word **not** comes between a **helping verb** and a **main verb**.

  We **could drive** up the driveway.
  helping   verb
  verb

  We **could not drive** up the driveway.
  helping   verb
  verb

Try It

A. Rewrite each sentence to make it negative. Add the word **not**.

1. Mom is outside. _____

_____

2. I am inside. _____

_____

3. I might shovel all the snow. _____

_____

4. Mom could help me. _____

_____

5. The snow is light and fluffy. _____

_____

6. It may take me all day to shovel. _____

B. Answer each question with a negative sentence. Use the word **not**.

7. There is a foot of snow on the roads. Are the roads plowed?

   _____

8. The electricity went off in the storm. Could you watch TV?

   _____

9. Your mom has a broken arm. Could she shovel the snow?

   _____

10. School is cancelled today. Could you go to school?

    _____

11. It is still snowing hard outside. Is the storm over?

    _____

Write It

C. What might you tell people about a big snowstorm? Complete the sentences. Use the word **not** to make your sentences negative.

12. Do _____.

13. I am _____.

14. People could _____.

15. Cars on the highway might _____.

16. The streets are _____.

D. (17–20) Write four sentences about a snowstorm or rainstorm. Use the word **not** to make your sentences negative.

   _____

   _____

   _____

   _____

   _____

31 How Do You Show That an Action Is in Process?

Use *Am, Is,* or *Are* Plus the *-ing* Form of the Verb.

- The **present progressive** form of the verb ends in **-ing**.
- Use **am, is,** or **are** plus a **main verb** with **-ing** to show that an action is in the process of happening. The **helping verb** must agree with the subject.

  Mom **is** go**ing** to work.

  I **am** go**ing** with her.

  She **is** show**ing** me her work.

  Her friends **are** tell**ing** me about their jobs, too.

Try It

A. (1–5) Write the correct present progressive verb to complete each sentence about career day.

We _____ a career day at school. Many parents
      am having / are having

_____ information about their jobs. I _____
is sharing / are sharing   **am listening / are listening**

carefully. My mom _____ her job as an engineer. She
      is describing / are describing

_____ about making computer software.
is talking / are talking

B. Write the present progressive form of the verb in parentheses.

6. Sonya's mom _____ about her job as a doctor. **(speak)**

7. I _____ close attention. **(pay)**

8. I _____ to be a doctor, too. **(go)**

9. My parents _____ me. **(help)**

10. They _____ me to follow my dream. **(tell)**

C. Complete the sentences about careers at your school. Use the present progressive to say what each person is doing.

11. The custodians _____.

12. The secretary _____.

13. My teachers _____.

14. Our principal _____.

D. (15–18) Write at least four sentences to tell where you would like to work someday. Use present progressive verbs.

_____

_____

_____

_____

_____

Edit It

E. (19–25) Edit the school newspaper report about career day. Use proofreader's marks to fix the seven present progressive verbs.

Career Day

Today, the students are learning about careers. Many parents is discuss their jobs. One dad is talk about his career as a city bus driver. He are telling about his route. Two moms are explain their jobs. They are police officers. They needed a lot of training.

"I is enjoying this career day," said student Jake Bloom. "It are help me decide what to do. As of today, I am think about a job with the city."

Proofreader's Marks
Change text:
Mom ~~am~~ is studying law.
See all Proofreader's Marks on page xi.

32 Use Subject Pronouns

Remember: The subject of a sentence can be a pronoun, but be sure the pronouns are clear.

- Use **I** when you talk about yourself.
- Use **you** to talk to one or more persons.
- Use **we** to talk about another person and yourself.
- Use **he**, **she**, **it**, and **they** to talk about other people or things.

Fix mistakes with subject pronouns. If necessary, rewrite your sentences to make them clear.

Joshua loves both New Hampshire and New York. It is where his grandma lives. Grandma is planning a family reunion at her house. They will be for the whole family.

Try It

A. Complete the sentences with subject pronouns if possible. Repeat a noun if needed for clarity.

1. My name is Joshua. _____ live in New Hampshire.
   I / You

2. My family and I are going to New York. _____ will attend a big family
   She / We
   reunion at my grandma's house.

3. My cousins Matthew and Ian look a lot like me. _____ even has a
   Ian / He
   similar birthmark.

4. Matthew and I both have blond hair and blue eyes. _____ looks more
   They / He
   like me than Ian does.

B. (5–8) Write the correct subject pronouns to complete the paragraph.

My grandma likes to garden. _____ grows beautiful flowers. "Joshua,"
she asks me, "would _____ like to learn about my flowers?" "Yes,
_____ would," I say. Her flowers are lovely. _____ smell sweet.

C. Answer these questions about the family reunion. Use subject pronouns in your answers.

9. Where is the reunion? _____

10. Whom does Joshua look like? Why? _____

_____

11. What does Joshua's grandma like to do? _____

12. How do you think Joshua's grandparents feel when their family comes to the reunion?

_____

D. (13–17) Write at least five sentences about your family's reunion. Who always comes? Whom do you look like? Use at least five subject pronouns.

_____

_____

_____

_____

_____

Grammar at Work

E. (18–25) Fix the six mistakes with pronouns. Fix the two incomplete sentences.

Dear Grandma,

    I a great time at the reunion. It enjoyed my time with Matthew and Ian. He both look different this year. The three of us look alike. They could be brothers instead of cousins!

    Grandma, it have beautiful flowers in your garden. Planted a strawberry plant and a rose bush in my yard. It already has berries. Mom helped with my planting. They loves gardens.

                        Love,

                        Joshua

Proofreader's Marks

Change text:

Grandpa and Grandma had a ~~Reunion. She~~ They invited the whole family.

See all Proofreader's Marks on page xi.

33 Use Helping Verbs

Remember: An action verb can have two parts: a helping verb and a main verb. **Am, is,** and **are** can be helping verbs. They must agree with the subject.

- Use the helping verbs **am, is,** or **are** plus a **main verb** with **-ing** to show that action is happening now.

   My neighborhood **is starting** a community garden. I **am helping**.
   People **are working** hard.

- You can use **helping verbs** to form **contractions**. You can join a pronoun and a helping verb or a helping verb and **not**.

You are planting.	Mom **is not** planting.	**She is** weeding.
You're planting.	Mom **isn't** planting.	**She's** weeding.

Try It

A. Write the correct helping verb to complete each sentence.

1. My neighbors _____ working on the garden today.
   am/are

2. Mr. Greene _____ planting flowers.
   is/are

3. I _____ digging the holes for him.
   am/is

4. You _____ doing a lot to help.
   is/are

B. Write the correct contraction to complete each sentence.

5. The flowers _____ blooming yet.
   isn't/aren't

6. _____ sprouting, though.
   They's/They're

7. It _____ raining much these days.
   isn't/aren't

8. _____ watering the plants every day.
   I'm/I's

C. Answer each question. Use helping verbs in all your answers. Use at least one contraction of a pronoun and helping verb and one contraction of a helping verb and **not**.

9. Is this flower blooming? No, _____.

10. Why are people planting a garden? _____

11. What is growing in this garden? _____

12. Are you planting a garden this spring? _____

D. (13–15) What would you plant in a garden? Write at least three sentences. Use helping verbs or helping verbs with contractions in your sentences.

_____

_____

_____

_____

Grammar at Work

E. (16–20) Fix the <u>four</u> mistakes with helping verbs. Two are in contractions. Fix <u>one</u> main verb to solve a problem in agreement.

> Our flower plot are looking beautiful.
> Some plants are starting to bloom. They's
> getting colorful flowers. Some bulbs blooms
> in early spring. The lilies bloom later. Those
> bulbs isn't blooming yet. I'm enjoying the
> community garden. Next year the neighbors
> am planning to plant vegetables, too.

Proofreader's Marks

Change text:
                            are
My friends ~~is~~ planting a
garden. ∧

See all Proofreader's Marks on page xi.

34 How Do You Use a Predicate Adjective?

After a Form of the Verb *Be*

- Most of the time, **adjectives** come before **nouns**.
  Scott is a **strong kid**. He makes **scary threats**.

- But if your verb is a form of **be**, you can put the adjective after the verb. The forms of **be** are **am**, **is**, **are**, **was**, and **were**.
  Scott **is tough**. Other kids **are afraid** of him.

Try It

A. Complete each sentence. Use a predicate adjective from the box.

lonely	certain	happier	mean	loyal
rude	stupid	unpleasant	tired	willing

1. Scott's friends were _____ last year.

2. They were _____ to do what Scott said.

3. But Scott was _____ to his friends.

4. "You guys are _____," he said.

5. "I am _____ of listening to Scott," said Marco.

6. "He is so _____."

7. "He is also _____," said Steven.

8. "We are _____ we can do without him," said Juan.

9. Scott's friends are _____ now.

10. Now Scott is _____.

B. Use a predicate adjective to complete each sentence.

11. Some kids at my school are _____ to other people.

12 I am _____ when I pass them in the hall.

13. Last year, one boy was very _____.

14. He said my friends were _____.

15. This year he is _____.

16. We are _____ to know him now.

17. He is _____ to know us, too!

Write It

C. Answer the questions about bullies. Use predicate adjectives in your answers.

18. Why do some bullies need to be in a group? They _____

_____.

19. How do you feel when a group of kids approaches you? I _____

_____.

20. How do your friends feel about bullies? _____

_____

D. (21–25) Think of a time when you or someone else was bullied. Write five sentences to describe what happened. Use predicate adjectives in your sentences.

_____

_____

_____

_____

_____

35 When Do You Use an Indefinite Adjective?

When You Can't Be Specific

- If you are not sure of the exact number or amount of something, use an **indefinite adjective**.

  There is **much** interest in martial arts today.
  A lot of people practice them.
  Many students take judo or karate lessons.
  Some kids try both of these martial arts.
  Several students become experts.

- **Many** and **much** are tricky.

  1. Use **many** before a noun, like **classes**, that can be counted.
     Many classes meet on weekends.

  2. Use **much** before a noun, like **excitement**, that can't be counted.
     Judo matches cause much **excitement**.

Try It

A. Complete each sentence with an indefinite adjective. More than one answer is possible.

1. _____ students take judo lessons.

2. Judo takes _____ different skills.

3. These skills require _____ practice.

4. Students take judo lessons for _____ reasons.

5. _____ girls and boys want to get stronger.

6. _____ students use judo to deal with feelings.

7. Judo is a way for _____ people to defend themselves.

8. _____ people report positive feelings because of judo.

B. (9–16) Complete the sentences. Use indefinite adjectives. More than one answer is possible.

Cole felt tired. He also did not have _____ physical strength.

_____ adults told him to try karate lessons. Cole's older brothers and

_____ friends agreed with the adults. It took _____

encouragement. Finally, Cole decided to take the lessons. Then he had to choose among

_____ kinds of karate. Karate started in _____ different

countries. Cole decided to take a form of karate from Korea. This decision gave Cole

_____ relief. He found karate to be a great way to build _____

strength.

Write It

C. Answer the questions about Cole. Use indefinite adjectives.

17. Why did Cole need encouragement to take karate lessons? Cole _____

_____.

18. What else could Cole do to build strengh? He could _____

_____.

D. (19–20) What are the best ways for kids to build strength? Write two
sentences explaining your opinion. Use indefinite adjectives in your
sentences.

_____

_____

_____

_____

_____

 **Can You Use an Adjective to Make a Comparison?**

Yes, But You Have to Change the Adjective.

- Use a **comparative adjective** to compare two people, places, or things.
  I used to live in a **rough** neighborhood, but this one is **rougher**.

- There are two ways to turn an adjective into a comparative adjective:

1. If the adjective is short, add **-er**. If it ends in **y**, change the **y** to **i** before you add **-er**.	**dark** **darker**	**clean** **cleaner**	**sunny** **sunnier**
2. If the adjective is long, use **more** before the adjective.	**comfortable** **more comfortable**	**thoughtful** **more thoughtful**	

Try It

A. Complete the sentences. Use comparative adjectives.

1. My mother was **happy** when we lived in Fairview. She is even _____ now in Bridgeview.

2. The people in Fairview were **kind**. The people in Bridgeview are _____.

3. The climate in Fairview was **mild**. It is even _____ here.

4. The pace of life in Fairview was **lively**. Life in Bridgeview is _____.

B. Write the comparative form of the adjective in parentheses.

5. Bridgeview people are _____ than in Fairview. **(busy)**

6. The stores in Bridgeview are _____ than in Fairview. **(nice)**

7. I was _____ in Fairview than I am in Bridgeview. **(nervous)**

8. My family has been _____ than some other families. **(lucky)**

9. Life in Bridgeview is _____ than life in Fairview was. **(pleasant)**

Write It

C. Compare the activity in your community with the activity in another community. Use comparative adjectives.

10. How busy is your neighborhood compared with another neighborhood you know?

In my neighborhood, _____

_____.

11. How do you feel about your neighborhood compared with how your parents feel?

I _____

_____.

D. (12–15) Now write four sentences that might change the amount of activity in your neighborhood. Use comparative adjectives.

_____

_____

_____

_____

Edit It

E. (16–20) Edit the journal entry. Fix five mistakes. Make sure comparative adjectives are in the correct form.

October 27

This afternoon, my brother and I heard loud music outside. The music got loud as it came more close. My brother was curious than I was. The music sounded lively. It was even lively as it passed by. We looked out the window. It was a parade! I was excited. My brother was even exciteder.

Proofreader's Marks

Change text:

faster

My heart beat ~~fast~~ than before.

See all Proofreader's Marks on page xi.

Can an Adjective Compare More Than Two Things?

Yes, But You Have to Use a Different Form.

- A **superlative adjective** compares three or more people, places, or things. To turn an adjective into a superlative adjective:

1. Add **-est** to a short adjective.	Ed is the **strongest** boy in the neighborhood.
2. Use **most** before a long adjective.	He is the **most energetic** kid around.

- Adjectives have different forms. Use the form that fits your purpose.

To Describe 1 Thing	strong	energetic
To Compare 2 Things	stronger	more energetic
To Compare 3 or More Things	strongest	most energetic

- Never use **more** and **-er** together. Never use **most** and **-est** together.

  Edgar is the ~~most~~ strongest boy in our neighborhood.

Try It

A. Complete each sentence with the correct adjective.

1. Ed says the _____ things about Stan.
   meanest / most mean

2. Then Joe says the _____ thing of all.
   insultingest / most insulting

3. Ed, Joe, and Stan get into the _____ fight ever.
   biggest / most big

4. Stan is the _____.
   more upset / most upset

5. Stan's _____ brother gets into the argument.
   oldest / most old

6. Then Stan's _____ brother does, too.
   youngest / most young

B. Complete each sentence. Use the correct form of the adjective in parentheses.

7. This is the _____ moment of Stan's life. **(difficult)**

8. It is also the _____ moment. **(scary)**

9. He knows that fighting is the _____ way to handle an argument. **(pointless)**

10. He also doesn't want to be the _____ kid in his neighborhood. **(cowardly)**

11. His heart is the _____ it has ever been. **(heavy)**

12. Maybe the _____ kids make the best choices. **(tough)**

13. Stan must make his _____ choice ever. **(hard)**

Write It

C. Answer the questions about arguments. Use comparative and superlative adjectives in your answers.

14. What should Stan do? Stan should _____.

15. When do you and your friends get into arguments? We _____
_____.

16. What are your arguments usually about? Our arguments _____
_____.

D. (17–20) How do you and your friends handle arguments? Write four sentences. Use comparative and superlative adjectives.

_____

_____

_____

_____

38 Which Adjectives Are Irregular?

Good, Bad, and Many

- These adjectives have special forms.

To Describe 1 Thing	good	bad	many
To Compare 2 Things	better	worse	more
To Compare 3 or More Things	best	worst	most

- How many things are being compared in these sentences?
  Diego wants his community to be **better** than it is.
  His community has the **worst** park of all the parks in the city.

Try It

A. Complete each sentence. Use the correct adjective.

1. Diego is _____ at finding solutions.
   good / better

2. He has _____ ideas about cleaning up the park than his friends do.
   more / most

3. The litter is _____ in summer than in winter.
   bad / worse

4. His _____ plan is to hold a weekly cleanup in summer.
   good / best

5. _____ volunteers join his cleanup crew.
   Many / Most

B. (6–12) Complete each sentence. Use forms of **good**, **bad**, or **many**.

The park was _____ than in summer. Then the _____ thing

happened of all. Diego's _____ friend found the _____ problem

ever. It was a box of kittens. There were _____ kittens than the boys had ever

seen. Then an animal shelter offered a _____ reward. The winner must find the

_____ homes for the kittens.

C. Answer the questions. Use forms of **good**, **bad**, or **many** in your answers.

13. What do you think about Diego's ideas? I think _____

_____ .

14. What else could Diego do to improve the park? He could _____

_____ .

15. How do you think Diego felt when his best friend found the kittens? I think he _____

_____ .

D. (16–20) Imagine that you are Diego. What would your next community project be? Write five sentences. Use forms of **good**, **bad**, or **many** in your sentences.

_____

_____

_____

_____

_____

Edit It

E. (21–25) Edit the letter. Fix the five mistakes. Make sure adjectives are in the correct form.

Dear J.T.,

The litter in our park is worse than ever. Sometimes worst things happen to better creatures. Yesterday, I heard the worse news. Four newborn kittens were left in the better section of the park. I am most upset now than before.

Your cousin,

Tanya

Proofreader's Marks

Change text:

The ~~bad~~ worst thing happened today.

See all Proofreader's Marks on page xi.

39 Why Do You Need Adverbs?

To Tell *How, When,* or *Where*

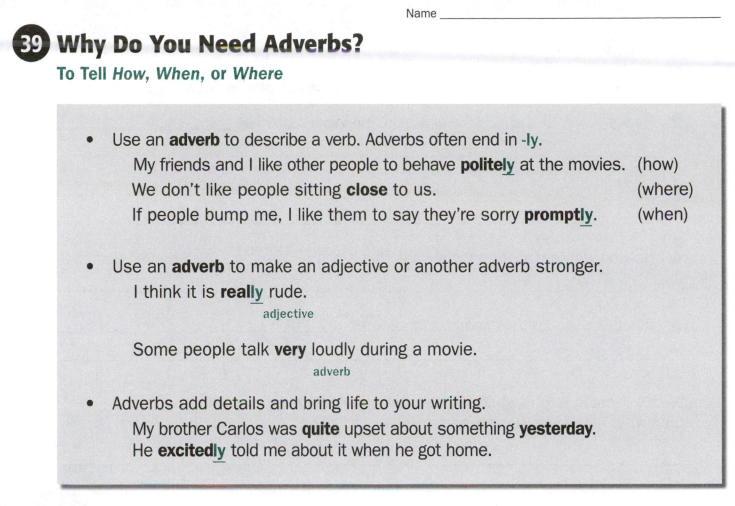

- Use an **adverb** to describe a verb. Adverbs often end in **-ly**.
  My friends and I like other people to behave **politely** at the movies.   (how)
  We don't like people sitting **close** to us.   (where)
  If people bump me, I like them to say they're sorry **promptly**.   (when)

- Use an **adverb** to make an adjective or another adverb stronger.
  I think it is **really** rude.
          adjective

  Some people talk **very** loudly during a movie.
              adverb

- Adverbs add details and bring life to your writing.
  My brother Carlos was **quite** upset about something **yesterday**.
  He **excitedly** told me about it when he got home.

Try It

A. Complete the sentences. Use adverbs to add details.

1. Carlos was at a _____ crowded basketball game.

2. He heard someone yelling _____.

3. Carlos looked _____.

4. A man was being _____ rude.

5. He yelled _____ mean words.

B. (6–11) Use adverbs to complete the story.

The man waved his arms _____ and refused to sit
_____. The people nearby watched _____. Someone
_____ asked the man to be quiet. The man refused. A security guard
_____ removed the man. Everyone applauded _____.

C. Answer the questions about Carlos's story. Use adverbs in your answers.

12. How do you think Carlos felt when the man was rude? He _____

_____.

13. What if the man were still there? What might happen? The other people _____

_____.

14. How do you feel about people who offend others? _____

_____

15. What can you do if someone offends you? _____

_____

D. (16–19) Think of a time when someone was rude. Write four sentences about what happened. Use adverbs.

_____

_____

_____

_____

Edit It

E. (20–25) Improve the letter. Use six adverbs to make the sentences more interesting.

Dear Jo,

We had an upsetting time at the movies yesterday. Thanks for telling that guy in the movie to sit. He talked and it made me mad. Some people can be thoughtless. They should think about how behaving bothers others.

Your friend,

Todd

Proofreader's Marks
Add text: very He was rude. ∧
See all Proofreader's Marks on page xi.

40 What Happens When You Add *Not* to a Sentence?

You Make the Sentence Negative.

- The word **not** is an adverb. Add it to a sentence to make it negative. If the verb is an **action verb**, change the sentence like this:
  I **help** my friend Ed. I **do not help** my friend Ed.

- If the verb is a form of **be**, just place **not** after the verb:
  He **is** very smart. He **is not** very smart.

- When you shorten a verb plus **not**, replace the **o** in **not** with an apostrophe (').

  1. Ed **does not** speak politely.

  Ed **doesn't** speak politely.

  2. He **is not** easy to like.

  He **isn't** easy to like.

Try It

A. Make these sentences negative.

1. Sometimes Ed says the right thing. _____

_____

2. Ed is always polite. _____

_____

3. Most people enjoy his rudeness. _____

_____

4. I know whom to invite to my party. _____

_____

5. I want to invite Ed. _____

_____

6. Most of my friends like him. _____

_____

B. Use the verbs in parentheses to make each sentence negative.

7. Some people _____ it is cool to be polite. **(think)**

8. They _____ about other people's feelings. **(care)**

9. But others _____ to be around rude people. **(like)**

10. They _____ to be offended. **(want)**

11. Most people _____ rude behavior. **(respect)**

12. They _____ meeting rude people. **(enjoy)**

13. A rude person _____ the rules. **(obey)**

14. We _____ the problem. **(overlook)**

Write It

C. Imagine that one of your friends is saying mean things about your other friends. Use **not** to make some of your sentences negative.

15. How does it make you feel? It _____

_____ .

16. What do you do about it? I _____

_____ .

D. (17–20) Think about someone you know who is rude. Write four sentences telling how other people react to this person's rudeness. Use **not** to make some of your sentences negative.

_____

_____

_____

_____

_____

41 Can You Use an Adverb to Make a Comparison?

Yes, But You Need to Change the Adverb.

- Adverbs have different forms. Use the form that fits your purpose.

To Describe 1 Action	soon	loudly	well	badly
To Compare 2 Actions	sooner	more loudly	better	worse
To Compare 3 or More Actions	soonest	most loudly	best	worst

- Think about how many things are being compared in these sentences:
  Some people speak **more carefully** than others.
  Kind people may speak the **most carefully** of all.

Try It

A. Complete each sentence with the correct adverb.

1. Some people try _____ than others to be kind.
   harder / hardest

2. Telling the truth works _____ than telling lies.
   best / better

3. People can learn to speak _____.
   nicely / most nicely

4. Kind people may speak _____ of all.
   well / best

B. Complete each sentence. Use a comparison form of the adverb in parentheses.

5. Maya acted _____ of all her friends. **(honestly)**

6. She spoke _____ than her friend Zoe did. **(boldly)**

7. Zoe thought _____ than Maya did about hurt feelings. **(hard)**

8. The truth hurts _____ when words are unkind. **(badly)**

9. Maya is behaving _____ now than she did before. **(well)**

Write It

C. Answer the questions about honesty. Use comparison adverbs.

10. Why do you think some people find it hard to be completely honest? They _____

_____.

11. Why is being kind and honest harder than just being honest? It is _____

_____.

D. (12–15) Do you think it is good to be completely honest even if it hurts someone? Write four sentences explaining your opinion. Use comparison adverbs in your sentences.

_____

_____

_____

_____

_____

Edit It

E. (16–20) Edit the journal entry below. Fix the five mistakes. Make sure adverbs are in the correct form.

> May 15
>
> I am worried that I treated Ayla badly. She wanted my opinion of her dancing. I said she danced gracefully than Renate. That isn't what I real think. I will tell her the truth. A person who speaks honestly behaves gooder than a person who lies. Of all my friends, she's the one I want to speak to the more honestly. I will act best than I did before.

Proofreader's Marks

Change text:
            more
I spoke most harshly than before.

Add text:
            most
You sang the beautifully of anyone.

See all Proofreader's Marks on page xi.

42 Can a Verb Act Like an Adjective?

Yes, When It Is a Participle

- Verbs have **four principal parts**. For example:

Present	Present Participle	Past	Past Participle
drive	driving	drove	driven
excite	exciting	excited	excited

- Many **verbs** are made up of a **helping verb** and a **participle**.
  Present Participle: My mother **is driving** to the store again.
  Past Participle: She **has driven** around all morning getting supplies.

- A **participle** can act as an adjective to describe a noun or pronoun.

  Mr. Powell is a **driven** man who always helps his neighbors.

- Insert a comma (,) after a participle that begins a sentence.

  Excited, the neighbors look forward to the block party.

Try It

A. Combine sentences. Move the <u>participle</u> **to tell about a noun or a pronoun in the other sentence. Write the new sentence.**

1. Warm weather brings the neighbors outside. They are <u>waiting</u>.

   _____

2. The neighbors set up tables and chairs. They are <u>excited</u>.

   _____

3. The block party includes new and old neighbors. It is <u>welcoming</u>.

   _____

4. The children greet their friends. They are <u>running</u>.

   _____

B. Complete each sentence. Use the present participle or the past participle of the verb in parentheses as an adjective.

5. _____, the children form a large group. **(dance)**

6. _____, Betsy asks Joey to perform. **(smile)**

7–8. _____, Joey sings. **(thrill)** The _____ crowd listens. **(please)**

9. _____, the neighbors praise Joey's performance. **(clap)**

Write It

C. Answer the questions. Use present and past participles as adjectives.

10. What yearly celebration or tradition do you enjoy in your community? _____

_____

11. How do people feel about the celebration? _____

D. (12–15) Now, write four sentences that tell more about the community event. Use participles as adjectives.

_____

_____

_____

Edit It

E. (16–20) Edit the letter below. Fix the five mistakes. Use present or past participles.

Dear Nora,

Today, our neighborhood had an excite street fair. We thought it might be ruined by the drive winds. Grin, Mr. Pearson said not to worry. A band played boom rock music. We got there early. Exhaust, we finally left at 5 o'clock!

Your pal,

Ali

Proofreader's Marks

Change text:

Shouting
~~Shout~~, he called me over.

See all Proofreader's Marks on page xi.

43 What Are Participial Phrases?

Phrases That Start with a Participle

- A **participle** is a verb form, but it can act like an adjective to describe a noun or a pronoun. It can stand alone or come at the start of a **phrase**. A participle often ends in **-ing**.

  Working, Maria helps clean up trash in the neighborhood.

  Seeing the activity, Thomas joins the people **cleaning the neighborhood**.

- You can create a **participial phrase** to combine two sentences. If the phrase begins a sentence, use a comma (,) after the phrase.

  Maria helps with the clean-up. Maria works hard.

  Helping with the clean-up, Maria works hard.

- Place a participial phrase close to the noun or pronoun that it describes.

  Not OK: Thomas picks up soda bottles **bending over the curb**.

  OK: **Bending over the curb**, Thomas picks up soda bottles.

Try It

A. Use a participial phrase to combine sentences. Write the new sentence. Don't forget the comma after a participial phrase at the start of a sentence.

1. Mr. Rummel organizes the clean-up. Mr. Rummel assigns the jobs.

_____

2. Mrs. Rummel greets each neighbor. Mrs. Rummel hands out garbage bags.

_____

3. Thomas roams the neighborhood. Thomas gathers bottles and cans.

_____

4. Maria watches the scene. She sees people picking up the trash.

_____

5. Delia smiles as she works. Delia plants many flowers.

_____

B. Choose from the participles in the box to complete each sentence.

exhausted	giggling	helping	looking	resting	sweeping

6. _____, Mr. Rodriguez sleeps in a chair.

7. Mrs. Rummel watches the children _____ with the clean-up.

8. _____ the sidewalk, Mrs. Bianco meets her neighbors.

9. She notices the whole neighborhood _____ much better.

10. _____, the adults admire the successful clean-up.

11. _____, the children race around the tidy playground.

Write It

C. Answer the questions about keeping neighborhoods clean. Use participial phrases in your answers.

12. Is there a clean-up in your neighborhood every year? _____

_____

13. What jobs do people do in a neighborhood clean-up? _____

_____

14. Why should people work together to keep their neighborhood looking nice? _____

_____

15. How does having a clean neighborhood make life better for the people who live there? _____

_____

D. (16–20) Write five sentences about how people can keep their neighborhoods clean. Use participial phrases in your sentences.

_____

_____

_____

_____

44 What Is an Appositive?

A Word or Phrase That Renames a Noun

- An **appositive** is a noun or noun phrase that identifies or explains the noun or pronoun that comes before it.

  Frankenstein, **a classic novel**, is considered early science fiction.

  Jules Verne, **a nineteenth century writer**, started the sci-fi craze.

- You can use **appositives** to combine sentences. Appositives are usually set off with commas.

  My teacher told us to write a sci-fi story. My teacher's name is Ms. Yang.

  My teacher, **Ms. Yang**, told us to write a sci-fi story.

Try It

A. **Use an appositive to combine the sentences. Write each new sentence.**

1. My story is about a trip to the stars. My story is called "The Milky Way."

_____

2. The main character is a 12-year-old boy. His name is Punch Miller.

_____

3. His starship soars through space. The starship is a flying saucer.

_____

4. Punch's little sister is also aboard. Her name is Sara.

_____

5. Sara always talks to her cat. The cat is named Twinkle.

_____

6. Twinkle is very mischievous. She is a green-eyed tabby.

_____

B. Use an appositive to combine the sentences. Write each new sentence.

7. Punch is very famous. He is an excellent pilot.

_____

8. His starship is also famous. It is called the _Silver Circle_.

_____

9. The _Silver Circle_ passes Jupiter. Jupiter is the largest planet in our solar system.

_____

10. The ship delivers cargo to a distant galaxy. The cargo is milk and cheese.

_____

11. The co-pilot drinks all the milk. The co-pilot is a thirsty cat named Twinkle.

_____

12. Ms. Yang read my story aloud to the class. She is a wonderful teacher.

_____

Write It

C. Write sentences of your own, using the appositives.

13. _____ , my best subject, _____ .

14. _____ , my favorite book, _____ .

15. _____ , an unusual hobby, _____ .

16. _____ , one of my favorite places, _____ .

D. (17–20) What kind of stories do you like to read? Write four sentences using appositives.

_____

_____

_____

_____

45 Use Adjectives Correctly

Remember: You can use adjectives to describe or compare people, places, or things.

- How do you know which adjective to use?

To Describe 1 Thing	safe	unpleasant	good	many
To Compare 2 Things	safer	more unpleasant	better	more
To Compare 3 or More Things	safest	most unpleasant	best	most

Some conflicts are **more unpleasant** than others. **Many** people think that a life without conflict is a **better** life. However, even the **most unpleasant** disagreement might be helpful. Conflict may be a **good** way to solve a problem.

Try It

A. Complete each sentence. Use the correct adjective.

1. There are _____ reasons for disagreement.
   many / much

2. All the reasons may be _____ .
   good / better

3. _____ reasons may be better than others.
   Much / Some

4. Don't make a disagreement _____ than it is.
   worse / worst

5. Let's make the world a _____ place.
   gooder / better

B. (6–10) Complete each sentence with an adjective. More than one answer is possible.

_____ people accept disagreement as a part of life. _____ people do not want _____ conflict in their life, however. Still others believe that all conflict is _____ . The _____ attitude of all says that we can work out our conflicts.

C. Answer the questions about disagreement. Use adjectives in the correct form.

11. How do you think living in constant disagreement might affect people? People _____

_____.

12. Do you think disagreement can be a good thing? I think _____

_____.

D. (13–16) How do you think the world would be different if people didn't accept violence? Write four sentences. Use adjectives in the correct form.

_____

_____

_____

_____

_____

_____

Grammar at Work

E. (17–20) Fix <u>three</u> mistakes with adjectives. Fix <u>one</u> mistake with subject pronouns.

June 10

This week I had more disagreements with my sister than usual. My sister gets everything! It really rules our whole household. Much people wouldn't put up with her. If someone would speak to her, I would be happiest. Home should not be such a worse place!

Proofreader's Marks

Change text: better

We will feel best than before.

See all Proofreader's Marks on page xi.

46 Use Adverbs Correctly

Remember: You can use adverbs to describe and compare actions.
An adverb can also make another adverb or adjective stronger.

Describe	Compare	Make Stronger
I did not speak **kindly** to my grandmother.	I know I should behave **better** around her.	I acted **very** badly.
My parents taught me to treat her **respectfully**.	I should treat her **more carefully**.	My grandmother is **really** upset.

Try It

A. Use an adverb from the box to complete each sentence.

more wisely   nervously   quietly   really   softly

1. My grandmother entered the room _____.

2. I looked _____ at her.

3. I was _____ embarrassed.

4. She spoke _____ to me.

5. "You should speak _____ than you did," she said.

B. (6–10) Complete each sentence with an adverb. More than one answer is possible.

My grandmother said I should choose my words _____ in the future. I understood her _____. If I speak too _____, it can be _____ harmful. From now on I will treat people the _____ that I can.

Write It

C. Answer the questions about how to speak without hurting people's feelings. Use adverbs.

11. Why is it a good idea to think before you speak? *If you don't* _____
_____.

12. How do you think people should speak to each other? *I think* _____
_____.

D. (13–16) Think about a time your words hurt someone. Write four sentences to tell what happened. Use adverbs.

_____

_____

_____

_____

_____

Grammar at Work

E. (17–20) Edit the letter. Fix the <u>four</u> mistakes.

Dear Mike,

    I want to quickly ask your forgiveness for my behavior yesterday. I am much sorry that I spoke so rude to you. I know I hurt your feelings. I promise I will treat you gooder from now on. I is apologizing most sincerely. I hope you can forgive me.

               Your friend,

               Sam

Proofreader's Marks
Delete:
There is a lot of ~~much~~ conflict.
Change text: badly
She treated me ~~bad~~.
See all Proofreader's Marks on page xi.

47 Combine Sentences

Remember: You can improve your writing by combining sentences.

- You can use a **participial phrase** to combine sentences.
  We will be on vacation. We are starting next week.
  Starting next week, we will be on vacation.
      participial phrase

- You can also use an **appositive** to combine sentences.
  Appositives are usually set off with commas.
  My father carefully planned our trip. My father is an excellent driver.
  My father, **an excellent driver**, carefully planned our trip.
      appositive

Try It

A. Use a participial phrase to combine each pair of sentences. Write the new sentence.

1. We are driving to my aunt's house. We will pass through several states.

_____

2. We will leave on Saturday. We will arrive the following Monday.

_____

3. My brother helped plan the trip. He studied the maps.

_____

B. Use an appositive to combine each pair of sentences. Write the new sentence.

4. My cousins will be happy to see us. Their names are Jo and Sam.

_____

5. Jo is my oldest cousin. She is a college student.

_____

6. Sam is my age. He is a very tall sixth-grader.

_____

C. Use each participial phrase or appositive in a sentence about a vacation or trip.

7. Looking for someplace to stay, _____ .

8. Arriving early, _____ .

9. _____ , my favorite game.

10. _____ , a good friend of mine.

11. Running to the _____ , _____ .

12. _____ , my favorite food.

D. (13–17) Where would you like to go on a family vacation? Write five sentences. Use a participial phrase or an appositive in each sentence.

_____

_____

_____

_____

Grammar at Work

E. (18–20) Combine <u>two</u> pairs of sentences, using a participial phrase and an appositive. Fix <u>one</u> mistake with a pronoun.

Dear Anya,

   Our vacation is wonderful! Aunt Pearl makes incredible meals. She is a great cook. My uncle even took us to the lake one day. Sam was feeding the ducks. Sam slipped and fell into the water. My father and my uncle both started to laugh. Them said it was a good thing Sam could swim!

Love,

Sara

Proofreader's Marks

Add text:
                    to
We went ˄ the park.

Change text:
            was
Our day ~~were~~ fun!

Do not capitalize:
The lake was Ⱡold.

Capitalize:
the ducks looked at Sam.

See all Proofreader's Marks on page xi.

48 How Do You Show That an Action Already Happened?

Add -ed to the Verb.

The **tense** of a verb shows when an action happens.

- Action in the **present tense** happens now or on a regular basis.
- Action in the **past tense** happened earlier.

Past ← **Earlier** ● **Now** ● **Later** ○ → **Future**

Past Tense
show**ed**

Present Tense
show, shows

Add **-ed** to most verbs when you talk or write about a past action.

1. Today, Marina **shows** me a picture.
   She **showed** me a picture yesterday.

2. Today, she **asks** me what is different.
   She **asked** me that yesterday, too.

Try It

A. Complete the sentence with the past tense form of the verb in parentheses.

1. Last summer, Marina _____ a big change. **(want)**

2. Marina _____ her friend Kate. **(call)**

3. They _____ a new hair style. **(pick)**

4. Then Marina's mother _____ her hair. **(curl)**

B. Complete the sentences. Choose verbs from the box and write them in the past tense.

act	explain	point

5. Her friends _____ as if they did not notice her curls.

6. Marina _____ out the new style.

7. Then they _____, "You are still the same Marina to us."

C. Answer the questions about someone you know who changed his or her appearance. Use verbs that end in **-ed**.

8. How did the person change his or her appearance? _____

_____

9. Did you like the change? Explain. _____

_____

10. Did this change affect your relationship with this person? _____

_____

D. (11–12) Now write two sentences about when you wanted to change something about yourself. Use verbs that end in **-ed**.

_____

_____

_____

_____

Edit It

E. (13–15) Edit the journal entry. It should be in the past tense. Fix the three mistakes.

May 19

The heavy frames of my glasses bothered me. So I ask the eye doctor for new glasses. She checks my eyes. Then she helped me pick out new frames. I walked home quickly. Then I look in the mirror a few times. I wished my new glasses were here already!

Proofreader's Marks

Change text:

The glasses change~~d~~ my appearance.

See all Proofreader's Marks on page xi.

49 Can You Just Add -*ed* to Form a Verb in the Past?

Not Always

Most verbs end with **-ed** to show the past tense. Sometimes you have to change the spelling of the verb before you add **-ed**. Follow these rules:

1. If a verb ends in silent **e**, drop the **e**. Then add **-ed**.

   Brianna lik**ed** her new drum. **(like)**

   She hop**ed** people would enjoy the sound. **(hope)**

2. Some one-syllable verbs end in one vowel and one consonant. Double the consonant before you add **-ed**.

   Brianna patt**ed** her drum gently. **(pat)**

   Then she slipp**ed** on her jacket. **(slip)**

Try It

A. Complete each sentence in the past tense. Use the verb in parentheses.

1. Brianna _____ on time for the parade. **(arrive)**

2. She _____ some band members up front. **(notice)**

3. Mrs. Doyle _____ a flag on Brianna's collar. **(pin)**

4. They both _____. Brianna was ready. **(nod)**

B. Complete the sentences. Choose verbs from the box and write them in the past tense.

beg	dance	like	stop

5. Brianna _____ the parade route.

6. The band _____ several times to play.

7. Children _____ in the street.

8. People _____ for more.

C. Answer the questions about a parade you were in or saw, either live or on TV. Use verbs with **-ed**.

9. What did you like most about the parade? Why? I _____ because

   _____.

10. What did you notice about the people in the parade? I _____

    _____.

11. How did other people react to the parade? Why? People _____

    _____

    _____.

D. (12–15) Write four sentences that tell more about what happened. Use verbs with **-ed**.

_____

_____

_____

_____

Edit It

E. (16–20) Edit the journal entry. It should be in the past tense. Fix the five mistakes.

September 10

Last year, a new boy moved into my neighborhood. He introduce himself as a great piano player. One morning, I skip my drum lesson to listen to him. I love his sound! He drum on the piano! From then on, we talked a lot about pianos, drums, and music. Last summer, we decide to invent a drum-piano or a piano-drum!

Proofreader's Marks

Change text:

He ~~smile~~ smiled at me.

See all Proofreader's Marks on page xi.

50 Can You Just Add -ed to Form a Verb in the Past?

Not Always

Most verbs end with **-ed** to show the past tense. Follow these rules for adding **-ed** to words that end with **y**.

1. If a verb ends in a vowel and **y**, just add **-ed**.

   stray + -ed = strayed   Bob **strayed** from the group.

2. If a verb ends in a consonant and **y**, change the **y** to **i** before you add **-ed**.

   hurry + -ed = hurried   Then Bob **hurried** to catch up.

   deny + -ed = denied   He **denied** the whole thing.

Try It

A. Complete each sentence in the past tense. Use the verb in parentheses.

1. Bob _____ his father's elephant models in the auditorium. **(display)**

2. The models _____ the whole stage. **(occupy)**

3. Bob _____ about people's reactions. **(worry)**

4. He _____ his friends would not laugh at the exhibit. **(pray)**

B. Complete the sentences. Choose verbs from the box and write them in the past tense.

stay	reply	vary

5. The reactions _____.

6. Bob _____ calm.

7. He _____ to everyone with a smile.

Write It

C. Answer the questions about a time you wanted to please someone or a group of people. Use verbs with **-ed**.

8. Whom did you want to please? I _____ to

_____.

9. What did you plan to do? I _____ to

_____.

10. How did the person or group respond to your actions? _____

_____

_____

D. (11–12) Write two sentences that tell more about what happened. Use verbs with **-ed**.

_____

_____

_____

Edit It

E. (13–15) Edit the journal entry. It should be in the past tense. Fix the three mistakes.

> November 30
>
> Last spring, lots of kids in my neighborhood started to play basketball together. We play every Saturday morning for months. Then we try to find other teams to play against. The Rovers portray themselves as unbeatable. They were not!

Proofreader's Marks

Change text:

studied
We ~~study~~ the teams.

See all Proofreader's Marks on page xi.

51 When Do You Use *Was* and *Were*?

When You Tell About the Past

The verb **be** has special forms to tell about the present and the past.

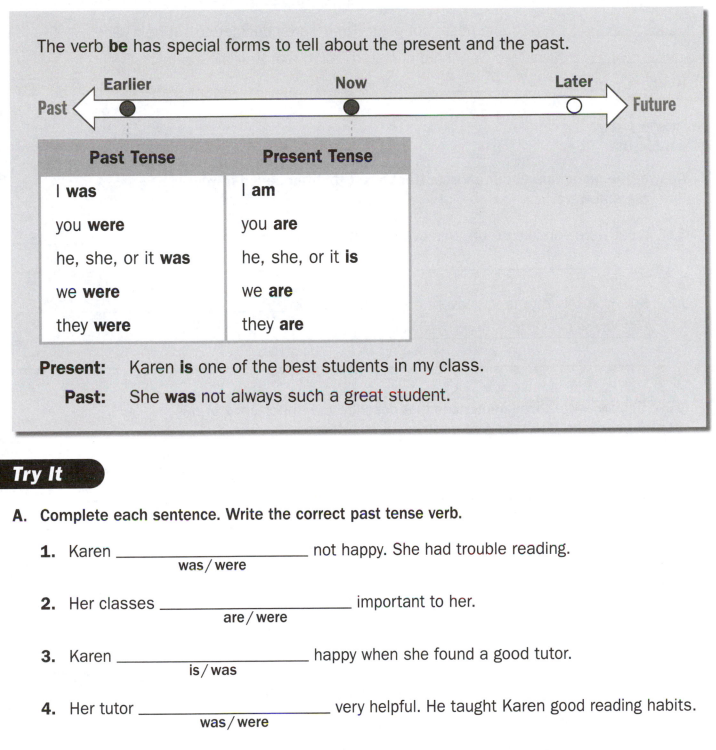

Past Tense	Present Tense
I **was**	I **am**
you **were**	you **are**
he, she, or it **was**	he, she, or it **is**
we **were**	we **are**
they **were**	they **are**

Present: Karen **is** one of the best students in my class.

Past: She **was** not always such a great student.

Try It

A. Complete each sentence. Write the correct past tense verb.

1. Karen _____ not happy. She had trouble reading.
    was / were

2. Her classes _____ important to her.
    are / were

3. Karen _____ happy when she found a good tutor.
    is / was

4. Her tutor _____ very helpful. He taught Karen good reading habits.
    was / were

5. Karen _____ pleased with her progress.
    am / was

6. Her tutor _____ determined to help Karen. Today, she is a great student.
    was / were

B. (7–10) Complete the sentences about how Karen became a better student. Use the correct past tense form of **be**.

A few years ago, Karen _____ a poor student. Her teachers

_____ afraid she might not pass. Then Karen decided to get help. She

_____ ready to work hard and study a lot, too. Karen got a tutor. Over

the next year, they _____ together a lot.

Write It

C. Answer the questions about an important event that happened in your life. Use **was** and **were**.

11. What were you like before this event happened? At that time, I _____

_____.

12. How was this moment or event important to you? _____

_____

_____

D. (13–15) Now, write three sentences that describe the importance of this moment or event. Use **was** and **were** in your sentences.

_____

_____

_____

Edit It

E. (16–20) Edit the letter. It should be in the past tense. Fix the five mistakes.

Dear Raul,

   I'm sorry I missed you at the game yesterday. My family and I were at a concert before the game. We are sorry to be late. We was so late that the game is already over. I am really disappointed. Then I saw you. You are very far away.

                   Talk to you soon,

                   Ben

Proofreader's Marks

Change text:
       was
He were there.

See all Proofreader's Marks on page xi.

52 When Do You Use *Had*?

When You Tell About the Past

The verb **have** uses special forms to show the present and the past.

	Earlier	Now	Later

Past ← ⬤ — ⬤ — ○ → **Future**

Past Tense	Present Tense
I **had**	I **have**
you **had**	you **have**
he, she, or it **had**	he, she, or it **has**
we **had**	we **have**
they **had**	they **have**

Present: I **have** a great story about the drama club.

Past: Last year, I **had** a chance to act in a play.

Try It

A. Read each sentence. Then write it in the past tense.

1. The drama club has many members. _____

_____

2. Some of them have fears about acting. _____

_____

3. Each student has a chance to act in a play. _____

_____

4. Most of the actors have some belief in their talents. _____

_____

5. I have faith in myself. _____

B. Complete the sentence. Use the correct form of have.

6. Last year, I _____ a new math class.

7. I _____ trouble with some of the work.

8. The teacher _____ great ideas about how to help me.

9. Then, I _____ to work very hard to succeed.

10. Today, I _____ trust in my math skills.

11. My teacher also _____ trust in me today.

12. Last year, I _____ a lot of homework every night.

13. Today, I still _____ a lot of homework, but I sail through!

Write It

C. Answer the questions about how a class has improved your life. Use the past tense of have in your answers.

14. How did a class you had in the past improve your life? _____

_____

15. What ideas, knowledge, or skills did you have before you took the class? _____

_____

16. How did those ideas, knowledge, or skills change? _____

_____

D. (17–20) Now, write four more sentences about a class that helped a friend. Use the past tense of have in your answers.

_____

_____

_____

_____

_____

53 How Do You Show That an Action Already Happened?

Change the Verb.

Add **-ed** to most verbs to show that an action already happened.
Use special past tense forms for **irregular verbs**.

Present	Past	Example in the Past
do, does	did	Hailey **did** her best on all her science projects.
go, goes	went	Last year, she **went** on a trip to the Science Museum.
get	got	She **got** excellent grades after that.
have, has	had	Last month, her class **had** a science fair.
meet	met	Hailey **met** her science team members.
take	took	She **took** a chance with a new challenge.
tell	told	Hailey **told** her teacher what she wanted to do.

Try It

A. Read each sentence. Write the sentence again, changing the verb to the past tense.

1. Hailey wants to run for leader of her science team. _____

   _____

2. The team tells Hailey to learn new skills. _____

   _____

3. Instead, they take a vote for Ben. _____

4. Ben has great leadership skills. _____

5. The team meets every afternoon for the whole month. _____

   _____

B. Complete the sentences. Choose from the verbs in the box. Use the past tense.

do	get	meet	take	tell

6. Hailey _____ a chance to be part of a real team.

7. Before, Hailey _____ everything by herself.

8. This time, Hailey _____ orders from the team leader.

9. She _____ new friends and team members.

10. Her friends _____ Hailey about her success.

Write It

C. Write three sentences about a time you learned something about yourself from participating in a group. Use the past tense.

11. Tell about what you did. _____

_____

12. Tell about the person or people that you met. _____

_____

13. What did you get from the experience? _____

_____

D. (14–15) Now, write at least two more sentences about the experience. Use the past tense.

_____

_____

_____

_____

_____

_____

54 How Do You Show That an Action Already Happened?

Change the Verb.

Add **-ed** to most verbs to show that an action already happened.
Use special past tense forms for **irregular verbs**.

Present	Past	Example in the Past
see	saw	Paul **saw** the sign for the class elections.
sit	sat	He **sat** down on a bench.
feel	felt	He **felt** uneasy about the elections.
run	ran	Paul **ran** down the street.
know	knew	He **knew** what Morgan would say.
say	said	Morgan **said**, "I think you should run for class president."

Try It

A. Complete each sentence. Write the past tense form of the verb in parentheses.

1. Morgan and her friends _____ they would help Paul. **(say)**

2. He _____ he could trust his friends. **(know)**

3. In the end, Paul _____ for class president. **(run)**

4. Everyone _____ Paul's name on the list. **(see)**

B. Complete each sentence in the past tense. Write the correct form of the verb.

5. Paul and his friends _____ election posters.
   make / made

6. On election day, the students _____ that it was time to vote.
   know / knew

7. The principal _____, "I counted the votes, and Paul is
   says / said
   our new president."

C. Use the questions to help you write about a time you tried something new. Use irregular past tense verbs.

8. What new thing did you try? _____

9. How did you feel about trying it? _____

10. What did you think after you tried it? _____

11. Did you learn something new about yourself? _____

_____

D. (12–14) Write three sentences that tell more about when you tried something new. Use irregular past tense verbs.

_____

_____

_____

_____

E. (15–20) Edit the letter. Fix the six mistakes.

Dear Sonrisa,

Last month, I ran for class president. At first, I feel nervous. My friends say, "We believe in you." They know I needed them. My friends sit with me on election day. Together, we wait for the final results. Guess what? I won! I make a promise to be a good president.

Your friend,

Paul

Proofreader's Marks

Change text:

I sit with my friends.

See all Proofreader's Marks on page xi.

55 How Do You Show That an Action Was in Process?

Use *Was* or *Were* Plus the *-ing* Form of the Verb.

- Sometimes you want to show that an action was happening over a period of time in the past. Use the past progressive form of the verb.

- To form the past progressive, use the helping verb **was** or **were** plus a main verb that ends in **-ing**. The **helping verb** must agree with the subject.

  Liam **was running** our class recycling project.

  Janice **was helping** him.

  They **were taking** ideas from different students.

Try It

A. Complete each sentence. Use the past progressive form of the verb in parentheses.

1. Liam _____ for new ideas. **(look)**

2. He _____ everyone to join him. **(ask)**

3. The teachers _____ to help Liam. **(plan)**

4. Liam _____ down all the ideas. **(write)**

5. He _____ a good manager. **(become)**

B. Complete the sentences with verbs in the past progressive tense.

6. The teachers _____ Liam suggestions.

7. Students _____ good ideas, too.

8. Liam _____ pride in how he managed the details.

9. He _____ good about his role in the recycling project.

C. Describe a project you worked on. Use the past progressive or past tense.

10. Describe what you were doing. _____

_____

11. Tell why you chose this project. What were you hoping would happen? _____

_____

12. Describe how you felt at the end of the project. _____

_____

D. (13–15) Now, write three sentences that tell more about the project. Use the past progressive or past tense.

_____

_____

_____

_____

Edit It

E. (16–20) Edit the paragraph. Fix the five mistakes in the past progressive tense.

One summer, I tried to organize a terrific vacation for my grandfather. I were planning a lot of activities. I was hoped to catch the biggest fish ever. I were wishing for sunny weather. The first night, my grandfather kept me up late. He telling me stories about his life. The next night, I kept him up late. I were snoring. Today, we still laugh about that funny trip.

Proofreader's Marks

Add text:
                    was
            I ∧ helping my grandfather.

Change text:
                    were
            We ~~was~~ wishing for a
            change. ∧

See all Proofreader's Marks
on page xi.

56 How Do You Tell About the Future?

Use *Will* Before the Verb.

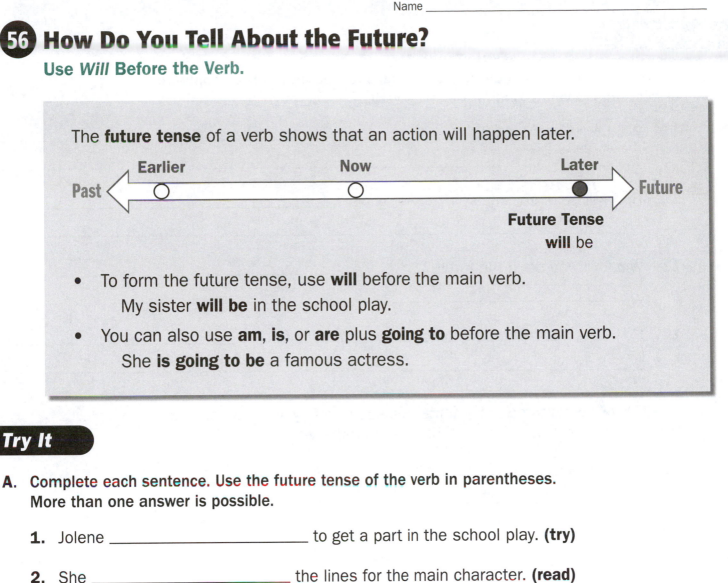

The **future tense** of a verb shows that an action will happen later.

Past ← Earlier ○ —— Now ○ —— Later ● → Future

Future Tense
will be

- To form the future tense, use **will** before the main verb.
  My sister **will be** in the school play.
- You can also use **am**, **is**, or **are** plus **going to** before the main verb.
  She **is going to be** a famous actress.

Try It

A. **Complete each sentence. Use the future tense of the verb in parentheses. More than one answer is possible.**

1. Jolene _____ to get a part in the school play. **(try)**

2. She _____ the lines for the main character. **(read)**

3. The director _____ carefully. **(listen)**

4. Other students _____ there. **(be)**

5. She _____ everyone. **(surprise)**

B. **Read each sentence. Then change it to the other form of the future tense.**

6. Some students will dance on stage.

   _____

7. The director is going to watch all the performances.

   _____

8. She will look for excellent dancers.

   _____

C. Answer the questions about a friend's plans for the future. Then compare his or her plans to yours. Use future tense verbs.

9. What will your friend do? _____

_____

10. How will he or she reach his or her goals? _____

_____

11. What will you do in the future? _____

_____

12. How does your future compare with your friend's future? _____

_____

D. (13–15) Now write three more sentences about what your future or your friend's future is going to be like. Use the future tense.

_____

_____

_____

_____

_____

E. (16–20) Edit this letter to a friend. Fix the five mistakes with future tense verbs.

Dear Juanita,

My sister Jolene is going to get the lead role in the school play. I be so proud of her. Our whole family help her learn her lines. She is become a star. We is see her dream come true. I is so excited for her!

Marissa

Proofreader's Marks
Add text:
will
I help them.
Change text:
will
He is be happy.
See all Proofreader's Marks on page xi.

57 Use Verb Tenses

Remember: You have to change the verb to show the past tense.

Add **-ed** to most verbs. Sometimes you need to make a spelling change before you add **-ed**.

Present Tense	Past Tense
walk, walks	walked
ask, asks	asked
hop, hops	hopped
save, saves	saved

Use special forms for the past tense of **be** and **have**.

Forms of *Be*	
Present Tense	**Past Tense**
am, is, are	was, were

Forms of *Have*	
Present Tense	**Past Tense**
have, has	had

Try It

A. Complete each sentence. Write the correct verb.

1. Every Monday, I _____ on a recycling project.
   work/worked

2. Last week, people _____ old cell phones.
   donate/donated

3. My teacher _____ surprised by the number of phones.
   is / was

B. Read each sentence. Write whether it uses present or past tense. Then rewrite the sentence and change the tense.

4. We mail the phones. _____

5. The company returned some money. _____

6. We contribute to charities. _____

7. I was proud of our project. _____

C. Answer the questions about how you see yourself. Use the correct verb tense.

8. What do you like most about yourself? I _____ my _____.

9. What opinions do your friends have of you? _____

_____

10. Have you changed how you see yourself compared with a year ago? Explain. _____

_____

D. (11–15) Now, write five sentences about one thing you wish you had changed about yourself. Use the past tense.

_____

_____

_____

_____

_____

Grammar at Work

E. (16–20) Fix the **four** mistakes with verb tenses. Fix **one** mistake with an adjective that compares.

August 8

Yesterday, we had our camp talent show.
I dance a folk dance from Mexico. I am
nervous! Then people want me to do it
again. My heart skipped a beat, but I hops
up to dance a second time. It was the more
exciting show ever!

Proofreader's Marks

Change text:

clapped
They clap for me.

See all Proofreader's Marks on page xi.

Name _____

58 Use Verb Tenses

Remember: You have to change the verb to show when an action happens. The action can happen in the **present**, **past**, or **future**.

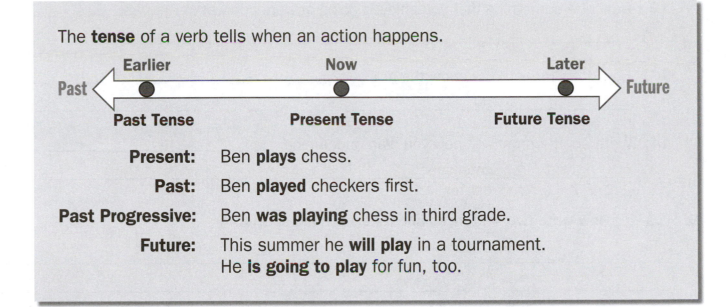

The **tense** of a verb tells when an action happens.

| | Earlier | Now | Later | |
| Past | Past Tense | Present Tense | Future Tense | Future |

Present:	Ben **plays** chess.
Past:	Ben **played** checkers first.
Past Progressive:	Ben **was playing** chess in third grade.
Future:	This summer he **will play** in a tournament. He **is going to play** for fun, too.

Try It

A. Read each sentence. Write a new sentence. Change the verb to the tense in parentheses.

1. Ben also likes sports. **(past)** _____

2. I see Ben at a judo match. **(past)** _____

3. He kicked very well. **(past progressive)** _____

4. Ben takes music lessons soon. **(future)** _____

B. (5–11) Write the missing forms of each verb in the chart.

Present	Past	Past Progressive	Future
learn		was learning	
take			will take / is going to take
	wrote		

Write It

C. Use the questions to help you write about your skills. Use three different verb tenses in your sentences.

12. Describe something that you enjoyed doing or were good at in the past. _____

_____

13. How does this activity show the real you? _____

_____

14. Write about something new you plan on learning. _____

_____

D. (15–16) Now write two sentences about how you are special.

_____

_____

_____

Grammar at Work

E. (17–20) Fix the **three** mistakes with verb tenses. Fix **one** mistake with adverbs that compare.

Dear Dan,

   I like to write words and music for songs. Last week, I meeted a famous songwriter. He listened more careful to my songs than anyone else. Then he sayed very nice things about them. He telled me to write a new song every day!

                     Your friend,

                     Mark

Proofreader's Marks

Change text:

     took
I ~~taked~~ piano lessons.

See all Proofreader's Marks on page xi.

59 How Do Nouns Work in a Sentence?

They Can Be the Subject or the Object.

- Nouns can be the **subject** of a sentence.

  Bruce is good friends with Dan.
  subject

- Nouns can be the **object** of an action verb. To find the object, turn the verb into a question like: "Plays what?" Your answer is the object.

  Bruce **plays baseball** with Dan.
              verb   object

- Many English sentences follow this pattern: subject → verb → object.

  Bruce hits the **ball**.
  subject verb   object

  Dan wears a **glove**.
  subject verb   object

Try It

A. Read each sentence. Decide if the <u>noun</u> is a **subject** or an **object**. Write **subject** or **object** on the line.

1. The boys both enjoy <u>sports</u>. _____

2. Dan has other <u>interests</u>, too. _____

3. <u>Dan</u> plays the drums in a jazz band. _____

4. The <u>band</u> enjoys jazz music. _____

B. Write a subject or an object to complete each sentence.

5. My best _____ plays the saxophone in a band. **(subject)**

6. Another band member plays the _____ . **(object)**

7. One _____ plays sports after band rehearsal. **(subject)**

8. Some kids do many _____ . **(object)**

Write It

C. Answer each question. Use an object in your answer. Underline the object.

9. What instrument do some people play? _____

10. What sport do some people play? _____

11. What equipment do players need for that sport? _____

12. What activity do your friends enjoy? _____

D. (13–15) Write three sentences about activities that students do at school. Use a subject and an object in each sentence. Circle the subject. Underline the object.

_____

_____

_____

_____

_____

Edit It

E. (16–20) Edit the paragraph. Add two subjects and three objects.

The enjoy different activities. Kristen plays. She shoots balls into the hoop. Victor enjoys. He plays the guitar in a band. My two best write for the school newspaper. Chris writes. Craig writes movie reviews.

Proofreader's Marks

Add text:

Pamela meets ^friends at school.

See all Proofreader's Marks on page xi.

60 Why Are There So Many Pronouns?

Some Work as Subjects, and Some Work as Objects.

- Use a **subject pronoun** as the subject of a sentence.

  Marissa likes math. **She** is in the math club.

subject

- Use an **object pronoun** as the object of the verb.

  Marissa has a **brother**. She helps **him** with math.

object

- The pronouns **you** and **it** stay the same no matter how they are used.

Pronouns	
Subject	**Object**
I	me
you	you
he	him
she	her
it	it

Try It

A. Write the correct pronoun from the chart to complete each pair of sentences. Then underline the noun it refers to.

1. Math is a difficult subject. _____ is hard for Tom.

2. Tom likes English. _____ writes well.

3. The English homework confuses Marissa. Tom helps _____ .

4. Marissa appreciates Tom. Marissa thanks _____ .

5. Marissa finishes her English homework. _____ helps Tom with math.

B. (6–10) Complete the paragraph. Write the correct pronouns from the chart.

Tom writes a play. Marissa helps _____ . The play solves a

problem. _____ is a math mystery. The main character is Snoopy

Sue. _____ is a detective. Mr. Math helps _____ .

_____ is a math professor.

Write It

C. Answer each question. Use either a subject pronoun or an object pronoun in each answer.

11. What school subject do you like the best? _____

_____

12. Who helps you with hard schoolwork? _____

_____

13. Is math easy or hard? Why? _____

_____

14. Whom do you help? How do you help him or her? _____

_____

D. (15–16) Write two sentences about helping someone. Use one subject pronoun and one object pronoun.

_____

_____

_____

_____

Edit It

E. (17–20) Edit the paragraph. Fix the four mistakes with pronouns.

Mr. Marques is a math teacher. Him is a great teacher. All the kids want him for math. I do not have he this year. Next year, me will, though. This year, I have Mrs. Plummer. Her is a good teacher, too. I like her a lot.

Proofreader's Marks

Change text:

Mrs. Plummer helps ~~I~~ me

See all Proofreader's Marks on page xi.

61 Which Pronouns Refer to More Than One?

We, You, They, and *Us, You, Them*

With so many pronouns, how do you know which one
to use in a sentence?

- Use a **subject pronoun** as the subject.
  Carla's **parents** had dreams. **They** followed
  their dreams.   subject

- Use an **object pronoun** as the object of the verb.
  Now Carla has **dreams**. Carla follows **them**.
                                           object

  We all have our own dreams. Our dreams inspire **us**.
  subject   object

Pronouns	
Subject	**Object**
we	us
you	you
they	them

Try It

A. **Write pronouns from the chart to complete the sentences.**

1. Carla's parents are teachers. _____ teach at the middle school.

2. Carla loves her parents. Carla respects _____ , too.

3. Carla has different dreams, though. Carla shares _____ with her parents.

4. " _____ both are teachers," Carla says to her parents. "I want to dance."

B. **(5–9) Complete the paragraph. Write the correct pronouns from the chart.**

Carla's friends take dance lessons. Carla takes _____ , too. Carla's
parents help the girls. _____ drive _____ to dance classes.
"We thank _____ both so much," say the girls to Carla's parents. "You
really help _____ ."

Write It

C. Answer each question. Use either subject or object pronouns from the chart in each answer.

10. How do people accomplish their dreams? _____

_____

11. What are your dreams? _____

_____

12. Do you think kids follow their dreams? Why or why not? _____

_____

D. (13–15) Carla's friends all take dance lessons together. Write three sentences about things you do with your friends. Use one pronoun from the chart in each sentence.

_____

_____

_____

_____

_____

Edit It

E. (16–20) Edit the letter. Fix the five mistakes with pronouns.

Dear Grandpa,

My dance classes are so much fun. I enjoy they a lot. My friends take they, too. Us all go together. My parents drive we. Our dance teachers are great. Them know many new dance steps. My dream is to be a dancer. I will work hard and follow my dream.

Love,
Carla

Proofreader's Marks

Change text:

We
~~Us~~ can dance!
︿

See all Proofreader's Marks on page xi.

62 What's an Antecedent?

It's the Word a Pronoun Refers To.

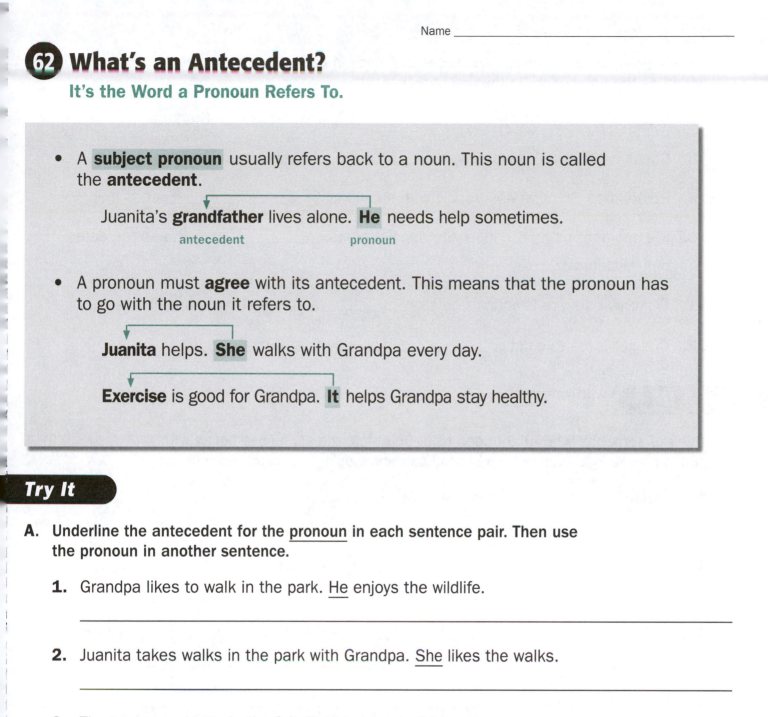

- A **subject pronoun** usually refers back to a noun. This noun is called the **antecedent**.

  Juanita's **grandfather** lives alone. **He** needs help sometimes.

      antecedent   pronoun

- A pronoun must **agree** with its antecedent. This means that the pronoun has to go with the noun it refers to.

  Juanita helps. **She** walks with Grandpa every day.

  Exercise is good for Grandpa. **It** helps Grandpa stay healthy.

Try It

A. Underline the antecedent for the <u>pronoun</u> in each sentence pair. Then use the pronoun in another sentence.

1. Grandpa likes to walk in the park. <u>He</u> enjoys the wildlife.

   _____

2. Juanita takes walks in the park with Grandpa. <u>She</u> likes the walks.

   _____

3. The trees are pretty in the fall. <u>They</u> have colorful leaves.

   _____

4. Today a squirrel is collecting nuts. <u>It</u> has a mouthful of food.

   _____

5. Juanita's dad picks up Juanita after the walk. <u>He</u> visits with Grandpa, too.

   _____

6. The two men like each other. <u>They</u> are father and son.

   _____

B. Write a pronoun to complete the second sentence in each pair. Then underline the antecedent in the first sentence.

7. Grandchildren visit Grandpa. _____ play chess with Grandpa.

8. Chess is Grandpa's favorite game. _____ is a game of strategy.

9. Sometimes Grandpa has trouble with his memory. _____ needs help.

10. His daughter helps Grandpa with appointments. _____ marks the dates on the calendar.

11. Two gray cats are Grandpa's pets. _____ keep him company.

12. One cat loves to cuddle. _____ sleeps on Grandpa's lap.

Write It

C. Think of someone who might need help. Complete the sentences below with nouns as needed. Then write a second sentence, using a subject pronoun.

13. Today _____ has an appointment. _____

_____

14. _____ takes _____ to the doctor. _____

_____

15. _____ and _____ go out to lunch after the appointment. _____

_____

16. Lunch is delicious. _____

_____

17. The waitress is really nice, too. _____

_____

D. (18–20) Write three sentence pairs about what grandchildren do to help grandparents. Use antecedents and pronouns in your sentences.

_____

_____

_____

63 What's an Antecedent?

It's the Word a Pronoun Refers To.

- An **object pronoun** usually refers back to a noun. This noun is called the **antecedent**.

  Rachel babysits the **kids** next door. Rachel watches **them** .

antecedent   pronoun

- A pronoun must **agree** with its antecedent. This means that the pronoun has to go with the noun it refers to.

  Rachel reads a **book** to Paul. Paul likes **it** .

  Paul likes **Rachel**. Paul thanks **her** .

Try It

A. Underline the antecedent for the <u>pronoun</u> in each sentence pair. Then use the pronoun in another sentence.

1. Kids always like Rachel. Rachel likes <u>them</u>, too.

_____

2. Today Rachel babysits Henry. Rachel takes <u>him</u> to the playground.

_____

3. Henry goes down the slide. Henry likes <u>it</u> the best.

_____

4. Some friends come to the playground. Henry sees <u>them</u>.

_____

5. Rachel goes on the swings. Henry pushes <u>her</u>!

_____

6. Rachel gives Henry a sandwich. Henry eats <u>it</u>.

_____

B. Write a pronoun to complete the second sentence in each pair. Then underline the antecedent in the first sentence.

7. Rachel wants spending money. Rachel earns _____ babysitting.

8. Rachel babysits three afternoons after school. Rachel schedules _____ each week.

9. Rachel babysits one girl every Monday. Rachel walks _____ home from school.

10. Henry is Rachel's Wednesday job. Rachel always takes _____ to the playground.

11. Every Friday, Rachel babysits the twins. Rachel helps _____ with homework.

12. Rachel gets cash. Rachel counts _____ every Saturday.

13. Rachel saves money. Rachel spends _____ , too.

Write It

C. Imagine that someone you know needs to earn extra money. Complete each sentence below with a noun as needed. Then write a second sentence, using an object pronoun.

14. _____ wants more money. _____

15. _____ has some extra chores. _____

16. _____ takes the dog for a walk. _____

17. _____ needs help with yard work. _____

D. (18–20) Write three sentence pairs about how kids can earn money. Use antecedents and pronouns in your sentences.

_____

_____

_____

_____

64 How Do You Know Which Pronoun to Use?

Figure Out the Noun That It Refers To.

- Use a **subject pronoun** in the subject of a sentence. Use an **object pronoun** after the verb or after a preposition.

  Kids attend **camps**. **They** enjoy **them**.

  Louisa attends basketball **camp**. **She** loves **it**.

- All **pronouns** must agree with the **noun** they refer to. This noun is called the antecedent.
  1. If the noun names a male, use **he** or **him**.
  2. If the noun names a female, use **she** or **her**.
  3. If a noun names one thing, use **it** or **it**.
  4. If a noun names "more than one," use **they** or **them**.

Try It

A. (1–4) Write the correct pronouns to complete the paragraph.

Mike helps Louisa at camp. _____ teaches

He / Him

_____ to shoot basketballs. Other campers learn,

she / her

too. Then _____ play a game. The campers enjoy

they / them

_____.

it / them

B. (5–9) Write the correct pronoun in the space provided.

Hugo attends a robot camp. Kara is one of the counselors for the campers.

_____ teaches _____ about robots. The campers make

a robot. First _____ design _____. Will _____

work?

Write It

C. Answer the questions. Use pronouns that have antecedents in the questions.

10. Suppose Kara is a counselor at a summer camp by a lake. What could Kara teach Hugo? _____

_____

11. Suppose Louisa wants to make the soccer team next year. How could soccer camp help Louisa? _____

_____

12. Why do children go to different camps? _____

_____

D. **(13–15) What camp would you like to attend? Why? Write three sentence pairs. Use subject pronouns, object pronouns, and their antecedents.**

_____

_____

_____

_____

_____

Edit It

E. (16–20) Edit the journal. Fix the five mistakes with pronouns.

July 28

Camp today was fun. They was the best ever. Mara taught her young campers to paddle a canoe. Her showed they what to do. Then the campers put canoes in the water. Them paddled the canoes. Matt needed help. Mara helped he.

Proofreader's Marks

Change text:

The counselor helped ~~she~~ her.

See all Proofreader's Marks on page xi.

© National Geographic Learning, a part of Cengage Learning, Inc.

65 What's a Reflexive Pronoun?

A Word Used to Talk Twice About the Same Person or Thing

- Use a **reflexive pronoun** to talk about the same person or thing twice in the same sentence.

  Athletes express **themselves** in sports.

  In my family, **we** express **ourselves** that way, too.

- Match the **reflexive pronoun** with its antecedent.

  Mom drives **herself** to the gym every morning.

  Dad and **I** get **ourselves** to the park on Sundays for soccer.

Reflexive Pronouns	
Singular	**Plural**
myself	ourselves
yourself	yourselves
himself	themselves
herself	
itself	

Try It

A. **Write the correct reflexive pronoun from the chart to complete each sentence. Then underline the noun or pronoun it refers to.**

1. I look at _____ in the mirror and decide I need more exercise.

2. My friend and I see _____ winning ballgames.

3. Xavier is already getting _____ to the baseball diamond every Saturday morning.

4. Well, a baseball can't pitch _____.

5. I guess I should get _____ off this couch and go join him.

B. Read each sentence. Circle the correct reflexive pronoun. Then, underline the noun or pronoun it refers to.

6. When you're on a sports team, you need to apply **(itself/yourself)**.

7. Xavier and I prepare **(himself/ourselves)** for practice with some stretching exercises.

8. After all, even professional ballplayers can hurt **(themselves/himself)** if they aren't prepared.

9. Xavier forces **(himself/myself)** to play his best until the coach pulls us out for an inning.

10. Our coach yells to us, "Drink water. Don't dehydrate **(yourselves/itself)**."

11. When the game is over, we congratulate **(itself/ourselves)**. We won!

Edit It

C. (12–15) Edit the email. Fix the four mistakes with reflexive pronouns.

Hi Grandpa! We did it! Xavier and I formed a baseball team by myself. We even found a coach by itself. Last week, I asked himself, "Who would make a good coach?" Ask herself the same question, and I think you'll come up with the same answer. You bet! It's Dad. I thought you'd want to know.

Proofreader's Marks

Change text:

Ballplayers have to get ~~yourself~~ themselves in shape before the season opens.

See all Proofreader's Marks on page xi.

66 What's an Intensive Pronoun?

A Pronoun Used to Add Emphasis

- Use an 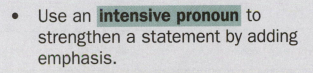 to strengthen a statement by adding emphasis.

  Child **hunger** **itself** is a human rights issue.

  I **myself** am concerned about the world's hunger crisis.

Intensive Pronouns	
Singular	**Plural**
myself	ourselves
yourself	yourselves
himself	themselves
herself	
itself	

- Use standard English by avoiding words like *hisself* and *theirselves*.

  themselves
  Many **adults theirselves** don't get enough to eat.
  ∧

  himself
  Our **Senator hisself** is going to speak to the President about it.
  ∧

Try It

A. Write the correct intensive pronoun from the chart to complete each sentence. Then underline the noun or pronoun it refers to.

1. I _____ read a lot of books about history.

2. The school library _____ cannot offer every book I want.

3. Even the public library _____ doesn't have everything.

4. Libraries and teachers _____ have a lot to teach us.

5. But in the end, we _____ must be in charge of our own education.

Write It

B. **Rewrite each sentence to make it stronger. Include an intensive pronoun in each sentence.**

6. What kind of books do you like to read? _____

7. I like to read novels. _____

8. My great-grandfather never learned to read. _____

9. Great-grandma never got to go to school. _____

10. We should be happy to have the opportunity of a good education. _____

_____

_____

Edit It

C. **(11–15) Edit the paragraph. Fix the four mistakes with intensive pronouns and the one mistake with an object pronoun.**

My father hisself is a reference librarian. He answers questions like this all day long: "May we ourselfs use the computers?" ("Yes," he says, showing they how.) "Can children theirselves check out books?" ("Yes," he says, "if they have a library card.") "Do we have to bring the books back on time?" ("Please do," he says kindly.) I himself can't imagine how he stays polite all day.

Proofreader's Marks

Change text:
Grandpa ~~hisself~~ himself got me interested in history.

See all Proofreader's Marks on page xi.

67 Use Pronouns Correctly

Remember: Use a subject pronoun as the subject of a sentence. Use an object pronoun as the object of a sentence. Use a reflexive pronoun to refer twice to the same person or thing in a sentence. Use an intensive pronoun to add emphasis.

Subject Pronouns	I	you	he	she	it	we	you	they
Object Pronouns	me	you	him	her	it	us	you	them
Reflexive and Intensive Pronouns	my-self	your-self	him-self	her-self	it-self	our-selves	your-selves	them-selves

My family loves day trips. Today, **we** took **ourselves** to the city. **We** went to the city park. **It** has a zoo with monkeys. **I** watched **them**. The monkeys **themselves** watched **me**, too. My brother saw a mother wolf. **He** liked **her**. **I** like the zoo. Do **you**?

Try It

A. Read the sentences. Then write the pronouns that stand for the underlined words.

1. My family took a train to the city. <u>The train</u> was fun. _____

2. My sister and I bought our own tickets. <u>My sister and I</u> had money from babysitting.

   _____

3. It felt good to pay with money we earned by <u>my sister and me</u>. _____

4. Our parents were proud of <u>my sister and me</u>. They thanked <u>my sister and me</u>.

   _____

5. The conductor collected tickets. I watched <u>the conductor</u> collect <u>the tickets</u>.

   _____

6. My father <u>my father</u> is a conductor, but it was my father's day off.

   _____

7. I love trains. I might work on <u>trains me</u> one day. _____

B. Write two sentences to answer each question. Use subject or object pronouns in your sentences. Challenge yourself by trying to include one reflexive pronoun or one intensive pronoun.

8. How would you get to a city you would like to visit? _____

_____

_____

9. Where would you go and what would you see in the city? _____

_____

_____

C. (10–12) Write three sentences about a trip you would like to take with your family. What would you do? What would you see? Use subject and object pronouns in your sentences. Also use one reflexive pronoun or one intensive pronoun.

_____

_____

_____

_____

_____

_____

Grammar at Work

D. (13–18) Fix the six mistakes with pronouns.

Today me went to the city yourself. They was so much fun. The animals theirselves in the zoo were the best. I really liked they. A woman juggled at an outdoor festival. I watched she. Maybe one day I will juggle like that!

Proofreader's Marks

Change text:

He
~~Him~~ enjoyed the city.

See all Proofreader's Marks on page xi.

68 How Do I Show Possession?

One Way Is to Use a Possessive Noun.

Use a **possessive noun** to show that someone owns, or possesses, something.

One Owner	Add **'s**.	**Maribel's** mother is a librarian.
More than One Owner	Add **'** if the noun ends in **-s**.	The **librarians'** days are full of work.

Try It

A. Rewrite the underlined words to include a possessive noun.

1. One of <u>the jobs of a librarian</u> is to put books back on the shelves. _____

2. Maribel restacks <u>the books of the library</u>. _____

3. Maribel answers <u>the questions of patrons</u>, too. _____

4. She also organizes <u>the magazines of teens</u>. _____

B. Rewrite each sentence to include a possessive noun.

5. Maribel likes the books of Joseph Bruchac. _____

_____

6. She studies the illustrations of the artists. _____

_____

7. The dream of Maribel is to be an illustrator. _____

_____

Write It

C. Answer each question. Use a possessive noun in your answer.

8. Whose job is it to check out books in the library? _____

_____

9. What could you do to help in a library room for patrons? _____

_____

10. When do you use the library at your school? _____

_____

11. What are some books by your favorite author? _____

_____

D. (12–14) Write three sentences about the library at your school or in your city or town. Use possessive nouns that name one and more than one owner.

_____

_____

_____

_____

Edit It

E. (15–20) Edit the journal entry. Fix the six mistakes with possessive nouns.

Today I found a child pair of glasses in the library. I put them in the librarys' lost-and-found. The lost-and-found has a lot of readers things in it. I decided to organize the lost-and-found. Guess what? I found Moms missing hat. There were three girls pairs of gloves. I even found one boy sneaker!

Proofreader's Marks

Add text:

I like this author͜books.

Add an apostrophe:

I like that authors books, too.

Transpose letters:

Which authors books do you like?

See all Proofreader's Marks on page xi.

69 How Is Possession Shown In Irregular Nouns?

It's Simple! Just Add 's.

Use a **possessive noun** to show that someone or something owns, or possesses, something.

More Than One Owner	Regular Plural Nouns	Add '	Most **libraries**' offices have a lost-and-found. Kids often leave bookmarks inside **books**' covers
Possessive Adjectives	Irregular Plural Nouns	Add 's	**People's** lost objects are often valuable. **Children's** bookmarks are not the only things lost.

Try It

A. Rewrite the underlined words to include a possessive noun.

1. Few things are left inside the covers of books. _____

2. Valuable things are often left in the purses of women. _____

3. Some lost things of people may not seem valuable. _____

4. But the rules of some libraries say to keep everything. _____

5. A teacher may return to get the artwork of her students. _____

6. The artwork of the children may be very valuable to them. _____

B. Answer each question in a complete sentence. Use a possessive plural noun in your answer.

7. What might you find in the lost-and-found box at a preschool? _____

_____

8. What items are most precious to small children? _____

_____

9. What are the things most often lost by men? _____

_____

C. (10–12) Write three sentences about things that you have found that belong to others. Try to use a possessive for at least one plural noun in your sentences.

_____

_____

_____

_____

Edit It

D. (13–16) Edit the email. Fix the four mistakes with possessive nouns.

Hey Lek! Guess what I found on the subway today. Mens' messenger bags don't get left behind. Right? Well, today, one was! Now, our parents advice has always been to be honest. So, I looked inside the man's bag for ID. Long story short, I called him. The man's sisters met me at the library so I could return the bag. Those womens' hearts are generous! They gave me a heroes reward.

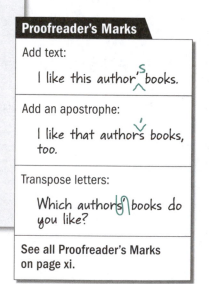

Proofreader's Marks

Add text:

I like this author's books.

Add an apostrophe:

I like that authors books, too.

Transpose letters:

Which authors books do you like?

See all Proofreader's Marks on page xi.

70 What's a Possessive Adjective?

It's an Ownership Word.

- Use a **possessive adjective** to tell who has or owns something.

I	→ **my**	I like Miguel. Miguel is **my** friend.
you	→ **your**	Do you know Miguel? Is Miguel **your** friend?
he	→ **his**	Miguel has a sister. **His** sister is my friend, too.
she	→ **her**	Do you know Miguel's sister? **Her** name is Rosa.
it	→ **its**	Miguel goes to school. **Its** name is Memorial School.
we	→ **our**	We go to school together. Memorial is **our** school.
they	→ **their**	Other students go to North. North is **their** school.

Try It

A. Write the correct words to complete the sentences.

1. Miguel plays travel soccer. Rosa plays on _____ team.

he / his

2. _____ team is having a tournament.

They / Their

3. " _____ team needs some help," Miguel says.

We / Our

4. "I will help _____ team," I tell Miguel.

you / your

B. Write the correct possessive adjectives to complete the sentences.

5. Miguel's mom is in charge of refreshments. She asks _____ friends to help.

6. I offer to help, too. Miguel's mom says, "Thank you for _____ help."

7. Then I watch Miguel play. _____ team plays well.

8. The teammates are happy. They win _____ game.

C. Answer each question. Use a possessive adjective in your answer.

9. What does Miguel need help with? _____

10. What does his mother need help with? _____

11. What do you sometimes need help with? _____

12. How do teachers help their students? _____

D. (13–15) Write three sentences about how you help people or how people help you. Use possessive adjectives in your sentences.

_____

_____

_____

_____

E. (16–20) Edit the journal entry. Fix the five mistakes with possessive adjectives.

May 26

Today I helped I friend Miguel. He soccer team needed help. I helped Miguel's mom, too. She needed help with she concession stand. Tomorrow Miguel is going to help me. My family is going away for the day. We need someone to walk its dog. Miguel will walk the dog. Miguel is a good friend. I am, too. Friends help they good friends!

Proofreader's Marks

Change text:

You need help with ~~you~~ *your* groceries.

See all Proofreader's Marks on page xi.

71 What's a Possessive Adjective?

It's an Ownership Word.

A **possessive adjective** identifies who owns or has something.

It comes before a **noun**. The possessive pronoun *its* does not have an apostrophe.

It's with an apostrophe means *it is*. Without an apostrophe, *it* owns something.

Possessive Adjectives	my	your	his	her	its	our	their

EXAMPLES   **My brother** and I are writing stories about space.
Our favorite **books** are science fiction.

Try It

A. Choose the correct words to complete the sentences.

1. My brother has already named _____ characters.
   his / him

2. I have named most of _____ characters, too.
   my / I

3. I am writing about a girl named Kalix-San and _____ family.
   she / her

4. The Kalix family loves _____ planet.
   they / their

B. Write the correct words from the chart to complete the sentences.

5. The Kalix family worries about _____ sun.

6. _____ light is not as strong as our sun's light.

7. In my story, I might have Kalix-San leave _____ planet.

8. She can come and visit me on _____ planet.

C. Correct the sentences. Use possessive adjectives.

9. I like the book <u>Stargirl</u>. I love it's characters.

_____

10. I like books by Clifford D. Simak, too. Him plots are funny.

_____

11. Me goal is to be a writer.

_____

12. What is the goal of you?

_____

13. Many people set goals in the youth.

_____

14. With hard work, we can achieve the goals.

_____

Write It

D. **(15–18) Think of a story you could write about space travel. Write at least four sentences about your story. Use a possessive adjective in each sentence.**

_____

_____

_____

_____

_____

_____

_____

_____

_____

_____

_____

72 What's a Possessive Pronoun?

It's a Word Standing For a Thing Owned and Who Owns It.

A **possessive pronoun** stands for something owned and who owns or has it. It stands alone. A singular possessive pronoun stands for one owner. The owner may own or have more than one thing.

Singular Possessive Pronouns			
mine	**yours**	**his**	**hers**
names that belong to me	names that belong to you	names that belong to him	names that belong to her

Those cleats are **mine**.
That ball is **yours**.
The goalposts are **his**.
Those kneepads are **hers**.

Try It

A. Write the possessive pronouns that stand for the underlined words.

1. Clarissa's ball is more colorful than <u>my ball</u>. _____

2. My cleats are more pointed than <u>her cleats</u>. _____

3. Our team scored more points than <u>his team</u>. _____

4. If you lose your kneepads, you can borrow <u>my kneepads</u>. _____

5. We can't find our goalposts, so may we borrow <u>your goalposts</u>? _____

6. Tarika forgot her snacks, so I'll share <u>my snacks</u>. _____

B. Rewrite the sentences. Use possessive pronouns instead of possessive adjectives.

7. Julio picked his team, and I picked my team.

_____

8. I made my team's banner, so when will you make your team's banner?

_____

9. Her game is on Saturday, but my game is on Sunday.

_____

10. If I bring my team's water, will you bring your team's water?

_____

C. Imagine that you are preparing for a game of pick-up baseball. You need help. Complete each question with a possessive pronoun.

11. If I bring my bat, will you bring _____?

12. Omar left his mitt at your house, so could you bring yours and _____?

13. Would you ask Paco to bring his ball because I can't find _____?

Write It

D. (14–15) Now imagine that you are preparing for a party. Ask for help. Write at least two questions. Use a possessive pronoun in each question.

_____

_____

_____

_____

_____

_____

_____

_____

_____

73 What's a Possessive Pronoun?

It's a Word Standing For a Thing Owned and Who Owns It.

A **possessive pronoun** stands for something owned and who owns or has it. It stands alone. A plural possessive pronoun stands for more than one owner. The owners may own or have more than one thing

Plural Possessive Pronouns		
ours	**yours**	**theirs**
names things that belong to us	names things that belong to you (plural)	names things that belong to them

Of all the science projects, I like **ours** best.
You all may like **yours**, but **ours** is really extraordinary!
Taft Middle School thinks **theirs** is better, but I haven't seen it.

Try It

A. Write the possessive pronoun that stands for the underlined words.

1. The model Mars Rover is <u>our model</u>. _____

2. Which of the science projects is <u>your project</u>? _____

3. The students from Taft did <u>their project</u> on why stars twinkle. _____

4. For <u>their model</u>, some high school students built a launch vehicle, but it didn't work. _____

5. Well, <u>our model</u> works! _____

6. I should say that <u>our model</u> sort of works. _____

B. (7–11) Write the correct plural possessive pronoun to complete the journal entry.

Most schools have submitted their projects, but other schools are still finishing
_____. We got _____ set up on the very first day. To get
extra points for early entry, you need to get _____ in today. Oh
my! The students from Central High are bringing in _____ now. It's a
working wind power generator. It might compete with _____.

C. (12–14) Compare something you have made in a group with something
made by another group. Write three sentences using plural possessive
pronouns.

_____

_____

_____

_____

_____

_____

Edit It

D. (15–20) Edit the journal entry. Fix the six mistakes with possessive pronouns

May 14

    Well, all the science projects have been judged, and our didn't
get first place. I was worried when Central High brought in
they're. I turned to my classmates. "If the decision were your,
which would you pick—our or theys?" "theys," they said,
frowning. Oh well, we're happy with second place.

Proofreader's Marks
Change text:
The solar cell is ~~theys~~. *theirs*
See all Proofreader's Marks on page xi.

74 What Do Prepositions Do?

They Show How Two Objects Or Ideas Are Related.

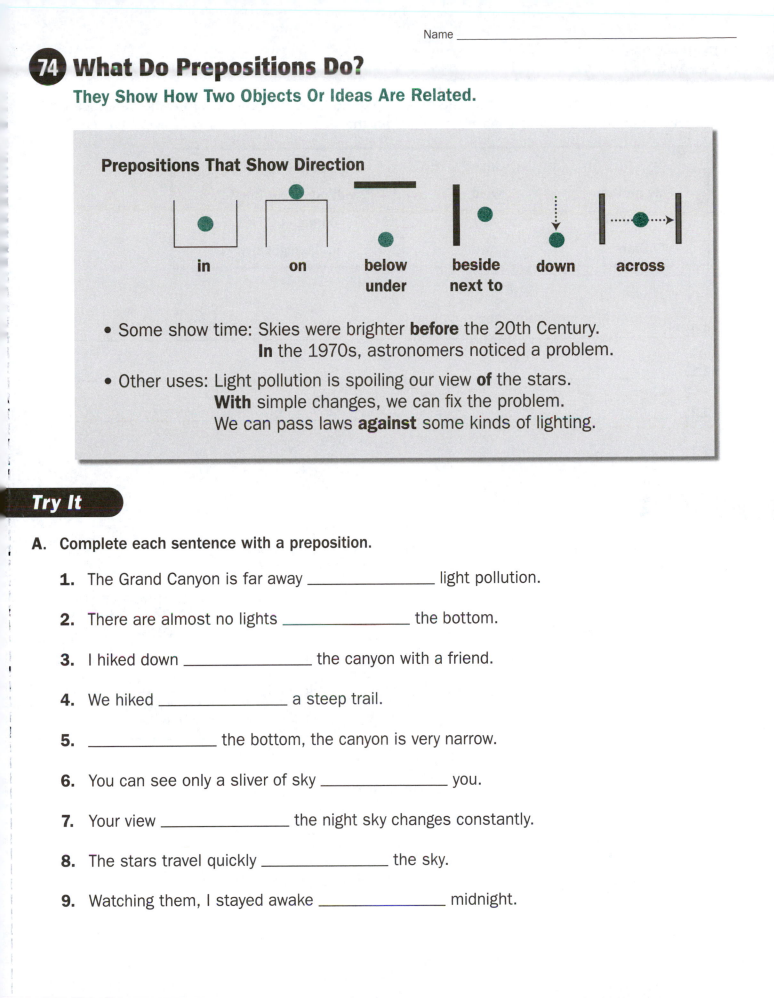

Prepositions That Show Direction

in   on   below under   beside next to   down   across

- Some show time: Skies were brighter **before** the 20th Century.
  In the 1970s, astronomers noticed a problem.

- Other uses: Light pollution is spoiling our view **of** the stars.
  With simple changes, we can fix the problem.
  We can pass laws **against** some kinds of lighting.

Try It

A. Complete each sentence with a preposition.

1. The Grand Canyon is far away _____ light pollution.

2. There are almost no lights _____ the bottom.

3. I hiked down _____ the canyon with a friend.

4. We hiked _____ a steep trail.

5. _____ the bottom, the canyon is very narrow.

6. You can see only a sliver of sky _____ you.

7. Your view _____ the night sky changes constantly.

8. The stars travel quickly _____ the sky.

9. Watching them, I stayed awake _____ midnight.

B. Use the words from each column and other words to build sentences. Write the sentences below. Then compare your sentences with a partner.

I	walked	into the forest.
My brother	went	with our scout master.
We	saw	during our hike.
Stars	glowed	in the night sky.

10. _____

11. _____

12. _____

13. _____

Edit It

C. (14–20) Edit the journal. Fix the seven mistakes with prepositions.

September 4

    Last night, I didn't sleep at our tent. On dinner, I lay outside, in the stars. With city lights, the stars are brilliant! The canyon is narrow. So, you only see a little bit to sky at a time. The stars seem to race of it. I felt like I was traveling during space with them.

Proofreader's Marks

Change text:

I hiked the canyon with ~~during~~ the day.

See all Proofreader's Marks on page xi.

75 What Is a Prepositional Phrase?

It's a Group of Words That Begins with a Preposition.

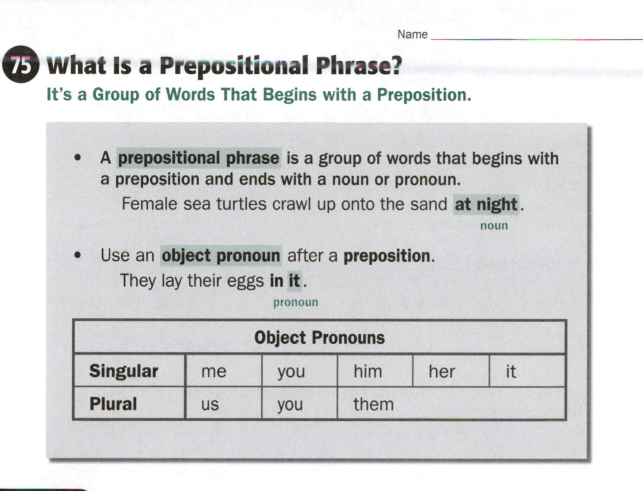

- A **prepositional phrase** is a group of words that begins with a preposition and ends with a noun or pronoun.

    Female sea turtles crawl up onto the sand **at night**.
    noun

- Use an **object pronoun** after a **preposition**.

    They lay their eggs **in it**.
    pronoun

Object Pronouns					
Singular	me	you	him	her	it
Plural	us	you	them		

Try It

A. Complete each sentence about endangered sea turtles. For each blank, choose the best prepositional phrase from the box.

of nesting beach	on the Caribbean Coast
in the 1960s	for green turtles

1. Tortuguero National Park is _____ in Costa Rica.

2. It is a very important nesting site _____.

3. The green turtles in Tortuguero almost disappeared _____.

4. The park now protects many miles _____.

B. What if you could watch sea turtles lay their eggs without harming them?
Complete each sentence with a preposition.

5. In Tortuguero, local guides take visitors to see the turtles _____

nesting season.

6. They leave very late _____ night.

7. The guides and visitors walk very carefully _____ the sand.

8. They use a special kind _____ red flashlight.

9. Lucky visitors get to see turtles dig holes _____ the sand.

10. _____ digging a hole, the turtle lays its eggs in it.

C. Learn more about sea turtles in Tortuguero. Add an object pronoun after the
preposition in the second sentence.

11. A green turtle doesn't lay just one or two eggs. She may lay 50 to 100 of

_____ .

12. To lay her eggs, the mother turtle crawls out of the sea. The hatchlings have to crawl

back to _____ .

13. Our tour began at midnight. But I didn't want the group to go without

_____ .

14. Imagine missing out! What if everyone got to go except _____?

Write It

D. (15–18) Think of an adventure you have gone on or would like to go on. Write
at least four sentences about it. Provide details in prepositional phrases.

_____

_____

_____

_____

_____

_____

76 In a Prepositional Phrase, Where Does the Pronoun Go?

It Goes Last.

- A **prepositional phrase** starts with a preposition and ends with a noun or pronoun. Sometimes, it ends with both. Put the pronoun last.

  Last week my friend Sarah got crutches. She taught a lesson **to my sister and me**.

- Avoid these common mistakes in a prepositional phrase:

  1. Use **me**, not **I**: Sarah explained to my sister and ~~I~~ me that she broke her leg.

  2. Put **me** last: Sarah seemed calm to ~~me and my sister~~ my sister and me.

Try It

A. Complete each sentence. Write the correct pronoun.

1. My father drives us to school each day. I ride in the car with my sister and
   _____.
   he / him

2. Sarah and her brother Tom walk to school. Their parents cannot give a ride to Sarah and
   _____.
   her / him

3. My sister and I see Sarah with Tom and other students in the mornings.
   We wave at Sarah and _____.
   they / them

4. Sarah began to use crutches. This made the walk to school very difficult for Tom and
   _____.
   she / her

5. My father and I invited Sarah and Tom to ride with _____. It is fun to
   we / us
   have everyone in the car together.

B. (6–12) Complete each sentence about a person with a physical challenge. Use **me**, **him**, **us**, or **them**.

I never knew a deaf person until I met Roberto. Roberto is a good friend to my brother Misha and _____. I am around Misha and _____ almost every day. We play video games together. It is fun for _____ and _____. Roberto usually wins. He and Misha play baseball with teammates. Misha likes to play baseball with Roberto and _____. Roberto is the star pitcher. After the games, Roberto makes dinner for my brother and _____. Misha clears the table, and Roberto helps _____. Roberto is a great teammate and a kind friend.

Write It

C. Answer the questions below about challenges with disabilities. Use prepositions and object pronouns.

13. Do you know someone with a disability? _____

_____

14. What activities are challenging for this person? _____

_____

15. What is the difference between how this person and other people view challenges?

_____

D. (16–20) Now, write five sentences that tell more about the way this person overcomes challenges. Use prepositional phrases with pronouns.

_____

_____

_____

_____

_____

77 Use Possessive Adjectives and Pronouns Correctly

Remember: Use possessives to tell who owns or has something. Possessive adjectives come before a noun. Possessive pronouns stand alone.

Possessive Adjectives	my	your	his	her	its	our	their
Possessive Pronouns	mine	yours	his	hers		ours	theirs

The Big Dipper is many people's favorite star pattern. It is **mine**. **My** little brother says it is **his**, too. **Its** seven stars shine brightly in **our** hemisphere. But the Big Dipper is only **our** name for these seven stars.

Try It

A. Add possessive adjectives and possessive pronouns to complete the sentences.

1. Other cultures have _____ own names for the Big Dipper.

2. *Akhsotha's* grandmother uses _____ name for it: Sky Bear.

3. The Greeks had _____ , too. Their name was Callisto.

4. As for the English, _____ name for it is the Plough.

5. Mr. Kwan says _____ name for it is the Northern Basket.

6. His wife is an astronomer, so _____ name for it is scientific: Ursa Major.

B. Write the correct possessive to complete each sentence.

7. Mrs. Kwan let Shen and me use _____ telescope last night.
  hers/her

8. "Should we set it up in my yard or _____ ?" Shen asked.
  your/yours

9. "Let's not set it up in _____ ," I said. "My yard has too many trees."
  my/mine

10. The Kwans' yard has fewer trees, so we set it up in _____ .
  theirs/their

C. Replace the underlined possessive adjectives and nouns with possessive pronouns.

11. Shen's favorite constellation is harder to find than <u>my favorite constellation</u>.

  _____

12. I tried for a long time, but I couldn't find <u>Shens' constellation</u>. _____

13. Maybe his eyesight is better than <u>my eyesight</u>. _____

14. Finally, I said, "<u>Your constellation</u> is impossible to find!" _____

15. "Maybe Mom's telescope isn't powerful enough," Shen said. "Next time, let's go to the observatory and use <u>their telescope</u>." _____

Write It

D. (16–19) Think about a time you did something with a friend. Write four sentences about what you did. Use a possessive adjective or a possessive pronoun in each sentence.

_____

_____

_____

_____

_____

_____

_____

78 Use Prepositions Correctly

Remember: Use prepositions to add details to your sentences.

> • Add a prepositional phrase to tell where or when.
>   We attended a family reunion.
>   We attended a family reunion **at a restaurant**.
>   We attended a family reunion **in the summer**.
> • A prepositional phrase can also show direction.
>   My relatives drove **across the state** to attend the reunion.

Try It

A. Add a preposition to complete each sentence. Choose a preposition from the box.

at	in	to	up

1. Our family gathered _____ the restaurant.

2. My aunt and uncle got _____ the restaurant early.

3. We arrived _____ noon.

4. I walked _____ a flight of stairs.

5. We went to my aunt's house _____ the evening.

B. (6–10) Read the invitation. Add a prepositional phrase to complete each sentence. Choose a preposition from the box.

at	up	in	on	through

You are invited to attend a family reunion. It will take place

_____. It will begin _____. Find the address on

the enclosed card. When you reach the restaurant, go _____.

Then go _____. The reunion will take place_____.

C. Answer the questions about an important family event. Use prepositional phrases.

11. When was the event held? The event was held _____.

12. Where was the event? The event was _____.

13. How long did the event last? It lasted _____.

14. What types of things did you see next to and around you? _____
_____

15. Who else came to the event? _____

D. (16–20) Now, write five sentences that describe more about the family event you attended. Use prepositional phrases.

_____

_____

_____

_____

_____

Edit It

E. (21–25) Edit the letter. Fix the **three** mistakes with prepositions. Fix the **two** mistakes with pronouns.

Dear Linda,

Thank you for coming to my party for Thursday. I hope it was easy for you to come at the evening! It was fun sitting next you. Me really appreciate the beautiful gift. Us always have so much fun together!

Your friend,

Kim

Proofreader's Marks

Add text:

The reunion was 1 PM.
^at

Change text:

We went to a party ~~for~~
^on
Sunday.

See all Proofreader's Marks on page xi.

79 Use Pronouns in Prepositional Phrases

Remember: You can use prepositions to add details to your sentences. If you need a pronoun in a prepositional phrase, use an object pronoun.

Sentences with Prepositional Phrases

- I like movies **about space and the future**.
- A trip to the movies is exciting **to me**.
- It's a special treat **for my brother and me**.
- Movies are important **to us**.

Object Pronouns	
Singular	**Plural**
me	us
you	you
him, her, it	them

Try It

A. Add a noun or an object pronoun to complete each prepositional phrase.

1. Science fiction is an exciting topic for my _____ and _____.

2. My parents read science fiction stories to _____ when we were little.

3. One afternoon, we acted out scary plays for _____.

4. That day was fun! We like to laugh about _____ now.

B. Complete each sentence. Use the correct pronouns.

5. My grandparents always like to hear about _____.

6. I try to write letters to _____ often.

7. My grandmother enjoys science fiction movies. My brother and I once made a video for _____.

8. She talked about _____ for years!

Write It

C. **Answer the questions about movies. Use prepositional phrases with object pronouns.**

9. For you, are movies very important? _____

    _____

10. What kinds of movies are special for you? _____

    _____

11. What other kinds of movies might be interesting for you to see? _____

    _____

D. **(12–15) Write four sentences about other activities that are important to you. Use prepositional phrases with object pronouns.**

    _____

    _____

    _____

    _____

Edit It

E. **(16–20) Edit the paragraph. Fix the three mistakes with prepositional phrases. Fix the two mistakes with pronouns.**

> My friend Manny says that movies are important to him. I agree! To we, the movie theater is a special place. The movies we see are so much fun for me and Manny. I like movies about space and the future. For I, these movies are the best. Manny prefers movies about animals and nature. That interests he very much. If we find some movies about animals going into space, we will see they.

Proofreader's Marks

Change text:

Books are interesting to you and I. me

See all Proofreader's Marks on page xi.

80 What's a Simple Sentence?

A Sentence with One Subject and One Predicate

- A sentence expresses a complete thought. It has a **subject** and a **predicate**.

    The students | are in the computer club.
    subject | predicate

    They | learn about computers.
    subject | predicate

- The most important word in a subject is the **noun** or **pronoun**. The most important word in the predicate is the **verb**.

    An older **student leads** the club.

    She knows everything about computers.

Try It

A. Write whether the underlined part of the sentence is the subject or the predicate. Then write the most important word in it.

1. Kichi is in the computer club. _____

2. The club members like computers. _____

3. Some students draw pictures on their computers. _____

4. Some play educational games. _____

5. I read all the sports news on mine. _____

B. Add a noun, a pronoun, or a verb to complete the subject or predicate of each sentence.

6. Mr. Marcus _____ us at computer club.

7. _____ is a wonderful teacher.

8. Mr. Marcus _____ us about computers.

9. The _____ of the club learn a lot.

Write It

C. Add a subject or a predicate to complete each sentence about school clubs.

10. My school _____.

11. _____ join one of the clubs.

12. My favorite club _____.

D. (13–15) What club would you like to join at your school? Why? Write three sentences. Draw a line between each subject and predicate. Then underline the most important word in each part.

_____

_____

_____

_____

_____

_____

Edit It

E. (16–20) Edit the rules for the computer lab. Fix five subjects or predicates.

Computer Lab Rules

1. Cannot eat or drink in the lab.
2. Students at their own computers.
3. No are allowed in the lab without a teacher.
4. All scrap paper in the recycling bin.
5. Every must be turned off at the end of the day.

Proofreader's Marks
Add text: use   We ∧ computers.
Do not capitalize: The L̸ab is on the first floor.
See all Proofreader's Marks on page xi.

81 What Is a Fragment?

It's an Incomplete Sentence.

A **fragment** is a group of words that begins with a capital letter and ends with a period. It looks like a sentence, but it is not complete. A subject or a verb may be missing.

Fragments	Sentences
1. Hears about a computer sale.	Mom hears about a computer sale.
2. Are very cheap.	The computers are very cheap.
3. The deal good.	The deal sounds good.
4. Buys a new computer.	Mom buys a new computer.

Try It

A. Write whether each group of words is a fragment or a sentence. If it is a fragment, change it to a sentence by adding a subject or a verb.

1. Mom the computer home. _____

   _____

2. Doesn't work. _____

   _____

3. Mom hears a news story about the computers. _____

   _____

4. Finds out that the computers were recalled. _____

   _____

5. The computer store takes back the computer. _____

   _____

6. Returns her money. _____

   _____

B. Underline the fragment. Then add a subject or a verb to the fragment. Write the new sentence on the line.

7. Many people computers. They use the computers in different ways.

_____

8. Some people to their friends on computers. They send messages.

_____

9. Many kids play games on computers. Play games online.

_____

10. Shops online. He does not like to shop in stores.

_____

Write It

C. Write a complete sentence to answer each question. Make sure your sentences have subjects and verbs.

11. Why do you think so many people use computers? _____

_____

_____

12. What do you use a computer for? _____

_____

_____

D. (13–15) Write three complete sentences that tell more about computers. Make sure your sentences have subjects and verbs.

_____

_____

_____

_____

_____

_____

_____

82 What's One Way to Fix a Fragment?

Combine Neighboring Sentences.

Writers may create a fragment by starting a new sentence when they shouldn't. These fragments are easy to fix. Just combine the fragment with the sentence before it.

1. ┌─── sentence ───┐   ┌──────── fragment ────────┐
   I have to save my money.   If I want to buy the computer game.
   I have to save my money if I want to buy the computer game.

2. ┌─── sentence ───┐   ┌──────── fragment ────────┐
   I can save my allowance.   And my money from doing chores.
   I can save my allowance and my money from doing chores.

Try It

A. **Find each fragment. Combine it with the sentence. Write the new sentence.**

1. I am saving money. Because I want to buy a computer game. _____

   _____

2. I can earn money. If I walk the dog. _____

   _____

3. I take my dog. And then get my neighbor's dog. _____

   _____

4. I earn more money. When I walk both dogs. _____

   _____

B. **(5–9) Draw a line to combine each sentence with a fragment.**

I ask my neighbors	to bring in his garbage cans.
Mr. Green hires me	if they need help.
I get Mrs. Fong's mail	and bring in her newspaper.
Mom will pay me	and put it in my money jar.
I count my money	if I clean my room.

Write It

C. Complete each sentence about money.

10. I need money because _____

_____.

11. I earn money when _____

_____.

12. I take all my money and _____

_____.

D. (13–15) Imagine you earned $25 or got it for a gift. Write three complete sentences that tell what you would do with the money.

_____

_____

_____

_____

Edit It

E. (16–20) Edit the note. Fix the five fragments.

Dear Parker,

   I saved all my money. That I earned from chores. I saved all my gift money, too. Now I am really happy. Because I can finally buy my computer hockey game. Mom is taking me to the store tomorrow. To buy my game. We can play. When you visit. We will have fun. Now I will save more money. And come visit you!

                       Jason

Proofreader's Marks
Do not capitalize:
We will play the ~~G~~ame.
Delete:
It will ⌒ be fun.
See all Proofreader's Marks on page xi.

83 How Are Phrases and Clauses Different?

A Clause Has a Subject and a Predicate.

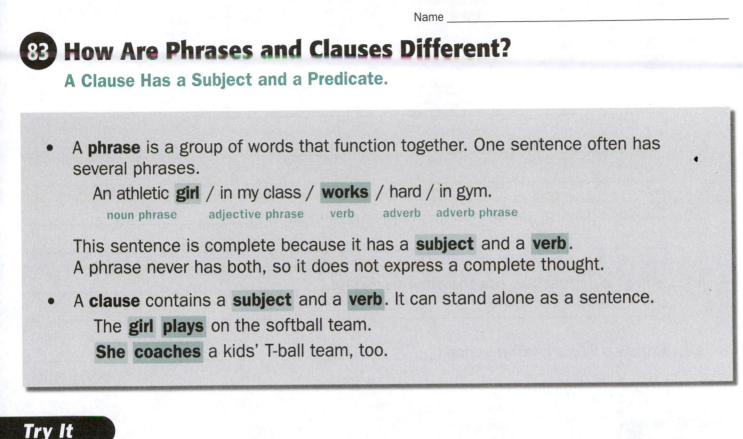

- A **phrase** is a group of words that function together. One sentence often has several phrases.

  An athletic **girl** / in my class / **works** / hard / in gym.
  noun phrase   adjective phrase   verb   adverb   adverb phrase

  This sentence is complete because it has a **subject** and a **verb**.
  A phrase never has both, so it does not express a complete thought.

- A **clause** contains a **subject** and a **verb**. It can stand alone as a sentence.
  The **girl plays** on the softball team.
  She coaches a kids' T-ball team, too.

Try It

A. Underline the phrase in each sentence. Then rewrite the sentence, using a different phrase.

1. Christina goes to my school. _____

2. She is my best friend. _____

3. Everyone in our school respects Christina. _____

   _____

4. Christina plays volleyball in the fall. _____

   _____

5. She practices in the gym. _____

6. Every Friday, Christina plays games. _____

   _____

7. I cheer for the team. _____

   _____

B. Write the sentences again. Add the phrases in parentheses.

8. Christina plays basketball. **(in the winter)** _____

_____

9. She is a guard. **(on the team)** _____

_____

10. Christina plays in games. **(on Mondays and Thursdays)** _____

_____

11. She goes to practice. **(On the other weekdays,)** _____

_____

12. Christina is busy. **(after school)** _____

_____

Write It

C. What do you do after school? Complete the sentences. Use at least one more phrase in each sentence.

13. After school, I _____.

14. Every Tuesday, I _____.

15. My favorite activity is _____.

D. (16–20) Imagine that you just met Christina. Write five questions that you would ask her. Use at least one phrase in each question.

_____

_____

_____

_____

_____

_____

_____

84 What's a Compound Sentence?

Two Clauses Joined by *And, But,* or *Or*

The words **and**, **but**, and **or** are conjunctions. They join the two clauses in a **compound sentence**. A comma (**,**) comes before the conjunction.

- Use **and** to join similar ideas.

  My parents need to rent an apartment. It must be near their jobs. ⎤ **My parents need to rent an apartment, and it must be near their jobs.**

- Use **but** to join different ideas.

  My parents find a nice apartment. It is too expensive. ⎤ **My parents find a nice apartment, but it is too expensive.**

- Use **or** to show a choice.

  My parents can rent it. They can find a cheaper apartment. ⎤ **My parents can rent it, or they can find a cheaper apartment.**

Try It

A. Use and, but, or or to make each pair of sentences one compound sentence.

1. My brother lives at home. He just got a job in a different state.

2. He needs to move. He wants a nice apartment.

3. A nice apartment will be expensive. He needs to rent one.

4. My brother can look in the paper. He can call a rental agent.

B. These compound sentences are missing and, but, or or. Fix the mistakes.

5. My brother sees one apartment it is perfect.

6. He wants to rent the apartment it is too expensive.

7. My brother can rent this apartment he can buy a car.

8. He rents the apartment he takes the bus to work.

Proofreader's Marks

Add text:

But
My brother will take his time.
he is ready to move.
∧

Add a comma:

My brother will take his time
but he is ready to move.

Do not capitalize:

My brother will take his time,
but He is ready to move.

See all Proofreader's Marks on page xi.

Write It

C. Complete each compound sentence about where you live.

9. ·I live _____ and _____.

10. _____ , but it is close to my friend's house.

11. She plays at my house, or _____.

D. (12–15) Imagine that you could have any home at all. Write four compound sentences that tell what it is like.

_____

_____

_____

_____

_____

Edit It

E. (16–20) Edit the list of apartment rules. Fix the five mistakes in the compound sentences.

Apartment Rules

You may have a dog, cats are okay, too.
You can pay the rent in cash you can pay by check.
You can have one parking space for free you can pay for a second space.
You can paint your apartment I have to approve the color.
Garbage collection is on Tuesdays. You have to put your garbage out on the curb.
You can have friends visit you must not be too loud.

Proofreader's Marks
Add text:
He found a place, he likes it a lot. *and* ^
Add a comma:
He can move Friday or he can move Saturday. ^
See all Proofreader's Marks on page xi.

85 How Do You Fix a Run-on Sentence?

Break It into Shorter Sentences.

- Some run-on sentences include too many phrases or clauses divided by **commas**.

    Yesterday my family ran out of fruit, cheese, and milk, and we needed them for dinner, and Mom went to the grocery store, and I went with her, and I couldn't believe how much it cost to buy just fruit, cheese, and milk.

- To fix run-ons, create shorter, more understandable sentences.

    Yesterday my family ran out of fruit, cheese, and milk, and we needed them for dinner. Mom went to the grocery store and I went with her. I couldn't believe how much it cost to buy just fruit, cheese, and milk.

Try It

A. Edit these run-on sentences. Break them into shorter sentences.

1. Groceries are expensive, and they are necessary and my family needs to grocery shop every week.

2. Sometimes we run out of bread or milk and need to shop more often than once a week, and this is a problem.

3. Sometimes we have a lot of food left over from dinner, and we have leftovers the next night, and my favorite leftover dinners are chicken potpie, beef stew, and enchiladas.

4. Sometimes Mom and Dad do not want to cook, and they take us out to eat, and we can go out to breakfast, lunch, or dinner.

5. I'm learning how to cook, and I will live on my own one day, and I will be able to make my own chicken potpie, beef stew, and enchiladas.

Proofreader's Marks
Add a period: I like lemons⊙She likes limes⊙
Delete: They sell fruit but and vegetables.
Capitalize: He likes cheese. he likes it cold.
See all Proofreader's Marks on page xi.

B. **Rewrite each run-on sentence. Break it into shorter sentences.**

6. Grandma just moved into an apartment near my family, and she needs to buy groceries, and I go to the grocery store with her.

   _____

   _____

   _____

7. Grandma buys a lot of groceries, and I help her put them away, and she invites me for dinner, and she makes my favorite meal, and it is delicious.

   _____

   _____

   _____

Write It

C. **Complete the sentences about shopping for groceries. Fix any run-ons.**

8. At the grocery store, I always want to buy _____ because _____

   _____.

9. Sometimes Mom says it is okay, _____

   _____.

10. Sometimes Mom says I have to pay for it myself, and I _____

    _____.

11. Groceries are expensive, but _____

    _____.

D. **(12–15) Imagine that you can buy all the groceries for your family for one week. What will you buy? Why? Write four sentences. Fix any run-ons.**

   _____

   _____

   _____

   _____

   _____

   _____

86 What's a Complex Sentence?

A Sentence with Two Kinds of Clauses

- A clause has a **subject** and a **verb**. An **independent clause** can stand alone as a sentence.

  My **friends** **like** school activities.
  <u>   </u>
  independent clause

- A **dependent clause** also has a subject and a verb. But it cannot stand alone because it begins with a **conjunction**.

  because the **activities** **are** fun
  <u>   </u>
  dependent clause

- You can use the conjunction to "hook" the dependent clause to an independent clause. The new sentence is complete, and it is called a **complex sentence**.

  My **friends** **like** school activities **because** the **activities** **are** fun.
  <u>   </u>   <u>   </u>
  independent clause   dependent clause

Try It

A. Draw a line from an independent clause to a dependent clause to make a complex sentence.

1. I play soccer	after Ann tried out.
2. Mara tried out for the play	when there is an art show.
3. Spike plays the drums	whenever there is a game.
4. Nick goes to basketball games	because soccer is fun.
5. Kim helps the art club	because he likes the drums.
6. I exercise after school	because he is in the pep squad.
7. Stella writes a sports story	because I want to be healthy.
8. Juan goes to the basketball games	after she sees a game.
9. Ann became student council president	after she won the election.

B. Use the words to make complex sentences. Punctuate your sentences correctly.

10. Stella / she wants to be team captain / because / works hard _____

_____

11. after / Stella will get a trophy / the season is over _____

_____

12. Spike puts on his uniform / he marches in the parade / before _____

_____

13. Kim sets up shows / she wants artists to share their work / because _____

_____

14. Ann sees her friends / after / the play _____

_____

Write It

C. Add a dependent clause to complete each complex sentence. Start your clauses with **because, when, before,** or **after.**

15. School activities are important _____.

16. I like to do activities _____.

17. Sports are fun _____.

18. Students act in school plays _____.

D. (19–21) Write three complex sentences about activities in your school. Tell who does the activities, why the students participate, and when they participate.

_____

_____

_____

_____

_____

_____

87 What's One Way to Create a Complex Sentence?

Use *Because* or *Since*.

- A **complex sentence** has one independent clause and one dependent clause.

    <u>My brother goes to high school</u> <u>because he is sixteen.</u>
    independent clause   dependent clause

- When a dependent clause acts like an adverb, it begins with a **subordinating conjunction**. It is called an adverb clause.

    Some subordinating conjunctions tell why.

- If the dependent clause comes first, use a **comma** after the dependent clause.

    He rides his bike **because** he doesn't like the bus.
    Since he doesn't like the bus, he rides his bike.

Try It

A. **Draw a line from an independent clause to a dependent clause to make a complex sentence.**

1. _____, my brother gets himself to school.

    since it was raining

2. _____, he rides his bike.

    because he wants to arrive on time

3. Chris leaves at 6:45 in the morning _____.

    Since he wants exercise

4. This morning he rode the bus _____.

    Because he is sixteen

5. Chris rides with a bike club _____.

    because he wants to meet friends

6. _____, Chris gets up early on Saturdays.

    because he gets up so early

7. _____, Chris can ride for 30 miles.

    Since the bike rides start at 7:00

8. Chris is tired in the afternoon _____.

    Since he is in good shape

B. Choose words from each column to build four complex sentences. You can use words more than once.

Chris works at a bike shop		he knows a lot about bikes.
He can get a new bike	since	my old helmet got too small.
I get a discount	because	he gets a discount.
I bought a new helmet		my brother works there.

9. _____

10. _____

11. _____

12. _____

Write It

C. Add an independent or dependent clause to complete each complex sentence. Start your dependent clauses with **because** or **since**.

13. Because riding a bike is good exercise, _____.

14. I like to ride a bike _____.

15. Since my school has bike racks, _____.

16. Some people ride on bike paths _____.

D. (17–20) Write four complex sentences that tell how you like to get exercise and why.

_____

_____

_____

_____

_____

_____

_____

88 What's Another Way to Create a Complex Sentence?

Use *When, After,* or *Before.*

The subordinating conjunctions **when, after,** and **before** tell when an action happens. They can begin an **adverb clause.**

- Use **when** if the action in the independent and dependent clauses happens at the same time.

  My big sister reads the newspaper **when** she eats breakfast.

- Use **after** if the dependent clause tells what happens first.

  After she eats breakfast, she gets ready for school.

- Use **before** if the dependent clause tells what happens later.

  My sister packs her backpack **before** she leaves.

Try It

A. Write an adverb clause to complete each sentence. Use **when, after,** or **before.**

1. _____ I get out of bed. **(When)**

2. I eat my breakfast _____. **(after)**

3. I watch the sports news _____. **(when)**

4. _____ I pack my lunch. **(Before)**

B. Use the conjunctions **when, after,** or **before** to combine each pair of sentences.

5. I talk to my friends. I wait for the bus.

   _____

6. The bus stops. I get onto the bus.

   _____

7. We have to sit down. The bus driver starts the bus.

   _____

Write It

C. Answer the questions about what you do. Use **when**, **before**, and **after** to write complex sentences.

8. What do you do before you go to school? _____

_____

9. What do you do after you get out of school? _____

_____

10. What do you do when you are in school? _____

_____

D. (11–14) Write four complex sentences that tell what you do on a weekend. Use **when**, **before**, or **after**.

_____

_____

_____

_____

Edit It

E. (15–20) Edit the journal entry. Fix the six complex sentences.

September 8

I went to school this morning, it was raining. It stopped raining I got to school. That's why I did not have my soccer clothes. Usually I pack them I leave. I thought tryouts would be canceled, though. I had to go home tryouts began. I was back at school tryouts started. I was really tired tryouts were over!

Proofreader's Marks

Add text:

I wear soccer cleats I play soccer. ^when

See all Proofreader's Marks on page xi.

89 Use Compound Sentences

Remember: A compound sentence includes two independent clauses joined by **and**, **but**, or **or**.

- Use **and** to join like ideas. Use **but** to join different ideas.
  Use **or** to show a choice.

  Do you like summer better than winter, **or** do you like winter better? I like school vacation, **but** I do not like really hot weather. I like the snow, though. I like to ski, **and** I like to play hockey.

- Don't overuse **and**.

  It is cold in the winter, and there is a lot of snow, and I can ski down mountains, and I can ice skate at the rink in the park.

Try It

A. Edit the sentences. Use and, but, or or to make each pair of sentences into a compound sentence.

1. It snowed on Friday. Dad took me skiing on Saturday.

2. I never skied before. I took lessons.

3. Would you like to ski? Would you rather snowboard?

B. Edit these run-on sentences. Break them into shorter sentences.

4. The rope tow pulled me up the small hill, and I skied down the hill, and I fell flat on my face, and I got up, and I tried again.

5. Later I took the chair lift, and I went to the top of a small slope, and I jumped off the lift, and I skied down the slope.

Proofreader's Marks
Add text: and I ski, I have fun.
Do not capitalize: Dad Skis, and I do, too.
Add a period: I like to ski
Delete: We ski ski together.
See all Proofreader's Marks on page xi.

C. Write compound sentences to answer the questions. Use **and**, **but**, and **or**.

6. What do you like to do in the winter? _____

_____

7. What choices do you make when you decide what to do? _____

_____

8. What would you like to do but have not done yet? _____

_____

D. (9–12) Do you like summer or winter better? Write four compound sentences to tell why. Fix any run-ons.

_____

_____

_____

_____

_____

Grammar at Work

E. (13–15) Edit the conversation. Fix <u>one</u> run-on sentence. Make <u>one</u> compound sentence by combining two shorter sentences. Fix <u>one</u> pronoun in a prepositional phrase.

Beth: I went skiing for the first time today, and I had fun, and I took lessons, and I learned to ski.

Bill: That sounds like fun. It sounds scary, too.

Beth: I was scared at first, but then I felt more comfortable.

Bill: Maybe I should learn to ski.

Beth: My dad and I plan to go next week. You can go with we!

Proofreader's Marks

Add text:
                                              but
Beth likes to ˆski I do
not.

Delete:
Dad is a̷ a good skier.

Do not capitalize:
Bill wants to L̷earn.

See all Proofreader's Marks on page xi.

90 Use Complex Sentences

Remember: Varied sentences make writing interesting. One way to create variety is to use adverb clauses to make complex sentences.

- Tell why by adding an adverb clause with **because** or **since**.

  Because this is the first day at my new school,
  I do not know anybody.

- Tell when by adding an adverb clause with **when**, **after**, or **before**.

  I will not know anybody **when** I go to lunch.
  Before I go to lunch, I want to meet someone to sit with.
  I will feel more comfortable **after** I meet new friends.

Try It

A. Write an adverb clause to complete each sentence. Use the subordinating conjunction in parentheses.

1. That first day, I worried _____. (**before**)

2. I was nervous _____. (**because**)

3. _____, I smiled at the kids. (**When**)

B. Use subordinating conjunctions to combine the sentences into complex sentences with adverb clauses.

4. I went to classes. I met with the guidance counselor.

_____

5. She introduced me to Jenny. I was in her office.

_____

6. I am glad I met Jenny. Now I know one person at my new school.

_____

C. Answer the questions about yourself and meeting new people. Use adverb clauses in your sentences.

7. How do you feel when you meet new people? _____

_____

8. Why do you feel that way? _____

_____

9. How do you feel after you meet new friends? _____

_____

D. (10–14) Write five sentences with adverb clauses. Tell what you would do on your first day at a new school.

_____

_____

_____

_____

Grammar at Work

E. (15–20) Combine sentences. Make <u>four</u> complex sentences. Make <u>two</u> sentences with participial phrases.

April 15

I felt relieved. I finished my first day at my new school. I went to school. I did not know anybody at all. I met Jenny. The guidance counselor introduced us. I felt better. I knew at least one person. I feel confident now. I am not worried about school tomorrow. I will find Jenny. She will be waiting for me at the front door.

Proofreader's Marks

Add a word:
               when
I laugh | I am really
nervous.

Change text:
            when
I laugh ~~after~~ I am really
nervous.

Delete:
I started. at a new
school.

Do not capitalize:
I make new /friends.

See all Proofreader's Marks
on page xi.